THE GIFT OF SCIENCE

just ideas

transformative ideals of justice in ethical and political thought

series editors

Drucilla Cornell, University of Cape Town

Roger Berkowitz, Bard College

Kenneth Michael Panfilio, Illinois State University

THE GIFT OF SCIENCE

LEIBNIZ AND THE MODERN LEGAL TRADITION

Roger Berkowitz

FORDHAM UNIVERSITY PRESS

NEW YORK   2010

Copyright © 2005 by the President and Fellows of Harvard College
First Fordham University Press edition, 2010

All rights reserved. No part of this publication may be reproduced, stored in a retrieval system, or transmitted in any form or by any means—electronic, mechanical, photocopy, recording, or any other—except for brief quotations in printed reviews, without the prior permission of the publisher.

Fordham University Press has no responsibility for the persistence or accuracy of URLs for external or third-party Internet websites referred to in this publication and does not guarantee that any content on such websites is, or will remain, accurate or appropriate.

Library of Congress Cataloging-in-Publication Data

Berkowitz, Roger, 1968–
  The gift of science : Leibniz and the modern legal tradition / Roger Berkowitz.
    p. cm. — (Just ideas : transformative ideals of justice in ethical and political thought)
  Includes bibliographical references and index.
  ISBN 978-0-8232-3191-1 (pbk. : alk. paper)
  1. Leibniz, Gottfried Wilhelm, Freiherr von, 1646–1716. 2. Science and law—History. 3. Jurisprudence—History. 4. Law—Philosophy. I. Title.
K457.l4B47 2010
340'.11—dc22
                                                                2009049375

12 11 10   5 4 3 2 1

Acknowledgments

I owe my greatest intellectual debts to Marianne Constable, Laurent Mayali, and Philippe Nonet, who were my teachers at the University of California, Berkeley. Marianne Constable is a valued teacher and mentor. Her integration of law, philosophy, and history is peerless, a model for my own interdisciplinary scholarship. Laurent Mayali first sparked my passion for legal history that led to my interest in German codification. His work and example have helped teach me the meaning of scholarship. Philippe Nonet has shown me what I know of thinking. There is no more generous or gifted teacher. His spirit and wisdom touch every page of this book, and his passion for truth remains an inspiration and aspiration. This book could not have been written without his support and guidance.

I have been undeservedly fortunate to have had more than my fair share of great teachers. Two deserve special thanks. Austin Sarat first quickened my interest in the "force" of law. Drucilla Cornell is a true friend and intellectual companion. The depth of her passion for life and justice inspires and awes.

Many friends and strangers have read or commented on parts of this book over the years of its gestation. Particular thanks go to Philippe Nonet, Marianne Constable, Laurent Mayali, Drucilla Cornell, Ellen Rigsby, Jesse Goldhammer, Shai Lavi, Karl Shoemaker, Rainer Maria Kiesow, Uday Singh Mehta, Tom Dumm, James Whitman, David Saunders, Joshua Hayes, David Carlson, Peter Goodrich, Paul Berman, Judy Berkowitz, and two anonymous reviewers at Harvard University Press who read and commented, often beyond the call of duty, on all or parts of this manuscript. Jenny Lyn Bader has read and reread every page of this manuscript and improved it immeasurably. She and Wyatt Mason, in particular, have offered me the greatest gift one could expect from readers: brutal honesty. While this book will never live up to their discriminating standards of expression, it owes what music it has to their discerning ears.

I have received generous and repeated fellowship support and other grants from the University of California at Berkeley, the Max-Planck-Institut für Europäische Rechtsgeschichte, and the Robbins Collection. The support of these institutions and the engagement of my colleagues around the world have been instrumental in allowing me to write this book. In addition, I benefitted from fellowships given by the Eduard-von-Schwartzkoppen-Stiftung and Amherst College.

Peter König and Klaus Luig, through their writings and intellectual conversations, deepened my understanding of Leibniz's codification projects. I thank Dr. Hartmut Rudolph at the Berlin Academy of Science for his help in locating microfilm originals of certain of Leibniz's texts. In addition, Bradley Ritter, my Latin tutor, proved heroic at helping me to decipher difficult passages of Leibniz. Finally, Michael Aronson believed in my book and shepherded me through the publication process.

My most heartfelt thanks and love go to Jenny Lyn Bader and Madeleine Chava Berkowitz. They, along with Howard, Judy, and Sandy Berkowitz, personify justice and give me hope. This study is dedicated to my parents. They were my first teachers. Everything good in this book reflects their openness and love.

Contents

Preface *ix*

Note on Terminology *xvii*

Introduction: Legal Codification, Positive Law, and the Question of Science *1*

I   From Insight to Science: Leibniz's Scientific Foundation of Justice

1   Beyond Geometry: Leibniz and the Science of Law *17*

2   The Force of Law: Will *28*

3   Leibniz's *Systema Iuris* *54*

II   The *Allgemeines Landrecht:* From *Recht* to *Gesetz*

4   From the *Gesetzbuch* to the *Landrecht:* The ALR and the Triumph of Legality *71*

5   The Rule of Law: The Crown Prince Lectures and the Grounding of Legality in Order and Security *87*

Contents

III From Science to Technique: Friedrich Carl von Savigny, the BGB, and the Self-Overcoming of Legal Science

6 From Reason to History: Savigny's *System* and the Rise of Social Legal Science   *109*

7 The *Bürgerliches Gesetzbuch* (BGB) of 1900: Positive Legal Science and the End of Justice   *137*

Conclusion   *159*

Note on Sources   *163*

Notes   *169*

Index   *211*

Preface

> Justice?—You get justice in the next world. In this world, you have the law.
>
> —William Gaddis, *A Frolic of His Own*

Justice has fled our world. We have not noticed, however, because law has taken its place. The CEO of a Fortune 500 company who pays a fine so that his company can dump toxic waste into a reservoir, or moves its corporate address to the Bahamas with the intent of avoiding taxes, does not say: "I am acting legally if also unjustly." On the contrary, the very legality of the act is seen as proof of its justness. The divorce of law from justice informs our modern condition. Lawfulness, in other words, has replaced justice as the measure of ethical action.

What does it mean that law—the institutional embodiment of mankind's highest ideals—has become a tool wielded by lawyers and their clients in the pursuit of strategic interests? How is it that law—the rational feeling, as Kant teaches, of man's connection with the ideal of justice—has come to stand for obedience to rules? And what does it mean that this debasement of law into an instrument of politics and economics no longer shocks us?

We are not shocked because we are in denial. We have not yet stared in the face the hard truth that the pale word "justice" has lost its fire. Judges, lawyers, and law professors all speak vociferously of justice. When they speak of justice, however, they do not mean Antigone's burial of Polynices, or God's divine judgment that struck Ananias dead.

Instead, they say that justice is fairness, an objective standard of playing by the rules; they say that justice is efficiency, a cold measure that equates economic gain with moral rectitude; or they say that justice is legitimacy, thus reducing justice to whatever is believed to be just or is accepted by the people. In all of its contemporary guises, justice today means something like a fair and efficient balancing of interests in a way that produces legitimate legal outcomes.

To think about justice beyond the calculations of fairness, efficiency, and legitimacy is hard. Justice resists precisely what modern man most craves: the certainty of definition. Whereas fair rules and efficient norms offer the promise of legitimacy, the imperative to act justly requires us to think. Active thinking—what Emerson, in *The American Scholar*, calls the one thing of value in the world—is irreducible to rules or laws.[1] Similarly, justice demands that man think and in thinking transcend the limits of his unique self and enter into an ethical community with others. The dream of justice, in other words, is the dream of transcendence.

Throughout the history of political thought, the thoughtful activity of justice has been understood as an individual's moving beyond himself to a higher realm. This transcendental activity of justice has been characterized in different ways: Plato's turn from the shadows in the cave to the light of the sun; the religious believer's entry into a *unio mystica* with God; Rousseau's citizen losing himself in the general will; Kant's rational finding of oneself to be an inhabitant of the kingdom of ends; Nietzsche's rapturous self-overcoming into the ethical world created by the work of art; Whitehead's "ingression"—his entry into and actualization of abstract eternal truths; or, perhaps most fundamentally, Heidegger's openness to the event of the *Ereignis*[2]—the binding relation between man and being that first opens the possibility of law. Justice, within the tradition of Western thought, is the ethical activity of an individual's transcendence into a unified whole.

The distinction between transcendent justice on the one hand and modern conceptions of social justice based upon rules on the other is clear to anyone who has seen the final minutes of a basketball game.[3] Players on the trailing team foul their opponents to stop the clock. The foul is good strategy; it is also, however, a violation of the rules. As a wrongful act, it is punished according to the rules. Yet sports fans say it is fair to foul as long as the player accepts his penalty. Fairness requires nothing more than playing the game according to the rules. The foul reflects a calculation: stopping the clock is worth the pain of the penalty. What is more, basketball players, coaches, and fans not only expect and condone the strategic violation of the rules, but believe that such a violation is justified.

As in the sports arena, a similar logic of rule-bound wrongdoing has infiltrated the field of law. Consider the case of a landowner whose creek and soil are polluted by a mill owner a few miles upstream.[4] The law calls such an intrusion on one's property a nuisance and grants the landowner legal rights against the mill owner. At one time, those rights included the possibility of an injunction that would require the mill to stop polluting the stream or cease operation. Enjoining a polluter, however, is no longer considered an efficient approach to the problem of nuisance. Instead, the law now imposes a fine on the polluter that compensates the wronged landowner for his loss.[5] In essence, the law permits wealthy polluters to purchase a license to continue in their wrongdoing. Much as the basketball player chooses to foul when it serves his interest, the mill owner calculates that it is preferable to pay damages to his neighbor or fines to a regulatory agency than to change his practice. And just as basketball fans applaud players who foul strategically, shareholders and other interested parties demand and expect that corporations will use the law to maximize profit.

The basketball player who fouls and the polluter who "pays to play" are, as they would insist, playing by the rules. They follow the rules imposed upon them and pay the penalties prescribed for their actions. What makes these examples from sport and law notable is that mill owners and lawyers have, as have basketball players, internalized the injunction to play according to the rules as the first principle of justice. Fouling and polluting when the perpetrator accepts his penalty are not simply legally permitted; rather, they are considered to be just because they are legally permitted. In law, as in basketball, the players have internalized an ideal of "justice as fairness":[6] the rule of law has come to mean the equal application of the law as rules.

While the reduction of justice to rules may respond to our need for certainty and security, it overlooks a different way of understanding justice. As the examples above make clear, acting justly may require that one think beyond the rules. A basketball player may decide not to foul even though he knows that fouling is to his advantage within the rules set out by the game. To the extent a player does not foul strategically, he plays like a sportsman. A sportsman plays to win, yet he knows that there is more to the game of basketball than winning. The ideals of sportsmanship, whether or not they change the way we live and play in the world, are a reminder to the athlete that there is another score being kept, one that does not add points according to fixed rules.

Similarly, we know that there is more to being a neighbor than paying for the damage one does. Only one who understands that he is enmeshed in a moral world keeps his promise even when it is convenient, efficient, and legal to break it. Beyond simply following the rules, right action requires attention to oneself and to others that responds not only to laws but also to an "already presupposed ethical world" or an attunement to "the original morality of a society."[7] Beyond the rule of law, in other words, is the call of justice.

What unites the good sportsman and the upright neighbor as just actors is a vision of their involvement in an ethical project larger than themselves. It is because of his commitment to the spirit of the game itself that the sportsman refrains from widely tolerated but unjust violations of rules. From the perspective of justice instead of the perspectives of fairness or legitimacy, law requires that an individual sacrifice his rights, his pride, and even his self to something bigger and ultimately more meaningful. In this sense, law is the insightful bond that one sees with the mind's eye when one acts lawfully; or, law is the experience of friendship and mutual reciprocity that, as Aristotle writes, inspires the acts of grace that unite a plurality into a unity.[8]

Of course, no legal system has ever been or could ever be wholly organized around an idea of transcendent justice. Throughout human history, different legal orders have been inspired, in varying degrees, by such an insight into a unifying sense of the whole. At times—as in Homer's Greece, Numa's Rome, and Puritan New England—the close bond between law, tradition, and religion has supported the idea of justice as an obligation to an ideal of truth. At other times—as in Justinian's empire, Ignatius of Loyola's Christianity, and Napoleon's France—the intimate connection between law and order came to be more centrally located in the authority of manmade rules and statutes. The balance has shifted over time and place so that law that once was infused with the spirit of transcendent justice later seemed merely a means for the preservation of social order. It would be possible to tell the history of the world as a history of the struggle between transcendental justice and law understood as manmade rules. But that would be another book.

Instead, *The Gift of Science* tells another story. This book is written out of the sense that we are living through a time unique in history. With the reduction of law to a mechanism of legitimate decision making and justice to fairness, we are—to a degree until recently impossible to conceive—in danger of dissolving law's once sacrosanct bond to the ethical activity of life. Beyond the waxing and waning of the felt actuality of justice that persists through history, modern society is witnessing the silent, unacknowledged extinction of justice. How this happened is a complex and multilayered story. There is no single explanation that can account for such a world-transforming event as the separation of law from justice. And yet, if the cause of the great divorce of law from justice is beyond our ken, it is nevertheless possible to highlight particular practices and movements that have accompanied the rise of modern law.

Within the rarefied world of the academy, the increasingly normalized divorce of law from justice is given the name *positive law*. Positive law names, most simply, the thesis that law has its ultimate source in will, not in reason. Since positive laws are grounded in nothing but the willful command of a sovereign, they are often denigrated as arbitrary and irrational. However, it is a mistake to think that positive laws are without reasons. Rather, positive laws are precisely those laws most in need of reasons; in other words, positive laws must be justified.

Given the need to justify positive laws with reasons, it is not enough for critics of positivism to dismiss it as an immoral doctrine that authorizes any law with the power to institute itself. Instead, a meaningful critique of legal positivism must take seriously the characteristic kind of justification offered by positivist thinking. Since positivist lawyers deny that laws can be justified by transcendent principles and values, they seek law's reason in societal norms like fairness, equality, and efficiency. By seeking to discover justice in social rules of behavior and social norms, positivist lawyers do not so much abandon justice as transform the nature of justice.

Justice today is sought as a knowable product of science. No event in recent legal history rivals in significance the rise of science as a way of knowing law. *The Gift of Science* asks how the reduction of law to knowable rules and the attendant rise of fairness, efficiency, and legitimacy to express the core of justice have overwhelmed the once transcendent ideals of law and justice. The answer, as the title suggests, is that the rise of legal science both reflects and advances changing ideals of law and justice. By exploring the philosophical and historical development of legal science beginning in the scientific revolution of the seventeenth century, I show that the advent of positive law cannot be understood apart from its grounding in a scientific worldview.

To open a connection between science and positive law, however, is in no way to call for a return to a pre-scientific practice of law. The impulse to think deeply and critically about whom we have become need not and should not be confused with the romantic longing for a return to a glorified past. Whether the past ever was as it seems from the present is, of course, beyond our ken. My hope, instead, is that articulating the original scientific impulse that grounds positive law might help open a path to a different future.

Similarly, my embrace of a non-positivist ideal of law does not signify a return to natural law, in either its conventional form as knowable first principles of justice or its recent reincarnation in the work of Germain Grisez, John Finnis, and Robert George. What makes these new natural lawyers "new" is their rejection of innate natural laws based upon a theory of human nature. Even so, the new natural law theorists insist that they can identify objective ethical laws through a science of practical reason. The return to a theory of objective or intersubjective ethical laws, however, depends on the adoption of the very scientific approach to both natural and positive law that leads to and furthers the subjection of law to calculating rationality.

In striving to rejuvenate an ideal of justice rooted in the ethical activity of thinking, *The Gift of Science* resonates in part with the ethical deconstructionist writing of Jacques Derrida and Drucilla Cornell. Ethical deconstructionists rightly resist every attempt to fix the content of the good. Insofar as ethical deconstructionists focus on the epistemological indeterminacy of law, however, they continue to understand law to be posited rules in need of certainty. The great virtue of thinkers like Derrida and Cornell is that they call attention to the ethical impossibility of the very positivist idea of law that they nevertheless accept as our fate. To say that "deconstruction is justice" or that "to be just, is to be in the throes of [a] paradox,"[9] is to insist, rightly, that law cannot be separated from an ideal of transcendental justice. Yet the critique offered by ethical deconstructionists relies upon a specifically modern understanding of law as posited commands in need of scientific and objective justifications. In this regard, and only in this regard, ethical deconstructionists embrace the same concept of law as do the legal positivists and normative legal theorists whom they so forcefully oppose.

In contrast to those who approach the problem of law as one of a failed epistemology, I seek to preempt the epistemological critique (i.e., law cannot be known with certitude) by asking the prior ontological question: what is law? To ask after the truth of the being of law, however, does not dispute the ethical deconstructionist argument that every abstract articulation of law is unjust. Rather, it suggests that much of the focus on the importance of epistemology and the so-called interpretive turn is misplaced. Lawyers and jurists have been well aware of the impossibility of true and certain interpretations of law since at least the time of ancient Rome; and yet, the ancient lawyers did not conclude that the indeterminacy of law implied its injustice. The inherent indeterminacy of law cannot in itself account for the claim that any statement of law is unjust. Something else, something beyond the mere indeterminacy of law, must account for the vehemence of the modern critique of law.

The precise form that "something else" has taken is a redefinition of the very nature of law. For what law itself *is* has in the modern era undergone a transformation. At the heart of the shift is law's transformation from an insightful knowing of justice into a product of scientific knowledge. As a product of science, law comes to be a justified rule that is knowable in advance and can be applied to particular cases. Only once law becomes a product of science—only once law is transformed into an entity that is willed, posited, and in need of scientific justification—does the indeterminacy of law come to be such a forbidding problem.

In bringing to light the metaphysical presuppositions of the scientific idea of law, *The Gift of Science* calls into question the modern conception of law as scientifically justified rules. In doing so, it holds out the possibility that law might actually *be*—that it might actually have an existence—outside of its posited existence in rules, norms, and conventions in need of scientific justifications and proofs of its validity.

Even today, the reduction of law to positive law is not absolute. That we can see the idea of transcendent justice that seeks a truth beyond mere rules is proof that the ideal of justice cannot be fully separated from law. Law, as Friedrich Carl von Savigny has suggested, can only retain its authority to the extent that it lays some claim to a transcendent and more-than-human source.[10] Nevertheless, it is difficult to deny that the current conventional wisdom—that justice is indistinguishable from the following of legal rules—reflects a historically unrivaled belief in the scientifically rationalized legitimacy of rules over the rule of justice. In modern times, the human will to clarify and to know has very nearly succeeded in severing law from its traditional and necessary connection to the ineffable. What positive law denies is law's unknowable origin in thinking that, because it takes its direction from a creative, thoughtful, and artistic insight, cannot but appear to others as "lawless caprice."[11] By laying bare law's need for scientific justifications, therefore, I work to recall—and call for—the struggle for justice beyond the reach of sociological and positivist understandings of law and of politics.

Note on Terminology

This study examines a transformation of the sense of law, a difficult topic made more so by a particular limitation of the English language. English, in contrast to many other languages, has only one word for law. Whereas the transformation in law from an insightful activity to calculated rule can be spoken of in German as the move from *Recht* to *Gesetz*, in French from *droit* to *loi*, in Latin from *ius* to *lex*, and in Greek from *dike* to *nomos*, English ambiguously overlooks the difference by speaking only of law. While the blurring of the distinction in English between *ius* and *lex* may have the practical advantage of lending to law as *lex* the moral authority of law as *ius*, it has the definitive disadvantage of concealing the significant fact that law is increasingly spoken of only in the sense of *lex*—the setting down of official rules governing behavior. This covering up of the declining significance of law as *ius*—that is, as a natural and accepted moral obligation—works to conceal the importance of what was once a meaningful part of law.

Since it is part of the work of this study to bring to attention the significance of the transformation from *ius* to *lex* and from *Recht* to *Gesetz*, the ambiguity of the English word "law" is an intransigent obstacle without any satisfactory solution. To speak simply of law, or to distinguish between "Law" and "law," would be to invite confusion. Similarly, to employ the English word "right" as the translation of *ius* and *Recht* and to reserve "law" as the translation of *lex* and *Gesetz* is to ignore the fact both that "right" has acquired a specific meaning in English and that "law" most certainly means more than *Gesetz*. Simply put, there is no adequate English-language solution to the problem of discussing the nature of law.

Note on Terminology

Many legal scholars have struggled with this dilemma, although most have simply ignored it. For the sake of clarity, throughout this book I distinguish between the differing meanings of law and positive law by using the Latin and German equivalents. In Part I, during the discussion of Leibniz's Latin texts, I use *ius* (law understood as justice) and *lex* (law understood as rule) to designate natural and positive law. In Parts II and III, in deference to the discussion of the largely German texts, I employ *Recht* to denote natural law and *Gesetz* to denote positive law. I hope that whatever initial strangeness that might be experienced as a result of the reliance on these foreign words will be more than compensated for by the added clarity they offer.

The following simple glossary may be helpful:

ius (pl. *iura*), *Recht* (pl. *Rechte*), *droit* (pl. *droits*): natural law; law as an activity of thinking; law as justice, where justice is understood as an insight into a transcendent unity.

lex (pl. *leges*), *Gesetz* (pl. *Gesetze*), *loi* (pl. *lois*): positive law; written law; law as justice, where justice has come under the sway of science; justice, therefore, as the calculated outcome of a rule.

THE GIFT OF SCIENCE

Ruthlessness toward the tradition is reverence before the past—and it is authentic only in the appropriation of this—the past—out of the *destruction* of that—the tradition. From here out must each actual historical work, which is something fully other than history in the usual sense, insinuate itself in the discipline of philosophy.

—Martin Heidegger, *Plato's Sophist*

Introduction: Legal Codification, Positive Law, and the Question of Science

> The order of Law as an institution of the social (or the cultural) is contemporaneous not to men, but to a time before men; it originates in mythical, prehuman time. The society finds its foundations outside itself in the ensemble of rules and instructions bequeathed by the great ancestors or cultural heroes, both often signified by the name of Father, Grandfather, or Our True Father.
>
> —Pierre Clastres, *Archaeology of Violence*

In a legal system, there must be some way that the law comes to be known. In English common law, the law traditionally was announced in the verdict: literally the truth-speaking of a jury. The practice is quite different in Europe, where the tradition of legislation, making laws known through writing, stretches back to Roman times. It is only since the late seventeenth century, however, that science—and specifically scientific legal codification—emerged as a third and distinct way of knowing the law. This book tells the largely unknown story of the origin of legal science and the European movement to codify law. It does so not from a merely historical interest in legal codes, but rather to reveal how their emergence manifests a shift in the essence of law itself: namely, the advent of positive law as the essence of all modern law.

The story of the rise of legal codification, from its philosophical foundation in the jurisprudential writings of Gottfried Wilhelm Leibniz to its purest official realization in the German Civil Code of 1900, gives voice to the most basic characteristic of positive law. Insofar as legal codes posit the entirety of law in a single act of legislative will, they embody the highest striving of legal positivism: the clear, certain, and knowable ex-

2 Introduction

pression of the valid law. Legal codes, as the paradigmatic manifestation of positive law, offer a window into positive law's fundamental nature.

At first glance, the choice to investigate the rise of positive law through the lens of legal codification might appear anachronistic. After all, the collection of laws in books or codices has persisted for millennia. King Hammurabi chiseled his laws in stone, Solon wrote his laws in verse, Justinian compiled the Roman law in fifty books, and English barristers collected judicial opinions in annual yearbooks. Given such a long and pedigreed history of the practice of collecting and writing laws, one might conclude that the need to codify law that came to fruition in legal codes throughout Europe, Asia, South America, and parts of the United States during the eighteenth and nineteenth centuries was simply a continuation of an ancient practice of securing the law in writing.

Against such a conclusion, this study argues that the movement to adopt civil law codifications is modern. More importantly, the proliferation of legal codes is symptomatic of important changes, not only in the way in which law is known, but also in the idea of law itself. Modern codes are not simply compilations of preexisting laws—as were premodern codes. Instead, the rise of codes in the wake of the scientific revolution is an outgrowth of the scientific compulsion to secure the knowledge of law through scientific calculation.

An inquiry into codification as an entrée into the birth of positive law also might appear misplaced, at least from an Anglo-American perspective. Neither England nor the United States ever codified its common law. Louisiana is the only state in the United States that codified its law on the model of the French *Code Civil,* and despite the impassioned efforts of David Dudley Field in New York and California, the United States overwhelmingly rejected the idea of codification.[1] While most American states now have legal codes, and the United States publishes regular updates to the United States Civil Code (U.S.C.C.), these codes are basically collections of valid, albeit unconnected, statutes. In that they do not aspire to a complete, systematic, and coherent presentation of law, these collections differ fundamentally from the scientifically driven legal codes that dominated European jurisprudence in the eighteenth and nineteenth centuries. Furthermore, even European jurists have largely abandoned codification and embraced *Dekodifikation.* As a result of decodification—the passage of supplementary statutes that exist outside of the scientific systems of civil codes and the increasing reliance on judge-made law that departs from the strict language of the codes—law in Europe looks more and more like the uncodified common law in England and the United States.[2] On both sides of the Atlantic, law is increasingly thought to be nothing more than a mixture of avowedly unsystematic statutes and judicial opinions. Legal codes, as systematic formulations of legal reason, are dismissed as irrelevant to modern law[3] or are ignored altogether.[4]

The near-universal belief that modern law has abandoned the scientific impulse underlying codification is not proof of the insignificance of the scientific approach to law exemplified in eighteenth- and nineteenth-century codifications. That so little thought is given to codifications and systematic thinking in law today is not because codes and systems have disappeared; rather, it is because the fundamental idea of law that codes support—that law, as willfully posited, must have scientific grounds and reasons justifying its existence—has become so commonplace as to obviate the need for a formal code. There is, in other words, no imperative for an articulated system of law today because the necessity and existence of a scientific ground of positive law is taken for granted.

An essential distinction separates the strenuous limits of codified systems from the so-called interpretive freedom of current legal practice: the systematic rationality of code law is conscious while that of modern positive law proceeds unconsciously. Admittedly, judges today are empowered to decide cases by weighing social and economic interests. Yet to say—as many do—that the reduction of law to the calculated balancing of costs and benefits is proof of man's mastery of law and thus proof of mankind's freedom from logical, scientific, and metaphysical constraints is to confuse freedom with the ever-increasing subjection of mankind to rules of utility and efficiency. It is because the metaphysical underpinnings of contemporary positive law remain unrecognized—and thus unthought—that positive law has been so difficult to identify, let alone to understand.

In turning to a study of the philosophical origins of positive law in scientific codification, I hope that what has been perceived as the weakness of codified law—its overtly conscious, albeit failed, attempts to be complete and systematic—might offer a window through which to glimpse the willful core of modern positive law. Given the overriding need of positive law to ground and justify its legal pronouncements, the focus on scientific codification in this study as a way of summoning the foundation of positive law is, despite initial appearances, neither anachronistic nor misplaced.

My argument that positive law is willful law that requires scientific justification may appear to differ from common uses of legal positivism prevalent in Anglo-American legal theory. This apparent difference results in large part from the tendency of nearly all contemporary legal scholars to approach positive law as a theory of legitimate adjudication. It is for this reason that Sophocles's *Antigone* has, for better or worse, become a paradigm for the distinction of positive law over and against natural law.[5] If Antigone's burial of Polynices is held up as an explicit following of natural law, Creon's judgment sentencing her to death is considered the epitome of legal positivism. Creon reflects the core teaching of the "sources thesis" of positive law—that the validity of law depends exclusively on facts that can be objectively determined without resort to moral argument.[6] For a legal positivist, "to adjudicate is to promote justice by being an instrument of the law."[7] As a theory of judgment, positivism claims to be agnostic about the question of law itself.

Yet positive law cannot be merely a theory of adjudication separate from an understanding of law. Creon, for example, cannot judge until he has determined which rule of law—Antigone's natural law or Creon's own proclamation—he is to submit to. The question of judging cannot be asked without implicating the question of knowing law, and the effort to know the law presupposes some conception of what law is.

Whether they acknowledge it or not, all positivists proceed from an understanding of what law is: namely, positive law is an expression of will justified or at least rationalized through science. If non-positive law is, as the anthropologist Pierre Clastres writes, "bequeathed by the great ancestors or cultural heroes, both often signified by the name of Father, Grandfather, or Our True Father," positive law is severed from its ancestral inheritance.[8] Deprived of natural and traditional sources of authority, positive law is in need of the kind of justification that non-positive law not only does not need but also disdains. In order to defend itself against the charge of arbitrariness, positive law must seek to authorize its power with a claim to justice.

Science, by providing positive law with an objective claim to justice, becomes a necessary element of all positive law. For positivist jurists, therefore, law is not simply the bare will of a sovereign. Even the omnipotent will of the sovereign is compelled to deck itself with the legitimating mantle of scientific justification. The variety of scientific justifications for positive law is enormous: H. L. A. Hart, the father of American legal positivism, justifies positive law on the basis of an accepted "rule of recognition," which he defines as a "social fact" that is discovered through social science research into the norms of legality;[9] Richard Posner, one of the founders of the study of law as economics, argues that positive laws should be based on the "scientific study of social rules" that "are designed to bring about an efficient allocation of resources";[10] normative legal theorists insist that positive laws be legitimated (if not also justified) by appealing to social norms like integrity, fairness, and procedural equality;[11] and most generally, the vast majority of modern legal theorists and judges demand that positive law be grounded by weighing the costs and benefits of different outcomes. While a few anti-positivist jurists may still dream of an objective and universal legal science, legal positivists accept that the universalist ambition of legal science has failed; every justification for law is acknowledged to be partial, interested, and political. The result is an unprincipled competition among divergent criteria of justice that has led to the widespread belief that "force, mitigated so far as may be by good manners, is the *ultima ratio*" of law.[12]

That might makes right has been a theoretical seduction since Thrasymachus; however, it is only in the modern era that law, as positive law, has come to be defined as the command of a sovereign backed by the threat of sanction.[13] As a command, law is a willful decision. That means not only that a judge decides a case according to laws—as judges have for millennia—but that law has come to be nothing but a willful decision.[14] Today's laws can be different from yesterday's, and their malleability makes them convenient instruments for the willful regulation of social and economic relations. Once law is severed from its connection to a higher truth, it is, as Oliver Wendell Holmes Jr. once quipped, whatever a judge says it is.[15]

While Holmes is correct to say that law is, as John Austin famously defined it, the command of a judge or sovereign backed by sanction, the claim that positive law is nothing but sovereign will does not escape the grounding claims of a scientific legal system. Instead, the radical reduction of law to will merely shifts the metaphysical grounds of the legal system from the pursuit of justice to the preservation of order. The recourse to fiat and to judicial decision as grounds for law sets law in the service of the orderly resolution of disputes. The embrace of sovereign and judicial will as the essence of positive law, therefore, is not a retreat from the scientific grounding of law in justice so much as it is a redefinition of justice as security.

By insisting that positive law be seen to have its essence in science, I am not arguing that science is the cause of positive law. Beyond any simple thesis of causation, this book shows that law becomes positive law at the same time that law becomes a science.

This connection between positive law and science has gone largely unnoticed. Since modern positivists assume that all law is by nature positive law, there has been no need to ask what made it necessary that positive law come to be seen as law. Against this ahistorical acceptance of the naturalness of positive law, this book argues that the rise of legal science and the rise of positive law are corollaries and that they are manifestations of the same basic phenomenon: namely, the loss of insight as the source of law. Only once lawyers and lay people alike lose their sense of knowing law as it originates in what Clastres calls a "mythical, prehuman time" does the need arise for law to be secured in written positive laws. And only when insight into law is replaced by positive formulations does science appear as a new way of lending potentially arbitrary positive laws the authoritative patina of scientific truth.

It is to raise the question of the relation between positive law and science that this study turns to the history of legal codification. By giving historical substance to the idea of positive law, the codification story deepens our understanding of positive law as law that seeks its authority in a code's scientifically guaranteed propositions. It tells how, beginning in the seventeenth and eighteenth centuries, legal thinkers embraced a natural science methodology in the hope that a more scientific and thus more certain way of knowing the law would reinvigorate the increasingly precarious traditional and religious insights that secured the authority of ancient and medieval law. But it also tells of the inevitable failure of this hoped-for gift of science.

Once law seeks to reassert its rightful authority through scientific guarantees of its certainty, the technique of law comes to overwhelm its morality.[16] As a product of science, law is severed from its natural authority so that law itself ceases to make a claim on us; instead, law's authority comes to depend fully on the purposes and ends for which it exists. The story of legal codification told here gives voice to the silent fear that, despite the vast and incomprehensible proliferation of laws that surround us, we are living through the age of the death of law.

This study of the rise of science as the source of modern law begins, in the three chapters that constitute Part I, with an inquiry into the codification efforts of Gottfried Wilhelm Leibniz. This will be a surprise to many who know Leibniz chiefly for his mathematical discoveries, his theodicy, and his metaphysical doctrine of monads. Even for those aware that Leibniz was a jurist who pursued his work on a legal code throughout his life, the claim that Leibniz presided over the birth of positive law must sound strange. For, if nothing else, Leibniz is known as one of the canonical thinkers of natural law.

Yet the claim that Leibniz is the first thinker of positive law is not necessarily inconsistent with his reputation as a natural lawyer. The distinctive aim of Leibniz's natural law thinking is the accurate knowledge of natural law through science. If law was traditionally understood as something authoritative, a claim of right that originated in what Clastres calls a "time before men," the enlightenment faith in human reason had put the authority of such a *ratio scripta* into question. Leibniz sought to revitalize law's power through a scientific approach to law that promised a true and certain knowing of natural law that would render its existence and authority beyond dispute. Against Leibniz's intentions, however, the turn to science and specifically the scientific legal code as a way of knowing law contributed to the very transformation of natural law into positive law that Leibniz sought to prevent.

The scientific approach to law arises precisely when and because law loses its natural claim to authority. The science of law insists that law must be justified, and law is justified only when it exists for a reason. At the heart of Part I, therefore, is the claim that Leibniz's metaphysics, and specifically his embrace of the principle of sufficient reason (*nihil est sine ratione*), shifted the inquiry into law from a knowing of law itself to a knowing of the reasons, grounds, and justifications for law. Law comes to be subordinate to its justification or rationalizations; in other words, law is emptied of any independent meaning and authority. Instead, law comes to be an instrument of a scientifically knowable principle of justice.

Despite his profound commitment to the instrumentality of law, Leibniz's scientific approach retains its natural law mantle because the ultimate ends of law are those given by the perfectly rational will of God. The science of law, or jurisprudence, is, Leibniz argues, ultimately indistinguishable from the science of the truth of God, or theology. Scientific legal codification is not incompatible with natural law because natural law is knowable with the certainty and clarity demanded by science.

At the same time, the roots of positive law grew out of Leibniz's natural science approach. Leibniz's development of a legal science that radically subordinates law to its justification in the true will of God reflects a distinctly modern understanding of law as something that at its core does not exist without a reason. It was, in other words, Leibniz's philosophical account of law as a product of theological science *(scientia Dei)* that paved the way for future jurists and legislators to substitute other ends—and other decidedly less rational wills—as the justifications and grounds of law.

Parts II and III of *The Gift of Science* show how Leibniz's determination to justify positive law through science was adopted and adapted by diverse movements of legal science over the ensuing 300 years. Part II shows how Carl Gottlieb Svarez, the chief architect of the Prussian Code of 1794, the *Allgemeines Landrecht* (ALR), sought to ground law not on scientifically derived principles of morality but on an explicitly political science governed by the overriding need for political and legal security. The ALR was the first successfully adopted modern legal code and the first of the so-called natural law codes. Following Leibniz, the authors of the ALR sought to secure Prussian law through science. They did not, however, share Leibniz's optimism that a transcendent insight into God's will could be known with the certainty necessary to ground a knowing of law. Their solution was to replace God's will with the will of a sovereign legislator—the Prussian king, Friedrich the Great—as the ultimate arbiter of legal certainty. In doing so, however, the ALR abandoned the conviction, still alive in Leibniz, that law is essentially connected to a transcendent understanding of justice. On the contrary, the ALR inaugurated what Max Weber has called the "reign of legality."[17] Law, as a science, must render reasons for its being, and the distinctive measure of the validity of law is the posited will of the legislator. It was in its establishment of the human will of a legislator as the measure of both positive and natural law that the ALR revealed itself as the historical moment of the transformation of law into positive law.

Part III traces the link between Leibniz's legal science; the German Historical School of law founded by Friedrich Carl von Savigny; and the German Civil Code of 1900, the *Bürgerliches Gesetzbuch* (BGB). Chapter 6 offers a novel interpretation of Savigny's importance in legal history. While Savigny is most widely known for his opposition to codification, as famously memorialized in his disputes with Anton Thibaut and G. W. F. Hegel, it is important to understand that Savigny's scientific approach to law did more to advance German legal codification than did the work of any other nineteenth-century legal figure. Like Leibniz, Savigny sought to reinvigorate the law of his time through science. And just as Leibniz unintentionally furthered the positivization of law that he feared, so too can Savigny rightly be seen as a founding father of positive law.

Chapter 7 shows how Leibniz's original legal science was altered once more to form the backbone of the BGB. Again legislation is imagined to be a science; however, while Leibniz, the ALR, and Savigny sought to scientifically know some substantive idea of law (be it divine reason, kingly will, or the will of the people), the legal science adopted by the BGB had no object other than the formal properties of law itself. Law has no content outside of its role as a handmaiden to the achievement of ends, so that law comes to name the purely formal technical means to the achievement of higher ends that lie outside of law itself. Since these ends are explicitly imagined to be the social and economic good of society, the BGB can rightly be seen as the transition to modern sociological and economic theories of law. All mainstream modern approaches to law—from legal realism to law and economics, from normative moral philosophy to rational choice theory—have their roots in Savigny's appropriation of Leibniz's radical reconceptualization of law as an object of science.

The focus on the ontological question of law raised by codification contrasts with the overwhelming trend of legal thought that ignores the question of law itself. Modern legal scholarship is largely occupied with the social scientific investigation of law's causes or its effects. For sociolegal scholars, law itself is nothing but a jejune abstraction.

Within the field of legal codification, the focus on law's effects is noticeable in the oft-repeated claim that codification is to be understood as a problem of politics.[18] Even Sten Gagnér, the only historian to attempt a philosophical account of codification, misses its essentially scientific character by concentrating too heavily on its politics.[19] What such a sociohistorical viewpoint overlooks is that codification is not simply a choice to be pursued by politicians when it is in their interests to do so. Rather, codification is a necessary consequence of the shift in the nature of law into a product of science. At the same time, codification, by systematically rendering reasons for law, advances the transformation of law from a moral entity into a technical object. The historical event of scientific codification that was centered in Germany from the seventeenth through the late nineteenth centuries is, in other words, both an effect and a cause of the increasing instrumentalization of law as will.

The emergence of a new form of law—law as a product of scientific reason—was both a symptom of and a purported cure for the crisis of authority that Friedrich Nietzsche later called the death of God. Nietzsche traced the death of God back to Socrates' ambitious but futile attempt to save a decaying Greek civilization by a new reliance on reason. However, just as Socratic reasoning proved to be another kind of sickness that invariably served to undermine further the very belief in truth it was meant to support,[20] so too have the social-scientific offspring of Leibniz's legal science ruthlessly refuted all grounds for legal authority. The science of law has even recognized that science itself is interested, subjective, and suffused with political and metaphysical presuppositions. The scientific cure for law, therefore, has failed to restore law's once-vibrant bond with justice.

That the scientific cure has failed does not diminish either its impact on law or its importance to us today. Shorn from its traditional and religious foundations, law remains dependent on science for the rational grounds of its authority—the only grounds that modern man is willing to recognize. Law continues to seek its justification in the ever-paling scientific notions of efficiency, objectivity, and legitimacy; even these diminished goals, though, are increasingly seen to be illegitimate. The gift that science bequeathed to law has proven unreturnable: the reduction of the activity of justice to the refinement of a technique, one that strives for little better than the pursuit of political, social, and economic ends.

PART I

From Insight to Science: Leibniz's Scientific Foundation of Justice

> The modern metaphysics (i.e., Leibniz) says the *securing* of the being of man out of himself for itself . . . [E]qually is Leibniz the founder of "life insurance."
>
> —Martin Heidegger, *The Overturning of Metaphysics*

"Your Imperial Majesty," Gottfried Wilhelm Leibniz (1646–1716) wrote to his emperor, Leopold I, in 1671, "I deem myself indebted and most subservient to report an intended plan for the raising up of jurisprudence and the common good, a task begun a few years prior and one that moreover is, praise God, not little advanced."[1] The project the twenty-five-year-old Leibniz most humbly referred to as a restoration of the Roman law *(Corpus Iuris Reconcinnatum)* is anything but humble. Even as he presents his legal reform as a mere guide to the Roman law (the *Corpus Iuris Civilis*), Leibniz attaches the none-too-subtle condition that its role should be limited only "as long as [the Roman law] ought to be maintained and unchanged."[2] Hardly a restoration, Leibniz aimed instead at a radically new code of laws. The *Codex Leopoldus*—as he soon thereafter began calling his code—was to replace fully the *Corpus Iuris Civilis* as the valid law throughout the Austro-Hungarian Empire and Europe.

Leibniz pursued his dream of gaining imperial sanction for the *Codex Leopoldus* throughout his life. At age 21 Leibniz composed his earliest proposal for a scientific reform of the Roman law, the *Nova Methodus Discendae Docendaeque Jurisprudentiae (A New Method for Learning and Teaching Jurisprudence)* as part of an application for a position as assistant minister of law at the Court of the Bishop Elector of Mainz, *Kurfürst* Johann Philip von Schönborn. He got the job. Within four years of the publication of the *Nova Methodus* in 1667, Leibniz would make the first of two attempts to persuade Emperor Leopold to adopt his new *Codex* as the law of the empire.[3] During two distinct periods later in his life, Leibniz resumed his work on a legal code, first from 1678 to 1682 and then again in the 1690s. In the final years of his life, Leibniz was writing letters to friends and jurists throughout Europe suggesting the need for a legal code and promoting his own efforts. At his death, Leibniz's *Nova Methodus* lay open on his desk, marked with marginal annotations.[4]

Although Leibniz's code was never enacted, the creation of a scientific code is one of the most lasting and most basic of the great thinker's intellectual efforts.[5] Leibniz himself claims that the effort to reform moral law was one of his most personal objectives: "My particular family origin commends me to the effort to reestablish morality, the basis of right, and equity with a little bit more clarity and certitude than they are accustomed to having."[6] In spite of Leibniz's broad interests, which ranged from philosophy to accounting and from history to calculus, it was the discovery of codification as a new method of legal science that remained his lifelong preoccupation.

That Leibniz would address the problem of law and politics is not surprising. Alongside the well-publicized social crises of the seventeenth century,[7] there arose a spiritual crisis of authority that touched politics and law every bit as much as philosophy and religion. The crisis of authority was a crisis of unity; man as a free individual increasingly asserted himself against the traditional authority of the church and the newly emergent state. Shorn of the veils of "faith, childish prepossession, and deception" by which medieval and early modern man had been "conscious of himself only as a member of a race, people, party, corporation, family or otherwise in some form of universality," the pillars of traditional legal and political authority were shaken.[8] Man, Hobbes insisted, must make his commonwealth himself, and seventeenth-century thinkers like Bacon joined Hobbes in thinking that science offered the potential for the creation of a "New Atlantis."

Leibniz was a leading figure of a generation that believed that the crisis of authority was to be overcome through enlightened reason and a "renewal of science."[9] A trained jurist who worked nearly his entire life in legal capacities at princely courts, Leibniz's commitment to ethical and legal science stands out in its breadth and depth from that of other seventeenth-century natural scientists. The sciences of ethics and law are not simply one part of Leibniz's thinking. Rather, they combine to form the pinnacle of his philosophy. Indeed, Leibniz's legal thought emerges from his all-encompassing understanding of law *(ius)* as the right and rational order of the world. *Ius* is not simply humanly made law *(lex)*; on the contrary, *ius* embraces the entirety of divine and human relations.

Despite the fact that Leibniz placed such an emphasis on jurisprudence and exerted so much time and effort on the development of a legal code, surprisingly little attention has been paid to his legal work. There is next to nothing written in English on Leibniz's codes themselves,[10] and the few essays in German are a halting introduction at best.[11] Philosophical commentaries on Leibniz routinely ignore the existence—let alone the importance—of his legal writing. While a few recent books address Leibniz's legal works—most notably Patrick Riley's *Leibniz' Universal Jurisprudence*, the only substantial English-language account relating Leibniz's legal thought to his philosophy—these books are largely focused on the meaning of justice in Leibniz's metaphysics.

At its best, the focus on Leibniz's theory of justice aspires, in Riley's words, to "relate [Leibniz's] central moral and political ideas to the structural principles of his first philosophy."[12] In the same way, Hans-Peter Schneider's similarly titled *Justitia Universalis*—although it provides an invaluable history of Leibniz's codification project—focuses on Leibniz's historical relation to the Aristotelian natural law tradition.[13] In the existing literature, Leibniz's jurisprudence is read more to illuminate his moral philosophy than to ask after the importance of his approach to legal questions.

Riley surely is correct that Leibniz's theory of justice is incomprehensible apart from his philosophy; yet Leibniz's jurisprudence is more than just one of many avenues into the heart of his overarching philosophy. On the contrary, the philosophical inquiry into Leibniz's jurisprudential thinking must be guided, as must any meaningful philosophical and historical inquiry, by an interest in a problem of the present.

Riley does not and cannot approach Leibniz from the perspective of the present because he reads Leibniz as a backward-looking romantic dreaming of a dead golden age. Leibnizian ethics are, for Riley, squarely antiquarian yet beguiling, and represent a past era gladly, if futilely, grasped after as a failed alternative to modern liberalism. Whereas the Leibniz scholar Leroy Loemker has rightly noted that Leibniz's problem, like our own, is the grounding of the moral, social, and intellectual worlds in scientific reason,[14] Riley firmly places Leibniz with the ancients (Plato, St. Paul, and Augustine) against the moderns (Hobbes, Descartes, and Spinoza). And whereas Kuno Fischer, in his classic and still unsurpassed account of Leibniz's place in the history of philosophy, understood that Leibniz was equally a master of the past and a founder of our present,[15] Riley treats Leibnizian jurisprudence monolithically as the "last flowering (or last gasp) of a long and distinguished Graeco-Roman-Christian tradition which was to be definitively overturned by Hume, Rousseau, and Kant no more than a half-century after Leibniz' death."[16] Leibniz, Riley writes, "epitomized a world view which was on the edge of extinction; Hegel might have been thinking of Leibniz' effort to reanimate Christian Platonism when he said that 'the owl of Minerva takes flight only with the falling of the dusk.'"[17] Riley's is a nostalgic Leibniz, one whose moralism is a shining example of what we might have been.

What is fatally absent in such an account is Leibniz the natural scientist and enlightened prophet of scientific and technological progress. Nowhere is Leibniz's scientific optimism more powerful and influential than in his striving to develop a legal code. To see Leibniz as the philosophical father of modern scientific legal codes and the rise of positive law, it is necessary to reject Riley's portrayal of him as a relic of the past. Instead, Leibniz's work to bring law within the new metaphysics activated by the scientific revolution has helped to bring about one of the central phenomena of our times: the near total acceptance of legislative and judge-made positive laws as the ultimate source of law.

The striving to ground *ius* in reasons of justice suggests—especially given the centrality of the principle of sufficient reason to Leibniz's broader metaphysics—that the concept of *ius* itself, and not simply justice, undergoes a radical transformation in Leibniz's work. Because Riley and others overlook the question of *ius* and focus instead on Leibniz's theory of justice, they leave this question unasked: why is it that suddenly in the late seventeenth century the problem of knowing *ius* through a scientific code becomes a central preoccupation for one of the century's greatest minds? Put in other words, the question that Leibniz's theory of justice provokes is not the age-old question of justice, but the specifically modern felt need of law, of *ius*, to transform itself into a *science of justice*. Or, if the question is inverted, the next three chapters ask the following questions: What changes in the being of *ius* occurred that made it necessary for Leibniz's jurisprudence—and all jurisprudence after him—to become a science of justice? How is it that all subsequent inquiry into the idea of *ius* has been framed as a science of justice?

The following three chapters interrogate the Leibnizian inclination to elevate justice over *ius*. They give voice to Leibniz's striving to bring *ius*, once the province of insight, within the realm of measurable scientific knowledge. By subordinating *ius* to a science of justice, Leibniz initiates the metaphysical transformation of law into a product of science. In accord with the first principle of science, nothing is without a reason *(nihil est sine ratione)*. Law too, as a product of science, must have a reason for it to exist as a valid law. Law, in other words, loses its traditional and natural connection to justice and comes instead to be a mere technical means to bring about whatever grounds and reasons are set for it.

Leibniz's attempt to know *ius* with the certainty offered by codification proceeds from the core requirement of legal science, that *ius* must be grounded in and derived from basic and systematic principles. As a result of the principle of sufficient reason, the highest principle of science, *ius* emerges from a single source, what Leibniz alternatively calls justice, happiness, and well-willing. *Ius*, this study argues, is transformed by Leibniz from an authoritative statement of a practice into a forceful product of the scientific knowing of justice; *ius*, in other words, must be knowable neither as the pure reason of natural law, nor as the pure will of positive law but as a hybrid form of rational or divine will. It is this scientifically decipherable rationality of *ius* as will that, in the course of the following centuries, proved to be the seed from which positive law would sprout.

As his letter to Emperor Leopold made clear, Leibniz hoped that his scientific renewal of legal science would occasion a political as well as legal rebirth. Only once the general crisis of authority that gripped the seventeenth century began to be felt in the tradition-bound world of law did the demand that laws ground their authority assume its modern and scientific scope. In giving law a sure foundation in a scientific system, Leibniz sought to recover the authority law once had but no longer enjoyed. In doing so, however, Leibniz unintentionally helped to bring about a transformation in the very idea of law itself, a transformation that, against Leibniz's own purposes, has led to an ever-increasing separation of law from morality.

Leibniz's gift of science to law, then, was bittersweet—as indeed all gifts are. (The archaic meaning of "gift," still present in the German *Gift*, a poison, points to the ambiguity inherent in all giving.) Although Leibniz saw the demand that law posit scientifically certain reasons for its being as a guarantee of the morality of law, his followers progressively employed the law's need for self-justification to make it subservient to the more earthly measures of sociological and economic jurisprudence. However opposed to Leibniz's original aims, the subservience of modern positive law to willfully posited grounds has its roots in his own universal jurisprudence.

Leibniz's codification project can be seen as a symptom of the general diminishing of law's authority that dominated seventeenth-century legal reform proposals and persists into the present. It is also, however, an attempted cure for the disauthorization of law, one that seeks to discover in what Leibniz called the science of happiness *(scientia felicitatis)*, a new and scientifically grounded authority for law. As a symptom and cure for the discredited law of church and tradition, Leibniz's code offers a glimpse into one way in which law was transformed in the early modern world from an insightful activity of justice into a measured knowing of rectitude.

CHAPTER 1

Beyond Geometry: Leibniz and the Science of Law

> Only those who know geometry may enter.
> —Saying inscribed above the entrance to Plato's Academy

In his essay "Law and Geometry: Legal Science from Leibniz to Langdell," M. H. Hoeflich argues that Leibniz is the undisputed founder of a modern geometric paradigm for law:

> It is not often one can say with some confidence that a particular paradigm which becomes widely accepted in a special area of study originates primarily in the work of one individual. With regard to the development of the geometric paradigm in law, however, it is relatively clear that one jurist [i.e., Leibniz] must be given principal responsibility.[1]

Hoeflich's bold thesis—attributing to Leibniz the discovery of the geometric approach to legal reasoning—appears convincing. Leibniz is, indeed, the earliest and the most philosophically insightful founder of a new and specifically modern legal science. Geometry, like mathematics more generally, proceeds from accepted axioms to provable theorems; it yields truths free from the vagaries of empirical investigation. As a rational method promising timeless truths, geometry was considered by Descartes, Leibniz, and other seventeenth-century thinkers to be a model for scientific thinking. Since Leibniz was the first of these scientific philosophers to take seriously the possibility of scientific legal reform, his jurisprudence does seem to be the origin of the geometric approach to law. Yet, although it is technically correct, Hoeflich's characterization of Leibniz's jurisprudence as geometric conceals as much as it reveals.

This chapter shifts the terrain of the investigation of Leibniz's legal thinking from geometry to science. While the certainty offered by the geometric paradigm is an important element of Leibniz's thinking, it is the natural scientific method that, more than geometry, is the source of his reconceptualization of *ius*.

Geometry and Science

Leibniz surely valued the precision and certainty offered by geometric reasoning, yet he recognized that geometry could not serve as the model for a worldly science like jurisprudence. Geometry can provide the laws governing a perfect circle, but it says nothing definite about the properties of actually existing circles. To the extent that geometry and with it arithmetic name simply the rational knowledge of extension, space, and number as well as their analytic and synthetic combinations, they have no substantial connection with the real world.

Precisely because of its supersensibility, mathematics was not fundamental to the metaphysics of ancient and scholastic philosophers. Aristotle, for example, follows Plato in explicitly separating mathematics from the real world.[2] For Aristotle, mathematics is separate and abstracted *(choristos)* from the world;[3] it exists in no place *(atopos)*,[4] and the mathematical has no influence on actual things.[5] Coming out of the scholastic tradition that conceived "science" on the model of mathematics, pre-modern legal scientists saw science merely as a method to organize legal rules into ever more abstract logical structures; scholastic legal science had not yet become a systematic way to know and justify law.[6] If Leibnizian jurisprudence had conceived of mathematics as only a supersensible science of analysis and synthesis, therefore, it would represent no meaningful departure from the approaches of ancient and scholastic jurists.

What Leibniz and the other natural scientists of the seventeenth century saw in science, however, was not simply a methodological paradigm for conceptual analysis and synthesis. More importantly, science offered a systematic way of knowing the world as it proceeds out of divine and rationally certain first principles. The grand insight of seventeenth-century natural scientists was not simply to rediscover Euclid and ancient mathematical reasoning; rather, it was to extend the mathematical

Beyond Geometry: Leibniz and the Science of Law

method from logical beings to actual beings in the world. The natural scientific conception of nature as a rational system—not geometry—is the foundation of Leibniz's philosophic jurisprudence.[7]

The Knowing of *Ius* as a Product of Science

Leibniz was the first jurist to think about law as a product of modern science. To shift the gravamen of Leibniz's jurisprudence from mathematics to science does not deny the importance of math and geometry for Leibniz and later jurisprudence. The priority of science, however, is required by the recognition that mathematics itself has its ground in a scientific metaphysics. Mathematics itself, Leibniz first came to see in the 1670s, has its basis in a scientific worldview, such that the geometric laws that Descartes and others believed could explain the movement of physical beings must themselves have a prior scientific and metaphysical grounding.

Leibniz's proof of the scientific grounding of mathematics and geometry is based on the same scientific metaphysics that governs his jurisprudence. The highest principle of science, Leibniz argues, is that all beings have their first cause and reason in "something" that is not itself a physical being; as a result of the principle of sufficient reason, any inquiry into the origin of beings must go beyond the geometrical paradigm according to which a thing is extended in space. The understanding of all beings, therefore, is necessarily dependent on a prior understanding of the initial reason for the existence of that being and, ultimately, of beings as a whole. This initial reason, which is the active ground of all beings, comes to be known, in Leibniz's later writings, as the *force (vis)* of beings. Since all substances are forceful and partake of God's reason, *ius* too must have a reason. *Ius*, as something that exists, is itself a forceful being; it not only obeys geometric laws but also conforms to the rational laws of the universe. It ought to be possible, therefore, to discover a "universal jurisprudence"—"a system of justice and law common to God and man."[8]

Leibniz's universal jurisprudence is a science of *ius* that addresses the entirety of *ius*—both positive and natural law—from out of its scientifically knowable principles of justification.[9] "Almost all of theology," he writes, "hangs in great part from out of jurisprudence."[10] And since the everyday world partakes of its divine provenance, Leibnizian universal jurisprudence addresses the entirety of the world, human and divine.

In accordance with the scientific demand to ground actual positive laws in a higher yet controlling idea of rational natural law, Leibnizian jurisprudence subjects the knowing of *ius* to science. As Leibniz writes of jurisprudence, "The prudential knowing of Ius *(iuris prudentia)* is the scientific knowing of justice *(scientia justi)*, whether the science of liberty and duty, or the science of *ius* in any case proposed or actual."[11] Leibniz, therefore, understands jurisprudence literally, as *prudentia iuris;* at the same time, he insists that jurisprudence become a science, a *scientia iuris*.

With this definition of jurisprudence, Leibniz signals the three guiding principles of his understanding of *ius* as a practical and epistemic science, that is, as both *prudentia iuris* and *scientia iuris*. First, Leibniz's inquiry into *ius*, though practical, is an attempt to know *ius* scientifically, that is, with absolute certainty. Leibniz thus departs from Aristotle's absolute distinction between practical knowledge *(phronesis)* and scientific knowledge *(episteme)*[12] and argues for the possibility of an epistemic knowing of practical knowledge. Second, the scientific inquiry is guided by the science of justice. Since all *ius* is to be derived from a scientifically deduced universal definition of justice, Leibniz's inquiry into justice forms the living kernel of his legal code. As the seed from which the body of the code grows, the definition of justice is the precursor to the *Allgemeiner Teil*, or General Part, that introduces modern legal codes. Third, and following from the first two principles, the practical and worldly knowing of *ius* as *iustitia* is to be knowable and measurable by universal and eternal laws valid for both man and God. The fundamental drive of Leibniz's science of *ius* is to know *ius* with such certainty through the science of justice that all natural liberties and duties and all civil claims and obligations can be fully expressed, without exception, in a single, systematically coherent code of laws.

The outward manifestation of the knowing of *ius* through science is the modern systematic legal code. While *system*, from the Greek word meaning to stand together, and code, from the Latin *codex*, meaning book or collection, are both concepts with ancient histories, they only assume their modern senses once they are absorbed by the scientific quest for universality and certainty: a system is a "collection of truths duly arranged in accordance with the principles governing their connections," as formulated by Christian Wolff.[13] The modern *codex*, as distinct from the old books of laws, strives not only to compile all valid laws but also to present the laws systematically so that all laws, past, present, and future, could be deduced from fundamental legal principles. The modern legal code that has its roots in Leibniz's scientific jurisprudence is, therefore, necessarily systematic.

To ask after Leibniz's project for a systematic codification is to raise the question of what happens to *ius* when *ius* is subjected to the scientific demand for certainty. Once it becomes a product of science, law, in its essence, is transformed. But what is law as a product of science?

A Scientific Knowing of *Ius:* From Insight to Knowledge

In the debate over whether *ius* proceeds from reason or will, Leibniz is generally recognized to be an enthusiastic proponent of natural reason and natural right.[14] The characterization of Leibniz as a natural lawyer follows the conventional distinction between natural and positive law. If positive law establishes the willful command of a legislator as the source of *ius,* natural law is "conceived as the ultimate measure of right and wrong."[15] Natural law, therefore, is thought to locate the source of *ius* in calculable first principles that follow entirely from human reason.

Yet the character of natural law is frequently obscured by the threefold sense of nature at work in Leibniz's writing.[16] Nature is first what is, or *physis:* natural laws are native; they grow from nature itself, in contrast to the transitory and posited law of sovereigns or gods. It is in this sense of a law that arises from the earth as a self-known need, and in this sense only, that natural law is understood as an insightful glance into the law.[17] Second, nature is what must be, or *logos:* natural laws conform to the necessary laws of logic grounded in the justice of divine intellect. Leibniz believes that the entirety of legal predicates (the laws) can be derived from an adequate knowing of the subject of natural law, that is, God's justice. Finally, nature is also what ought to be, or *ethos:* natural laws are not only necessary but also the ethically best laws.

Leibniz illustrates the idea of the moral necessity of natural laws with the example of Julius Caesar crossing the Rubicon. It is Caesar's nature, Leibniz writes, to cross the Rubicon, overthrow the Roman Republic, and install himself as perpetual dictator. All of this is "certain," since "we have assumed that it is the nature [in the sense of *logos*] of such a perfect concept of a subject to include everything, in fact so that the predicate is included in the subject."[18] Caesar's destiny as the future dictator of Rome "is based in his concept or nature," so that Caesar will in the future actually come to rule Rome.[19] In taking up his destiny, however, Caesar does not simply give in to a necessity of fate *(logos)*. It is, of course, conceivable that Caesar would halt at the Rubicon and leave Rome to Cicero.[20] Everything Caesar does, he does freely to the extent that he could logically have done otherwise. And yet, Leibniz maintains that for Caesar to have acted otherwise would have been irrational, wrong, and unnatural: "There is a reason in [Caesar's] concept why he has resolved to cross the Rubicon rather than stop there, and why he has won rather than lost the day at Pharsalus, and why it was reasonable and consequently assured that this should happen."[21] Nature, as the laws of development in the concept of Caesar, is not logically necessary in the world of contingent truths, but it is nevertheless certain in the sense that Caesar will indeed act according to his nature *(ethos)*. That he does so is a moral law, "that man shall always do, though freely, that which appears to him to be best."[22] And what appears best is indeed natural *(physis)* because Leibniz's principle of sufficient reason holds that all contingent and free facts of nature have reasons for being as they are, rather than otherwise. The moral necessity of the natural law is secured by the wisdom and charity of God, who wills the best of all possible natural worlds into existence and who therefore assures the logical inherence of Caesar's actual actions in his concept.

It is largely on the one-dimensional understanding of natural law *(logos)* as a set of logically and morally necessary maxims that Leibniz is rightly yet reductively understood to oppose the voluntarism of positive law. As a product of science, Leibniz's natural law is "entirely grounded in reason."[23] Positive law, on the contrary, is expressly posited through legislation. To the extent that Leibniz must choose between natural and positive law, he clearly prefers the former.

This opposition between rational–natural and willful–positive law is central to Patrick Riley's explication of Leibniz's jurisprudence. Riley contends that the "whole of what [Leibniz] opposes can be summed up in *stat pro ratione voluntas*, 'let will take the place of reason.' "[24] Indeed,

Leibniz argues that legislative will is dependent upon rational intellect. When Leibniz writes that "we make judgments not because we will but because something appears," and that "we will only what appears to the intellect,"[25] he transposes the question of *ius* into the question of reason. Natural law, Leibniz insists, partakes of the logical necessity that governs the lawful natural freedom (*ethos*) of rational willing beings. Leibniz's natural law, therefore, is fully under the sway of science: *iustitia* is *scientia Dei*.

Traditionally, Leibniz's legal writing is justifiably read as responding to the perceived threat from positivist lawyers.[26] Leibniz himself increasingly understood his work as a refutation of what he thought of as the dangerous theses of the voluntarists. He consistently opposes the voluntarist claim that right originates in will rather than in natural reason, a claim made forcefully by Samuel Pufendorf. For Pufendorf, law "is a command by which the superior obliges the subject to conform his actions to what the law itself prescribes."[27] Right, as positive right, has its origin in sovereign will.

Similarly, Hobbes argues that the "natural" ground of truth and justice is in the psychological mechanism of human will. It is the desire for self-preservation and consequently the "fear of not otherwise preserving himself" that Hobbes argues is the first cause that moves man to subject himself to another.[28] It is possible, Hobbes writes in *Leviathan*, to discover natural laws of justice simply by building out from the original, necessary, and materialist will for our "conservation and defense."[29]

So central was Leibniz's opposition to Hobbes's voluntaristic positivism that Riley suggests Leibniz's *Theodicy* might be profitably read as an "anti-Leviathan."[30] Indeed, Leibniz opposes the voluntarist claim that justice does not rest on man's natural reason but gains its currency only through the willful effects of sovereign command—God's in the natural world and a prince's in the civil realm. For Leibniz, those who mistakenly set will over reason as the source of *Recht* are confusing *droit et loi*.[31] While natural right, based on reason and wisdom, cannot be unjust, positive right, founded on power, can be, "for if this power lacks wisdom or good will, it can give and maintain quite evil positive rights."[32] Against the dangers of voluntarism, Leibniz embraces a natural law ideal separate from that of positive law.

And yet, in spite of Leibniz's undeniable antivoluntarism, it is also true, as Hartmut Schiedermair has suggested, that Leibniz had a highly ambivalent relation to positive law. In fact, Schiedermair notes that Leibniz's entire rationalist jurisprudence can be seen as an apology not only for the evil in the world, but for the positive laws *(leges)* as well. Because Leibniz enlists natural law as a support and justification for existing positive law, this implies that positive law has a preponderance *(Übergewicht)* over natural law.[33] Indeed, for Leibniz there is reciprocity between natural and positive law. Both natural and positive right condition and determine one another; without the natural law, the positive law of a state is like a body without a soul, and natural right alone is a phantom with neither actuality nor force.[34]

Attempts to understand Leibniz's idea of natural law have largely oscillated between the charged poles of antivoluntarism and a conservative justification of existing positive laws. Moving beyond these opposing viewpoints, it is necessary to see how Leibniz's uniquely scientific approach to *ius* transcends both natural and positive law. Specifically, through the science of *ius* that Leibniz develops, natural *(ius)* undergoes a transformation. The scientific approach to *ius* transforms its object, so that natural law *(physis)*, that which was previously knowable only through a free and active insight into an incalculable yet manifest sense of divine and human justice, increasingly assumes the character of an instrument of scientifically knowable will (divine and human) in the service of human happiness.

The shift in the concept of natural law is one from insight *(physis)* to knowledge *(ethos* governed by *logos)*, from practice *(phronesis)* to science *(episteme)*, from inclination to justification, from conceptual seeing to definitional speaking, and finally from custom to legislation. As a product of scientific knowledge, *ius* is neither reason nor will but a kind of rational will that—understood as practical reason—conforms to the certainty of science. Through what Leibniz calls a science of happiness *(scientia felicitatis)*, *ius* is made into a will guided by science and constrained by the principle of reason. *Ius*, as Rudolf von Jhering reformulated the original Leibnizian idea two centuries later, is a scientific instrument for human ends.

The relationship between insight and a scientifically guided will can be seen most clearly in Leibniz's ambivalent position toward the classical Roman jurists whose work is collected in Justinian's codification of Roman law, the *Corpus Iuris Civilis*. What Leibniz praises in the jurists

Ulpian and Paul is their insight into the truth of divine and human justice, their unwavering sense of right and wrong in the decision of particular legal disputes. As insightful as the classical jurists were, however, their insights suffer the ills of all insight: singularity and opacity. Insights lack clarity because they cannot be proven and tested against known measures.

Mathematical truths, on the other hand, can be tested against experience: 2 + 2 = 4 can be illustrated with counters, just as the Pythagorean theorem can be worked out on paper. Although math is not grounded in experience, it possesses a sure method and can be honed according to exact measures. Jurisprudential and metaphysical insights, however, have previously lacked the "faithful guide, experience," which might aid them in their steps "like the little wheeled device which keeps toddlers from falling down."[35] In order that insight not suffer the vagaries of willfulness, a science of *ius* that would give to ethical and legal thinking the certainty of method they lacked was necessary.

Jurisprudence and Leibniz's Legal Code

From his earliest writings—including his philosophical dissertation, the *Ars Combinatoria* in 1666, and his program for legal reform, the *New Method for Learning and Teaching Jurisprudence* in 1667—Leibniz set out to place jurisprudence—and metaphysics—on sound methodological grounds. At the core of Leibniz's early efforts were what he called the "elements of law," the building blocks of legal thinking modeled on Euclid's axioms and theorems. If jurisprudence and metaphysics have relied too much on insight and have lacked the clarity and sureness of mathematics, Leibniz writes, the remedy is the extension of the mathematical use of elemental principles as guides and measures to aid in the science of jurisprudence: "One of the chief ways of making jurisprudence more manageable, and of surveying its vast ocean, as though in a geographical chart, is by tracing a large number of particular decisions back to more general principles."[36] Just as in arithmetic large and complex numbers can be broken down into their component parts, and just as geometrical theorems can be traced back to their most fundamental axioms, so can the diffuse truths of juridical insight be based on a foundation of first principles and maxims.

It is precisely this task that Leibniz envisions for himself in 1671, when he claims in a letter to Johann Georg Graevius, a German classical scholar and professor in Utrecht, that the "labor I have undertaken for myself" is none other than the "reducing of all the Roman Laws both natural and civil to their own principles, which are few, and that in turn for all the laws to be deduced from these principles once they are found."[37] Leibniz was sure that the Roman jurists' insight into justice was as incisive as that of any jurists before or after them. At the same time, he was equally convinced that insight, the momentary vision of justice—the *Augenblick*—needs to be made knowable, calculable, and useful for the advancement of society.

While it is undeniable that geometric models and reasoning dominate Leibniz's early legal thinking, they quickly give way to his broader scientific metaphysics. Against the Cartesian axiom of insightful perception that *"illud omne esse verum quod valde clare et distincte percipio*—all things that I perceive very clearly and very distinctly are true"[38]—Leibniz erects an even more rigorous and more scientific criterion of truth. Since "what seems clear and distinct to men when they judge rashly is frequently obscure and confused," Leibniz argues against Descartes, the Cartesian axiom "is thus useless unless the criteria of clearness and distinctness which we have proposed are applied and unless the *truth of the ideas is established.*"[39] Truth, and also *ius*, must have clear and distinct criteria above and beyond Cartesian perception. Neither insight nor geometry alone is a sufficient measure of truth; instead, insight into truth must be rationally knowable and testable, at least theoretically, for humans as rational beings.

Leibniz's scientific optimism propels him forward toward an ever more exact measure and knowing of man and his world. Both the world of matter and the world of intellect conform to rational and therefore knowable natural laws. As a result, Leibniz imagines a science of happiness and a science of law that would reveal a certain path to self-knowledge and self-improvement. While we must be "content with the ordering of the past," as that which is willed as best by God, we must also live as free subjects by trying "to make the future, insofar as it depends upon us, conform to the presumptive will of God or to his commandments."[40] Free and contingent subjects are driven to act in such a way that enhances and maximizes their freedom, but only insofar as their freedom conforms to the concept of their nature as willed by God.

Beyond Geometry: Leibniz and the Science of Law   27

What is required for free action, therefore, is an ever more perfect knowing of one's nature. "Wisdom," understood as "the science of happiness or of the means of attaining the lasting contentment which consists in the continual achievement of greater perfection,"[41] becomes the measure not just of man, but of justice as well.

Justice, Leibniz famously writes, is the charity of the wise *(caritas sapientis)*. Christian charity, the feeling of benevolence *(bene-voluntas)* or well-willing, becomes an object of Leibniz's legal science to be made measurable and knowable through a science of happiness *(scientia felicitatis)*. It is Leibniz's determination to make jurisprudence—the prudential knowing of justice—into a *scientia juris*—an epistemic knowing of justice—is the source of his lifelong desire for a posited legal code in which the entirety of law would be set down in a few short pages.

CHAPTER 2

The Force of Law: Will

> With the growing claim of the principle of ground as one of the highest principles of thinking and knowing, a new interpretation of the being of beings unfolds . . . The principle of ground's growing claim to mastery says, accordingly, that being—namely as an objective-standing-against (will)—more decisively brings itself to mastery.
>
> —Martin Heidegger, *The Principle of Reason*

What does it mean that *ius* is knowable and measurable by a science of justice? What does it mean that *ius* comes to be an object of scientific knowing? If the first question addresses the epistemological question of how *ius* is known, it invokes the second query regarding the essence of *ius* itself. It is this latter inquiry into *ius* as a product of science that is the focus of this chapter. Law *(ius)*, this chapter argues, first acquired its modern characterization as will—what Leibniz within his metaphysics calls force *(vis)*—in Leibniz's efforts to work out a scientific legal code.

Leibniz's early codification efforts have their roots in his attempt to develop a scientific method through which a legal system could be deduced from simple elements. These elements of law *(elementa iuris)* are the precursors to Leibniz's famous monads. In tracing the connection between Leibniz's early attempts to build a legal code on simple elements of *ius* and his mature reconceptualization of substance in the monad, this chapter sets the transformation of *ius* into will within its proper historical and philosophical context.

A monad, from the Greek for "unit," is the word Leibniz employs within his general philosophy to name the simple and unifying formal substance that is the essence of every being. The monadology has roots in Leibniz's early thinking about the elements of law. More importantly, it is the driving force behind his codification efforts. Indeed, Leibniz reconceives law along the lines of the monad. Since all beings are, essentially, monads, law, as a being, must also proceed from an original, striving, appetitive, willful force. Leibniz names the force of law the force of justice. Justice, therefore, is the original and active essence of *ius*.

To say that *ius* is a willful force of justice is not to say that Leibniz conceives of *ius* as the arbitrary will of a sovereign. *Ius*, for Leibniz, remains natural law; thus, it is knowable by all rational beings, including God and, to a certain extent, man. And yet Leibniz's natural law is not inspired insight into *ius* that grows of its own accord *(physis)*. Instead, the knowledge of natural law is transformed into an object of science, an entity knowable according to principles of justice *(logos)*. The demand that *ius* have grounds and reasons, and its consequent dependence on knowable principles of justice, subordinates *ius* to a willed idea of the good. That Leibniz makes *ius* dependent on a scientifically knowable will is the first step in the emergence of positive law.

The Early Codification Project

The scientific approach to *ius* animates Leibniz's lifelong involvement with questions of jurisprudence and legislative codification. His masters' thesis, *Specimen Quaestionum Philosophicarum* (1664), as well as his dissertation *De Casibus Perplexis in Iure* (1666), are characterized by a philosophical and mathematical approach to a science of law. Especially in *De Casibus*, Leibniz expresses his ambition to discover a method for the determination of fundamental principles that would decide all legal cases, even the most difficult and perplexing ones, with certainty. His quest for the development of a science of law that would yield practically useful principles for the deciding of legal disputes continued after he joined the Court of Johann Philipp von Schönborn, the Elector, in Mainz. From 1669 to 1672 in Mainz, Leibniz wrote dozens of short works that laid the foundation for his newly conceived idea of a scientific legal code.

The code, as it was worked out by the youthful Leibniz, consisted of four parts. First came the *Elementa Iuris Naturalis*, which was to be a short work not formally part of the code, but preceding it. The size of the "Elements of Natural Law" would belie its importance, for "so much would be contained within, [and] with such clarity and brevity, that the most important questions of international and public law *(ius)* could be explained by any rational man, if he will only follow the method prescribed therein."[1] The "Elements of Natural Law" is an analytic deduction of laws from first principles; the work "contains demonstrations deduced from only the definitions of justice."[2] Given a definition of justice—for example, the just man is he who loves everyone—Leibniz writes to Louis Ferrand, all possible legal cases can be logically deduced. Since to love is to be delighted by the felicity of others, and since felicity is the state of lasting delight, and delight is a sense of harmony, Leibniz reasons that out of these definitions, he can derive the entirety of law.[3] The method of the "Elements of Natural Law," which Leibniz pursued in numerous plans from the years 1671–1672, is to determine a single fitting definition of justice from which "all legal rules" *(omnes juris regula)* could be deduced.[4]

Following the "Elements of Natural Law," Leibniz set out the "Elements of Civil Law," the *Elementa Iuris Civilis hodierni*. The "Elements of Civil Law" are to be given in a single table that would be about the size of a map of the Netherlands. This short table would contain "all the main rules, and thus all legal concepts, so that out of their combinations all given cases can be decided, and all actions, exceptions, and responses, etc. can be discovered simultaneously [by tracing their relations] with a finger."[5] The table of the elements of civil law *(ius)* is composed of those concepts that, as idealizations of civil law, can be bracketed out and set before the actual rules of civil law. The table of elements forms a collection of the shortest, clearest, and best concepts, which can serve as guides for the derivation of the lower rules of law.

Leibniz builds his table of legal concepts on four basic elements of civil law: subject, object, action *(actio)*, and concept *(iura)*. Derived from these four elements, the table of the elements of civil law promises to be so clear and simple that even an adolescent, in just a few weeks, "can be instructed with play and jokes, so that he can with no great labor define all offered cases from out of the table and can decide the most difficult controversies among jurists from a solid fundament."[6]

The "Elements of Civil Law" find their authentication and justification in the third and fourth parts of Leibniz's proposed code, the *Nucleum Legum* and the *Corpus Iuris*.[7] While the "Elements of Natural Law" and the "Elements of Civil Law" are comprised of abstract concepts and definitions, both the "Nucleus of Laws" and the "Body of Laws" include the laws themselves. The Nucleus and Body are derived from the "Elements," and at the same time, the literal words of the law "clearly strengthen" the "Elements."[8] Just as the doctrinal manifestation of Christian theology strengthens the natural bond of all men to one another by giving that bond a positive form, so too, Leibniz writes, do the words of the *Nucleum Legum* "dress the skeleton of the naked tables [of elements] as if with flesh,"[9] but only with the leanest meat—that is, only with those words taken from the *Corpus Iuris* that express truly natural law.[10]

Finally, the *Corpus Iuris* is composed of the literal words of valid laws, adding or subtracting nothing from them.[11] The *Corpus Iuris* presents valid *ius* according to the order and reasons of the elements and the nuclei from which it comes, so that "all laws *(leges)* are brought forth as conclusions, under their principles, and namely all *leges* . . . bring forth and are derived from a positive rule in the table of elements, on which they depend."[12] For the *Corpus Iuris* to conform to the clarity of the elements of natural and civil law, the Roman laws would have to be pared of extraneous, contradictory, and anachronistic passages and reordered in a more rational and systematic way under, as Leibniz suggests, nine general titles.[13]

Of the four parts of his proposed code, Leibniz clearly understands the work on the first and second parts—the *Elementa Iuris Naturalis* and *Elementa Iuris Civilis*—to be the most important and the most revolutionary. Writing to Ferrand, he concludes his account of the four sections of the code with a declaration of propriety concerning the elements: "I declare as my own the elements of natural law and the table of elements of the common law, while I am the assistant to Lasser in the "Nucleus of Laws" and the "Body of Laws."[14] While Leibniz considered the painstaking work of ordering the valid laws of the *Corpus Iuris* to be important, he understood that his work on the "Elements of Law" was what would distinguish his codification attempt from those of both his contemporaries and the ancients.

The work on the elements of natural and civil *ius* form the heart of Leibniz's early work in Mainz. Although his later codification efforts in

Hannover from 1678 to 1682 and then again in the 1690s would abandon the explicit thematization of the elements of *ius*, these elements continued to guide Leibniz's search for a general science of *ius*; the elements of *ius* remained essential for Leibniz's scientific effort to know *ius* as universally true and eternally certain. A deeper understanding of how Leibniz thought the elements of *ius* could transform jurisprudence, therefore, is an important first step in the inquiry into the Leibnizian grasp of *ius* as a product of science.

The Elements of *Ius*

Leibniz's approach to the elements of *ius* begins with the presumption that all science, in the spirit of Descartes, must be reducible to the certainty that predominates in arithmetic and geometry. His additional metaphysical insight is that every being is comprised of wholes (that is, unities) that in turn can be broken up into parts—smaller wholes, as it were. As a whole, every entity is one thing. Number, therefore, is a metaphysical property of being. Number itself is "something of [the] greatest universality," and thus, number—and with that all of mathematics—"rightly belongs to metaphysics, if you take metaphysics to be the science of those properties that are common to all classes of beings."[15] Number, as a quality of being, is grounded in the science of being, namely metaphysics.

Not only are number and thus mathematics grounded in metaphysics, but number also provides a model for metaphysics. Since number and oneness can be broken up with mathematical certainty into smaller wholes, and since being is numerical, mathematics offers the possibility for thinking about being through relations that can be measured and tested. Mathematics, in other words, can be applied to the science of being in ways that provide a level of certainty usually absent from traditionally inexact metaphysical speculations. Not only metaphysics but also every scientific discipline, insofar as it concerns relations of quantity among beings, can be illuminated by number, or "to speak accurately, mathematics."[16]

In perceiving the metaphysical basis of mathematics, Leibniz senses that the same certainty and universality that has allowed arithmeticians and geometers to deduce innumerable theorems from a set of axiomatic definitions, and natural scientists to deduce laws of physics, could be even more usefully employed in the metaphysical and legal realms. The scientific revolution of the sixteenth and seventeenth centuries granted man power over his world. The seas were being tamed, uniting once foreign lands, and the secrets of the heavens had been revealed, disclosing "to us new worlds and new species." Writing and history had defeated human mortality with paper monuments "more enduring than bronze" by which geniuses could guarantee the "eternity of fame." But although human will had achieved previously unforeseen powers that had elevated men to be "conquerors of the world," Leibniz laments that "everything remains clear to man but man." While science has revealed to man the true secrets of the mechanical and physical world, "we have not drunk from the true springs of equity and of good."[17]

The successful pursuit of happiness is possible only on the basis of a science of divine and human justice. "Since happiness consists in peace of mind," which comes, Leibniz argues, only with clear and distinct knowledge—that is, scientific knowledge—of the nature of God and the human soul, "it follows that science is necessary for happiness."[18] Human happiness *(felicitas)*, Leibniz writes in the "Elements of Natural Law," consists of two things: first, the power to actualize one's will, and second, the knowledge of what one ought to will.[19] The proposed elements of *ius* "suffice to sow the seeds of that science which shows how individuals should give way to the good of all if they wish happiness to revert to themselves, increased as by rebound."[20] By making knowledge of *ius* certain and easy—by presenting *ius* clearly, briefly, and sufficiently—the elements of *ius* and the legal code lay the ground for a world in which peace, justice, and piety might reign.

What Leibniz sought to actualize in his lifelong struggle to fashion a code was something altogether original, a work that "until now has never been attempted, let alone completed."[21] This is true despite Leibniz's choice of the genre of the *codex*, a legal form with an impressive and ancient lineage. By selecting from the manifold of often contradictory and unclear laws, and by establishing a new and limited legal universe, historical codifiers—from Solon and Justinian to Gratian and Emperor Friedrich II—strove to reverse the feared descent from polyarchy into anarchy. Past codifications of law sought to solve the evils of legal uncertainty by building an artificial dam with a book of laws. "So it seemed to wise men long ago," Leibniz writes, that the untamable mass of laws required mastery "with a better hand, which could not be better achieved than with the establishment of a new *codex*."[22]

But past codes had always proven mere temporary bulwarks, Leibniz argues, not least because they lacked an elemental method that could guarantee their comprehensiveness. Historical codifications, he complains, tended to return to the same uncontrollable girth as the legal regimes they were supposed to simplify. New laws inevitably were needed to address unanticipated events—Justinian and his followers appended the *Novellae* to the Digests, just as early modern glossators and commentators made room for local customs and imperial and royal statutes. The history of legal codification is littered with failures.

What is demanded, then, is a new approach to law, one that proceeds neither from tradition nor from the authority of willful positing, but rather that proceeds scientifically from the elements of law. Such a scientific remedy for the uncertainty of right and law, Leibniz says, had never before truly been attempted, countless reform and codification efforts over 500 years of scholastic legal history notwithstanding. "We have so many methods," he notes, but none of these methods had tried, let alone succeeded, in discovering the principles—the grounds and reasons—on which right and positive right depend. There is not one existing method, he writes,

> that might lead to the way in which every *lex*, proposition, decision or consequence would be brought under its ground and reason [*Grund und ratio*], out of which it flows, since such is the only way to separate as through a telescope the equally bountiful rays and therefore to arrive clearly at the core.[23]

The radical task Leibniz proposes as a remedy for the shortcoming of past codes will "make *ius* certain from uncertainty and finite from infinity."[24] Each positive law is to be brought under its *Grund und ratio* and traced back to a universal element of natural or of civil law.[25] Like a telescope that looks past a ray of light and focuses instead on its source, the jurist too must gaze past the individual *leges* to seek their foundational principles. Instead of the mass of laws, therefore, the scientific method of jurisprudence focuses instead on the principles of *ius*, or what Leibniz, following Euclid, names the elements of law.

The *Ars Combinatoria* and the Elemental Method of Law

The analogy between legal and geometric elements harbors a fundamental ambivalence regarding the application of the elemental method. Leibniz often writes as if the importance of the elemental method lay in its combinatorial or synthetic capacities—the practice of constructing complex propositions out of fundamental elements. Leibniz's clearest defense of such a synthetic use of the elements is found in his philosophical dissertation, the *Ars Combinatoria* (1666).[26]

The combinatorial art *(ars combinatoria)* is Leibniz's solution to the ancient jurisprudential problem, previously raised by Plato and Aristotle, of how to provide a state with "the best possible laws without defects, from the first."[27] The problem concerns judicial discretion. Since judges, either out of ignorance or corruption, cannot be counted on to interpret laws rightly and consistently, Leibniz considers it incontestable that "in any state whatsoever, a judicial matter is the better treated, the less is left to the decision of the judge."[28] One promise of Leibniz's *ars combinatoria* is to overcome the shortcoming of legislation—the gaps that are filled by judicial discretion.

In the *Ars Combinatoria,* Leibniz gives full scope to his earliest and most exhaustive jurisprudential ambition: the synthetic deduction of the entirety of legal rules out of a set of first principles, or legal elements. Although Leibniz will later abandon the synthetic approach to law, the effort to understand what he came to consider his youthful mistake is worthwhile. This is true not simply because it clarifies Leibniz's own intellectual development. More importantly, exploring the *Ars Combinatoria* exposes the erroneous belief in a deductive legal science based on the synthesis of laws from first principles, a belief that has proven irresistible to numerous legal thinkers since Leibniz, both youthful and mature.

The *Ars Combinatoria* contains the original kernel of Leibniz's elemental method and also of his later monadology. In it, he expresses his core belief: that ethical and metaphysical problems can be investigated with the same certainty as problems of mathematics and physical science. This is not simply an assertion; Leibniz grounds his claim in a provable theorem. The theorem at the heart of the *Ars Combinatoria* is a formula for the calculus of combinations—what Leibniz calls complexions—so that given a determinate set of terms, one can calculate how many different combinations of pairs, triads, and so forth of subsets of the terms can be created. Assuming five terms (e.g., five fruits: apple [a], banana [b], cantaloupe [c], durian [d], and eggplant [e]) calculated in complexions of triads (three fruits together), there would be ten possible combinations of those fruits in groups of three: namely, abc, acd, ade, bcd, bde, bea, cde, cea, dea, eab. Similarly, given five numbers (1, 2, 3, 4, 5) calculated in complexions of triads (three numbers in a series), there would be ten possible combinations. Leibniz expresses this conclusion in a combinatorial equation:

> 5/3 = 4/3 (123, 124, 134, 234) + 4/2 (12, 13, 14, 23, 24, 34) = 10.[29]

This equation is not as formidable as it seems, and it can be translated as such:

> The complexion (i.e., combinatorial possibilities) of 5 terms with the exponent 3 (i.e., into groups of 3) equals the sum of the complexion of 4 terms with the exponent 3 (i.e., 4) plus the complexion of 4 terms with the exponent 2 (i.e., 6) equals 10.

The rule is that the complexions of a certain number and its exponent (e.g., 5 with the exponent 3) arise from the sum of the complexions of the preceding number (i.e., 4 in the above example) with the same exponent (i.e., 3) and with the preceding exponent (i.e., 2). Consequently, the number of possible complexions of 5 terms with the exponent 3 is discovered by adding the complexions of 4 terms with the exponent 3 (i.e., 4) and with the exponent 2 (i.e., 6).

The development of an *ars combinatoria* not only represents an important precursor to Leibniz's codiscovery with Newton of differential calculus, but also has practical applications beyond mathematics. Given Leibniz's juristic training, it is not surprising that in his dissertation, while discussing instances of the use of the combinatorial method, he illustrates its usefulness with several jurisprudential examples.

In one of these, Leibniz demonstrates the purported usefulness of the combinatorial method with the example of the Roman contractual mandate.[30] A mandate is a kind of consensual contract in which one party gives to the other without remuneration some thing or some right that the other can exercise—for example, I can give you a sum of money,

The Force of Law: Will   37

and we can agree to a mandate that you will take that money, invest it, and return to me the principal and a return at a fixed rate. The Roman jurist Gaius claimed that the mandate contract could be analyzed in five ways: (1) in favor of the mandator (the giver of the mandate), (2) in favor of both the mandator and the mandatory (the receiver of the mandate), (3) in favor of a third person, (4) in favor of the mandator and a third person, or (5) in favor of the mandatory and a third person. If the mandate is exclusively in the interest of the mandatory, a sixth possibility that is similar to the Anglo-American common law doctrine of illusory promise, then the mandate is superfluous and cannot give rise to an obligation.[31]

Gaius's division can be checked, Leibniz suggests, through the *ars combinatoria*. Given the three interested parties (the mandator, the mandatory, and the third party), there are seven possible complexions of advantaged parties. These include, in addition to the six mentioned by Gaius, a mandate in favor of the mandator, the mandatory, and the third party. Since Gaius explicitly rejects the sixth possibility—and rightly so, Leibniz reasons, because there is no obligation there—there is a question as to why the seventh possibility, of a mandate in favor of all three parties, is ignored. Leibniz writes that he does not know, expressing his suspicion that Gaius simply overlooked the possibility of such a mandate. The omission, he suggests, was a mistake that an analysis according to the *ars combinatoria* would have avoided. To achieve more certain lawmaking, therefore, Leibniz recommends his combinatorial method to legislators as a tool that will allow the infallible calculation of all possible future legal cases.

What, if anything, is gained in this particular application of the *ars combinatoria* is highly questionable. Though Leibniz's method of discovering the missing seventh case was novel, he was not the first jurist to have noticed its absence. The late twelfth-century glossator, Johannes Bassianus, famous for his *Arbor actionum*, or "law tree," had made the same discovery simply by listing the various forms of the mandate. More significantly, the missing seventh case, in which all three participants benefit, may be logically important, but its legal significance is understandably left unremarked on by Leibniz. It may be, as Gerhard Otte has remarked, that the passing over of the seventh case ought to be seen as a strength rather than a weakness of Gaius's analysis.[32]

Leibniz, however, argues that the simple analysis of the mandate illustrates that the combinatorial method is valid for the more involved analysis of legislation in general. The *ars combinatoria*, he writes, allows the wise legislator to posit laws comprehensively in a way that leaves no room for judicial discretion. Indeed, from out of simple concepts—that is, elements—the jurist, like the geometer, can calculate a determinate number of complexions or cases of combination: "For as jurisprudence is similar to geometry in other things, it is also similar in that both have elements and both have cases. The elements are simples; in geometry, figures, a triangle, circle, etc.; in jurisprudence, an action, a promise, a sale, etc. Cases are complexions of these, which are infinitely variable in either field."[33] From the given geometric elements or simples *(simplicia)* arise a determinate number of combinatorial theorems. Similarly, from the elements of law, it ought to be possible to determine all possible legal cases (past and future) by deduction.

Jurisprudence, therefore, can be envisioned as a combinatorial "art of forming complex cases" from simple terms, an *"ars casuum formandorum."*[34] Once this elemental core of the body of law is discovered, one could, in an emergency, do without the laws themselves. Through the combination of the elements of *ius*, one could solve all cases that arise in accord with the common Roman law.[35] Thus the elements are the heart and soul of *ius*, and "contain the very soul of jurisprudence."[36] From the elements alone, Leibniz writes, all law can be logically and clearly derived out of the inner core, and all possible conflicts can be resolved without difficulty in full accord with the natural and positive Roman law.[37]

The Limitations of the Elemental Method

Leibniz's optimistic endorsement of the *ars combinatoria* as a synthetic art for the forming of laws from their simple elements is nevertheless tempered by nagging doubts. As powerful as the *ars combinatoria* may be as a means for the calculation of all possible legal actions, it is plagued, as Leibniz himself recognizes, by two serious limitations.[39]

One difficulty involves the potential multiplication of simple elements and consequently the production of an infinite number of possible cases that would render human comprehension of the whole virtually impossible. Leibniz is aware that other simple legal terms beyond his proposed four (person, object, *actio*, and *ius*) are possible. With a bit of effort and diligence, one might, as Bernardus de Lavintheta did in his *Ars Magna* of 1523, seek to list all of the conceivable simple terms of jurisprudence.[39] In addition to the person, thing, act, and right, Leibniz suggests an extraordinary list of simple terms that he admits might be expanded by the industry and attention of the reader. Within the simple term "person," for example, exist other simples, including man, woman, twin, monster, blind man, mute, invalid, embryo, child, youth, young man, man, and elder. There are also artificial persons, like corporations and *collegia*. Among things, there are movable and unmovable, divisible and indivisible, and corporeal and incorporeal. Particular things include animals (tame, wild, predatory, dangerous, etc.), horses, water, land, and even slaves. Actions include tenure, transfer, theft, violence, murder, and injury. Finally, concepts of law *(iura)* include rights in things *(in rem)* and rights based in persons *(in personam)*, as well as pure rights, delayed rights, and rights that are transferable. The list may even be extended. Leibniz cautions that one must take care when making the list of simple legal terms that the terms are truly simple—that is, they must not be formed through the combination of other simple terms.[40] Nevertheless, the number of simple terms that are conceivably part of the civil law is ultimately infinite, as are the possible combinations that arise from them.

The determination of a closed set of simple terms in jurisprudence is, as Leibniz at times acknowledges, at the least extremely difficult and likely humanly impossible. While there must be a first concept, only God can perceive all the intricate connections through which the entirety of jurisprudence proceeds out of a single concept.[41] The analysis of a synthetic jurisprudence in its fullness simply exceeds human capacity.[42]

Leibniz heroically attempts to deduce all jurisprudential propositions out of his fundamental definitions of justice—*iustitia est caritas sapientis* and *iustitia est habitus amandi omnibus*. These seductively simple principles of justice—"justice is the charity of the wise," and "justice is the habit of loving all things"—lure Leibniz into a labyrinth with no exit. From these definitions, he deduces the elements of justice: *sapientis* (wisdom), *caritas* (charity), *amare* (love), *felicitas* (happiness), *status* (status), *accidens* (accident), *praedicatum* (predication), *nomen* (noun), *optimum* (best), *bonum* (good), and *pernoscere* (knowledge); he combines these with the juridical modalities—*justum* (justice), *licitum* (legality), *illicitum* (illegality), *debitum* (obligation), and *indebitem* (non-obligation).[43] Leibniz calculates, in one fragment of the proposed *Elementa Juris Naturalis* from 1671, that from the elements contained in the first definition of justice, 1,485,600 combinations could be formed.[44] Even if one were to limit oneself to the most fundamental elements of natural law, as Leibniz assiduously attempted in numerous sketches and tables he worked out in the early 1670s, the fact remains that the application of the combinatorial art to jurisprudence simply produces too many cases.

The second difficulty concerns the problem of judgment. As the example of the mandate makes clear, the *ars combinatoria* alone is unable to discriminate between relevant and irrelevant combinations. In order to exclude from the code the sixth and seventh possibilities—the complexion to the advantage of the mandatory alone and that in favor of all three parties—a principle of selection beyond the mere calculation of the *ars combinatoria* is essential. Therefore, in particular disciplines—for example, jurisprudence—Leibniz is aware that the means of finding the useful and nonuseful rules formed from the elements depend on a presupposed scientific understanding of the discipline as a whole and not on the *ars combinatoria* itself.[45] Since judgment requires a knowing of the reasons behind the rules in order to select from the universe of possible rules, legislation cannot be reduced to a mere geometrical combination of simple terms.

It is because of the necessary incompleteness of the elemental legal method, Leibniz argues, that the Roman jurist Ulpian called jurisprudence "the science of divine and human things."[46] The knowing of law demands more than merely empirical or purely logical knowledge. Indeed, jurisprudence requires the scientific unification of man with the divinely rational world. "Without this preceding philosophical insight," Leibniz writes, "neither would jurists exist, nor could the scientific knowledge of justice and injustice be gained."[47] While both experience and geometry contribute to jurisprudence, the use of elements in the combinatorial method must incorporate a prior philosophical insight.

Leibniz points to the Roman jurists preserved in the Digests of Roman law as masters of philosophical legal insight. The Roman lawyers compare favorably with Euclid and Descartes because their many rules and utterances proceed as if from a single philosophical insight into the source of justice. The reasoning in the Digests is so insightful into the true nature of law that "one would have great difficulty telling [the Roman jurists] apart if their names did not head the selections; just as it would be hard to distinguish Euclid, Archimedes and Apollonius by reading their demonstrations about matters with which they all dealt."[48] Leibniz praises the Roman jurists because their judicial decisions manifest an insight into the coherence of justice beyond mathematics and any version of the elemental method.

Even as a youth, Leibniz sought to supplement the logical, mathematical method of elemental jurisprudence with the wisdom of the Romans:

> This is how it is then: All people now are working in competition on a law of nature to be passed down: and we lack clear demonstrations besides the few things of Aristotle and of Hobbes. The neglect of the old Roman Jurisconsulates spreads by degrees, but whoever still understands them will admit with me, I think, that there exists now no book in which more things concerning natural law have been demonstrated with greater elegance and clarity (for those who understand an erudite diction and old things). So that I believe neither Euclid nor Descartes, if they had applied themselves to this discipline, could have written more perfectly than either Ulpian or Papinian: So that whoever hopes to be a jurisconsult of the natural law and the law of persons without having read these things or understood them—he would have wandered far from the gate.[49]

What Leibniz saw in the Roman laws and in the profound insights of Ulpian, Papinian, and Paul was a scientific and philosophical method, one that recognized that the elemental and combinatorial method alone would never yield justice. In setting philosophy and jurisprudence above combinatorial geometry, Leibniz consciously distances his work from prior legal thinking and recognizes that "the considerations that I here set forth contribute to the contempt of philosophy by jurists, when they see how many instances of their 'ius' would be an unwieldy labyrinth without the guidance of philosophy."[50]

Nevertheless, as brilliant as the Roman jurists' philosophical insight was and as nearly as it approached scientific demonstration,[51] Leibniz is convinced that insight alone cannot yield the clarity and distinctness of knowledge that true thinking demands. If Leibniz's geometric and combinatorial method lacks the power of insight, the insight of the Romans is diminished by the absence of logical method and demonstrative certainty. Leibniz came to recognize that neither insight nor mathematical science offers a properly practical and scientific knowing of justice.

From Elements to Monads: Leibniz's Forceful Rethinking of Substance

Although Leibniz never fully abandoned his interest in an *ars combinatoria*, the purely combinatorial paradigm that dominated his early jurisprudential search for the elements of *ius* was gradually subsumed by his emerging systematic philosophy. The combinatorial art must aim not simply to produce an infinity of combinations, but rather to build a system of concepts founded on the insightful and true definitions of *ius* and *iustitia*. The actual usefulness of the *ars combinatoria*, therefore, is not to be sought in the synthetic art of forming cases from elements, but rather in the systematic ordering of legal concepts under the fundamental concept of justice, philosophically and scientifically understood. The elements of law are not abandoned in this shift but transformed; instead of analogizing the elements to geometrical ideas, Leibniz comes to see them as substantial forms.

Substantial forms, or monads, play a central role in Leibniz's jurisprudence. They are the first and essential building blocks not only of his system of knowledge, but also of his system of law. The monads are the simple and "true atoms of nature; in a word, they are the elements of things."[52] The shift from geometrical elements to monads is the crucial step in Leibniz's attempt to build a universal science from simple substances.

Leibniz's monadology is rightly, albeit rarely, understood as a continuation of his early interest in geometric elements and the *ars combinatoria*. While geometric laws continue to hold sway in explaining movement in the physical world, Leibniz's monads are governed by metaphysical laws of reason: "And we do in fact observe that everything in the world takes place in accordance with the laws of eternal truths and not merely geometric but also metaphysical laws; that is, not merely according to material but also according to formal reasons."[53] While the material, phenomenal, and extended world of space and time continues to obey geometric laws, the intellectual and moral worlds of monads are governed by the formal laws of reason. What is more, the metaphysical laws predominate over geometric laws; therefore, Leibniz concludes, "I was at length compelled to give up the law of geometric composition of inclinations *(conatuses)* which I had formerly defended when, as a youth, I was more materialistic."[54] The search for the universal principles of *ius* requires that jurisprudence transcend the geometrical analysis and synthesis of given laws; jurisprudence, Leibniz insists, must become a philosophical science.

Leibniz's critique of the geometric paradigm—and his turn to philosophical insight in jurisprudence—has important and enlightening parallels in his critique of the geometric paradigm in the natural sciences. The critical engagement with the geometric paradigm arises out of Leibniz's attempted solution to one of the oldest and greatest philosophical problems—namely, the nature of substance. Descartes famously and influentially defined body as absolute extension and mind as absolute reason but had struggled unsuccessfully to explain how the body can cause anything to occur in the soul or vice versa. Though Descartes, according to Leibniz, abandoned the search for a solution to this problem, his disciples sought to provide an answer with the system of occasional causes, otherwise known as the *deus ex machina*. Accordingly, the Cartesians believed that we sense qualities in bodies not as a result of the body's impression on us, but because "God causes thoughts to arise in our soul on the occasion of material movements." Similarly, when our rational soul wishes to move or influence material beings that are pure extension and thus deaf to our rational entreaties, God steps in and moves the body in accordance with the soul.[55]

Against Descartes' radical separation between body and mind, Leibniz argues that either a purely mechanical or geometric world has no beginning, which he believes is absurd, or there must be some non-physical cause inherent within each and every being. Since science demands a universal and true knowledge of its objects, the scientific method must presuppose a necessarily metaphysical conception of substance:

> *There are indivisibles or unextended beings*, for otherwise we could conceive neither the beginning nor the end of motion or body. The proof of this is as follows. There is a beginning and an end to any given space, body,

motion, and time. Let that whose beginning is sought be represented by the line *ab,* whose middle point is *c,* and let the middle point of *ac* be *d,* that of *ad* be *e,* and so on. Let the beginning be sought at the left end, at *a.* I say that *ac* is not the beginning, because *cd* can be taken from it without destroying the beginning; nor is it *ad,* because *ed* can be taken away, and so forth. So nothing is a beginning from which something on the right can be removed. But that from which nothing extended can be removed is unextended. Therefore the beginning of body, space, motion, or time—namely, a point, conatus, or instant—is either nothing which is absurd, or unextended, which was to be demonstrated.[56]

$$a \ldots e \ldots d \ldots c \ldots b$$

In this elegant and early proof, Leibniz expresses an idea that remained at the heart of his thinking throughout his life, a thought that has extraordinary importance not only in mechanics but also in metaphysics and jurisprudence. If motion and change are possible, the beginning of motion and change cannot be found among the aggregate of extended substances.

What holds for motion and change also holds for all things in the world and even for the world itself, because "a sufficient reason for existence cannot be found merely in any one individual thing or even in the whole aggregate and series of things."[57] Leibniz illustrates this point with the example of Euclid's *Elements of Geometry,* an example that reveals Leibniz's own dissatisfaction with the combinatorial method.

> Let us imagine the book on the *Elements of Geometry* to have been eternal, one copy always being made from another; then it is clear that though we can give a reason for the present book based on the preceding book from which it was copied, we can never arrive at a complete reason, no matter how many books we may assume in the past, for one can always wonder why such books should have existed at all times; why there should be books at all, and why they should be written in this way. What is true of books is true also of the different states of the world; every subsequent state is somehow copied from the preceding one (although according to certain laws of change). No matter how far we may have gone back to earlier states, therefore, we will

never discover in them a full reason why there should be a world at all, and why it should be such as it is.[58]

In all contingent or changing things, by which Leibniz means both objects of the natural and human sciences, there must be reasons for the existence of the objects outside of the series of objective things themselves. Every thing, insofar as it is, must have a formal—that is, non-physical—reason from which it proceeds. Within a substance, there must be a non-physical force, "something related to souls, which is commonly called a substantial form."[59] The formal reason for a thing is not the mere cause of the thing; the monad is not, therefore, simply a Spinozist unity.[60] Rather, the formal monad is the forceful source of all action. *Actio sine vi agendi esse non potest*;[61] Every thing has an active force from which it is driven to act out of itself.

Ius and the Force of Justice

The introduction of force—in Latin, *vis;* in French, *la force;* and in German, *die Kraft*—is central for an understanding of "the true concept of *substance,*" or being, as well as for Leibniz's jurisprudence.[62] There is, Leibniz concludes, something in the nature of every substance that cannot be determined and explained through mere physics and math, but that can be fully known only when its higher, non-physical determinative laws are understood. Those parts of substance that are beyond the physical world (that is, meta-physical) are what Leibniz calls "forces." Force is the unifying power, that "real unity" from which a multitude can derive its unity. Within seventeenth-century philosophy, the immediate importance of this distinction is the correction of the Cartesian error in the understanding of the relation and connection among physical and mental substances. Against the mechanical separation of intellect and body that characterized the Cartesian and Spinozist universes, Leibniz maintains that every body is a living body (a *leib* as against a *körper*).[63] Motion is not merely a mechanical or extensive property, but has an intelligible force that is the indestructible and indivisible point of beginning and end of every being.

The reconceptualization of substance as force in the natural sciences is an essential part of Leibniz's jurisprudential philosophy as well. The science of *ius* must investigate not merely the existing *ius* in a society, but also the principles of *ius*, "or what is the same thing," the "first reasons of justice."⁶⁴ All *ius* that is and that may be has a reason and ground in the principles of natural justice. *Ius* arises not simply from geometric elements but from the rational and substantial forms—that is, forces—that are the metaphysical fundament of all beings. The effort to know *ius* is the scientific inquiry into the formal forces of justice: "Jurisprudence is, then, the science of what is just," and takes as its object the "force *(vis)* of justice."⁶⁵

The identification of *ius* with the force of justice *(vis)* is, admittedly, rarely made explicit in Leibniz's writings. Leibniz hesitated to transfer his new metaphysical vocabulary into the tradition-bound legal world. For whatever reasons, at least in his published writings, he continued to characterize *ius* not as a force, but rather as a juridical power *(potentia)*. Indeed, Leibniz defines *ius* consistently throughout his writing as *potentia*—*ius*, he writes, is a specifically "moral power."⁶⁶ Or, as he formulates the same thought in the preface to the *Codex Iuris Gentium*, *ius* is a moral power of doing what is just.⁶⁷

Potentia—translated here as power—was employed throughout scholastic Aristotelian writings in a double sense. First, the potential power of the medieval scholastics was little more than a *propinqua*, a near-possibility of acting, yet one that depended on an "external excitation or a stimulus" in order to be transformed into action.⁶⁸ Second, active power was the simple faculty to act;⁶⁹ it can be described as the power or possibility of causing change in contrast to the act itself. Both potential and active power, as faculties, exist only as possibilities. They point, therefore, to the essence of things (potential power) and to the possible actualization of the essence of things (active power), but not to the reality of the thing itself.⁷⁰

The scholastics understood being *(esse)* as existence and believed that real things *(res)* or real rights *(ius)* are the real foundations for what is possible but does not yet exist. Like the Megarians Aristotle discusses in Book Theta of his *Metaphysics*, the scholastics conceived of a power as a faculty or possibility that is contrary to reality and thus nonexistent. Since a power or a possibility for action only exists in the actualization or enactment of itself—for example, since one's faculty for house building only exists when one is building a house—the scholastics and

Megarians argued that the power or faculty for house building does not exist at all, except in the act of building.[71] The power itself has no real existence; it only exists insofar as it is in action.

While Leibniz adopts the scholastic and juristic vocabulary of power *(potentia)* as possibility, he follows Aristotle in adapting the traditional terminology to his own purposes. Aristotle had objected to the Megarian claim that if a builder has the power or faculty for building and yet the faculty for building does not exist except when it is actualized, then it would be impossible for builders to exist except when they are building. This, Aristotle argues, is absurd: builders do not simply lose their faculty for building when they stop building. Further, if no builders exist when they are not building, there is no way that the art of building in general could be taught.[72] The power or faculty of building, Aristotle argues, must not be lost simply by one's ceasing to build; rather, the specific faculty of building must exist as something one *has*. The being of a power to act, Aristotle writes, is a having *(echein)*.

If a power to act exists as a having,[73] then the mere act of stopping from acting or building does not result in the loss or disappearance of that power.[74] More importantly, a power to act is—as a learning that is possessed—a faculty that at any time can be actualized; as a "having been learned," the having of a knowledgeable skill is always present and thus exists as a power. It is in this sense, following Aristotle, that Leibniz's *potentia* is active.

Against the scholastics, Leibniz's invocation of *potentia* is undertaken as a contrast, a foil to distinguish his own understanding of *potentia* as an active force. Active force is neither empty possibility nor pure act, but "contains a certain act or entelechy *(entelecheia)* and is thus midway between the faculty of acting and the act itself and involves a *conatus* [the word for "force" in Leibniz's early writing]."[75] The Greek word *entelecheia* means to have one's end—one's *telos*—in oneself. An *entelechy*, active force has its end *(telos)* in itself. "This can be illustrated," Leibniz writes,

> by the example of a heavy hanging body which strains at the rope which holds it or by a bent bow. For though gravity and elasticity can and ought to be explained mechanically by the motion of the ether, the ultimate reason for motion in matter is nevertheless the force impressed upon it in creation ... I say that this force of acting [*agendi virtutem*]

inheres in all substance [*omni substantiae inesse*] and that some action always arises from it, so that the corporeal substance itself does not, any more than spiritual substance, ever cease to act [*adeoque nec ipsam substantiam corpoream (non magis quam spirtualem) ab agendo cessare unquam*].[76]

Every being has this forceful character, a drive forward from out of itself, for which Leibniz reserves the word "force."[77] That every being has "its own pre-existent striving or power of action,"[78] means that every being is governed by an original force, which Leibniz calls the monad. Since every monad has its own perfection and forceful principle of development in itself, the monad has a certain self-sufficiency. That every monad develops according to its own internal force is the prerequisite for Leibniz's famous claim that the monad has no windows.[79] Against Descartes' assertion that the essence of bodies lies in extension, Leibniz concludes that every being has its essence in active force, or a monad.

Moving from metaphysics to jurisprudence, it is clear that Leibniz approaches law as a forceful object. *Ius*, therefore, is at once that which, as a *potentia*, exists as a subjective right *(ius)* or power to act and which, as a *potentia activa* or force *(vis)*, is the formal and forceful origin of the act itself—what "has been learned or acquired." *Ius*, in other words, harbors within itself its essential and active force of justice.[80]

However, the definition of *ius* as a moral *potentia activa* or force harbors a fundamental ambiguity characteristic of Leibniz's move from a geometrical *ars combinatoria* to a scientific system of *ius*. As will be seen in the discussion of his *Systema Iuris* in the following chapter, *ius* itself has a double presence within the Leibnizian system, both as the subjective force of rights and as the active force of justice that is the ultimate genesis of subjective *ius* itself. Despite this ambiguity, Leibniz will insist that the forceful origin of *ius* has metaphysical and legal priority over the subjective force of rights.

While jurisprudence, as the science of *ius*, does address its elements—now comprehended as forces—it does so not with the aim of attaining a geometrically complete list of all possible juridical combinations; rather, the science of *ius* seeks to know *ius* as a systematic philosophic doctrine. The effort to know the entirety of *ius* with certainty is not abandoned but transformed into a scientific project guided not simply by elemental terms but also by moral forces. The geometrical combination of elements itself is possible only within a system of *ius* guided by the science of justice.

The Principle of Sufficient Reason and the Willful Essence of Law

That *ius* is the force of justice is a consequence of Leibniz's metaphysical reconceptualization of substance as force. As a forceful substance, law too must, as Leibniz insists it must, follow internal laws of development. Law has, Leibniz sees, its end already in itself. And this end or *telos* is what he calls the force of justice.

In that law is, in its essence, a forceful and willful striving for justice, every law is simply an expression of the force of justice that exists at its core and enlivens it from within. Even positive law must be nothing but the external manifestation of an original force of justice. That is why the system of *ius* described by Leibniz combines the entirety of *ius*, both natural and positive, into a single *Jurisprudentia universalis*. The universal science of *ius*, therefore, has two parts. First, the "scientific knowledge of the natural law," and second, the "experiential knowing of the positive law."[81]

If natural law concerns the real or possible world, positive law is the *ius* that actually exists in a society. "Positive law," Leibniz writes, is disclosed in experience *(perita)* and "is a fact rather than *ius*." It is *lex* set out as a *lex posita* by the needs of the state *(notitia rerumpublicarum)* as a vulgar law *(vulgò Ius publicum)*.[82] Despite their different realms, a definite harmony ought to exist between natural and positive law. The two sciences of *ius* stand in close relation, embraced by the characterization of the science of arbitrary law *(scientia juris arbitrarii)* as that which gathers together *(conferre)* the existing laws and everyday court actions and joins them into a unity with the laws of the best republic.[83]

By the principle of sufficient reason, existing law must have a reason why it is rather than why it is not. For the existing positive *iura*, out of all the possible *iura* in the real world, to have been actualized specifically through God's will, there must be a sufficient reason—namely the wisdom and power of God. Since "this sufficient reason for the existence of the universe cannot be found in the series of contingent things," it must be "outside of this series of contingent things and is found in a substance which is the cause of this series or which is a necessary being bearing the reason for its existence within itself; otherwise we should not yet have a sufficient reason with which to stop. This final reason for things is called *God*."[84] Behind the need of positive law for a ground and reason stands the "noblest of all" metaphysical principles: *Nihil est sine ratione*.[85]

The principle of sufficient reason and the formal forces it necessitates are the keys to Leibniz's systematic philosophy. Since all that exists in the world must proceed from one beginning, the totality of beings must form a unified system that has as its beginning and end the all-encompassing creative power, intellectual wisdom, and will of a single omnipotent being. The first sufficient reason of the natural as well as the ethical worlds is the rational will of God.

The very limitation that experience places on our knowledge is the source of Leibniz's optimism. That no sufficient reason exists in the realm of sensible things is proof that there must be a prior cause outside this realm, namely a metaphysical ground on which all things in the world rest and on which a certain and universal science of *ius* might be constructed:

> It follows from the supreme perfection of God that He has chosen the best possible plan in producing the universe, a plan which combines the greatest variety together with the greatest order; . . . For as all possible things have a claim to existence in God's understanding in proportion to their perfection, the result of all these claims must be the most perfect actual world which is possible. Without this it would be impossible to give a reason why things have gone as they have rather than otherwise.[86]

The forceful initiation of the actual world in God's will is the free, and thus rational, cause of all that exists. God is not brought in by Leibniz as *Deus ex machina* but rather as an actual being that is the first and formal cause of the system of the actual world. "We therefore have the ultimate reason for the reality of essences as well as existences in one being . . . [and] not only the existing things which compose the world but also all possibilities have their reality through it. But because of the interconnection of all these things, this ultimate reason can be found only in a single source."[87] God's rational and thus, in principle, also knowable will is the guarantor of the scientific system, the ultimate ground that provides the sufficient reason for the possibility and the existence of all things and of all *ius*.

The force of the *principium rationis* works in both natural and positive law. In natural law, the principle of sufficient reason guarantees the possibility of justice. Even more important, however, is that the principle of sufficient reason works to justify positive law as well. If nothing is without a reason, then every positive law—no matter how evil or inexplicable it may seem—also has its sufficent ground. Leibniz already recognized the fatalist force of the principle of sufficient reason in his *Studies in Physics and the Nature of Body* from 1671: "That *there is nothing without a reason*. The consequences of this principle are that as little as possible should be changed, that the mean is to be chosen between contraries, that *whatever* is added to one thing need not even be subtracted from another, and many other things that are important in *civil science* as well."[88] The need to justify the existing world as God's creation necessarily privileges God's freedom over human freedom and universal justice over worldly justice as the standards and measures of human will.

Leibniz's introduction of the principle of sufficient reason into jurisprudence promised to give law the scientific grounds for its authority that it so dearly desires. The gift of scientific justification, however, brought with it unintended consequences. The principle of sufficient reason is a metaphysical thesis concerning things and how they exist. The principle says that nothing is without a reason. Stated affirmatively, it says that every thing that is has a reason. In one of his most important formulations of the principle of reason, Leibniz names it the "principle of giving back reasons" *(principium reddendae rationis)*.[89] Since nothing exists without a reason, nothing exists unless reasons are given for it. All things, therefore, only exist insofar as they have a reason. Similarly, law too must have a reason posited for it if it is to exist. Law, in other words, does not exist in and of itself as a natural or traditional insight into what is right and fitting. A custom may develop or a statute may be announced, but the custom and the statute are only valid law insofar as they are justified.

The result of Leibniz's scientific understanding of law is that law is subordinated to its reasons and justifications. Law is thereby freed from its traditional mooring in custom and insight. But the price for law's scientific freedom is heavy. As law retreats behind reasons and grounds, it loses its natural connection to any ideas of truth and justice except those that are given as its justification. Law threatens to become merely a means to any rational ends that legislators posit. As a product of science, law is limited only by the limits of scientific justification.

It is important, however, not to make too much of Leibniz's transformation of law into a product of science. For example, Luc Ferry asserts that Leibniz's introduction of force and thus willfulness into metaphysics means that Nietzsche says the same thing as Leibniz if you consider Leibniz's philosophy but subtract harmony and God.[90] While Ferry's argument—that a willful impulse underlies both Leibniz's divinely harmonious world and Nietzsche's chaotic multiplicity—harbors an important insight, it certainly does not do justice to Leibniz. As Patrick Riley has argued, "Leibniz minus preestablished harmony between substances and minus God leaves zero, not Nietzsche"; since Leibnizian monads must be "imbedded" in the mind of God before they are "translated" into existence as parts of a harmonious order, it is not possible to separate Leibniz's necessarily willed world from the best and most rational world.[91] While Leibnizian man is "a little God," he is free only to one specific end, namely the end set by the wisdom and love of God. He is free neither to become God, as Nietzsche imagines, nor to do evil—as he will be within Schelling's system[92]—but instead is free only to will the concept of himself positively contained in his God-given subject. The subject, therefore, as subject, serves as the constraining "reason" that at once inclines the will without necessitating it, and which serves as *a priori* proof for the rationality of every existing being—and every existing *ius*. Since existing *ius*, like all existing beings, adheres to the rationality of God's will, *ius* must be knowable and comprehensible within a system.

And yet, it is not simply, as Riley believes, a "fashionable trick"[93] to highlight the parallels between Leibniz and philosophers of the will like Kant, Hegel, Schelling, and Nietzsche. As strongly as Leibniz clings to his view of the world as secured by a preestablished harmony, there is no doubt that his reintroduction of force into philosophy and his resurrection of the Aristotelian idea of *entelecheia* strongly prefigures the demise of the created and prefigured world that Leibniz's theological commitments require him to hold. While Leibniz without God may indeed be an oxymoron, so indeed is the next 200 years of German idealism without the central Leibnizian concepts of force and will.

Leibniz is the first thinker in the Western tradition to join will and thinking (appetite and perception) such that transcendence—that is, apperception, the perception of myself as a thinking and willing being—is determined by a perceiving of the willful force at the center of being. The essential paradox at the heart of human freedom is that man is free to stand on his own willful and appetitive ground even as that ground necessarily must seek to justify itself according to some higher scientific end or rational purpose. This means that the traditional distinction between theoretical and practical knowledge disappears: as *ius* becomes a science, so too does science become *ius*. Science, in other words, becomes legislative.

Universal jurisprudence, as the science of the laws governing the ethical universe, has as its object happiness or the good, that for the sake of which the world exists. In the Leibnizian universe, man exists for the sake of the best of all possible worlds willed by God. The distance between Leibniz and modern positive law, however, is not so great as his divinely ordered world might suggest. For Leibniz's natural law and modern positive law share the fundamental presupposition that man exists for the sake of a willed and posited conception of the good. While it would certainly be wrong to conflate God's divine will with the human will of modern positivist legal science, the basic characteristic of positive law—its being for a willful and posited ground—is rightly understood as the gift of Leibniz's legal science.

CHAPTER 3

Leibniz's *Systema Iuris*

> The highest rule of *ius* in which the use of the science of charity consists is that the *maximum general good must be sought.*
> —Gottfried Wilhelm Leibniz, *Concerning the Three Rules or Grades of Ius*

Leibniz's codification work is concentrated into three stages, distinguished both temporally and substantively.[1] The work on the elements of law began in Mainz, where he worked from 1667 through 1671 with Herman Andrew Lasser in the service of the Elector of Mainz, *Elector* Johann Philipp von Schönborn. After a hiatus in Paris, Leibniz relocated to Hannover as a court counselor in the service of Herzog Johann Friedrich. From 1677 to the mid-1680s, Leibniz resumed his work on the new code, first asking that his earlier notes be forwarded to him in Hannover and later enlisting his friends—Johann Lincker and the emperor's court councilor, Johann Paul Hocher—to win over jurists in the emperor's court for his proposed *Codex Leopoldus*.[2] Finally, Leibniz again returned to his codification project in the early 1690s. Building on his inquiries into the elements of law as well as into the nature of justice, Leibniz's second and third stages of legal work aim to compose an all-inclusive system of law, combining natural and civil law, from which the entirety of law could be clearly determined.

Leibniz began to conceive of the science of *ius* explicitly as a system of *ius* shortly after he resumed his work on the *Codex Leopoldus* in 1677. According to his systematic method, the plurality of *leges* must be set into such an order that the entire system can account for all possible legal matters, without exception. In the system of laws, Leibniz writes, the *leges* are like the stones with which we build an edifice and must be cut so that they can fit together among themselves without difficulty. So that no place remains empty and concerning the coordination of the *leges,* so that they do not fight one another and therefore so that no legal matter is left in doubt. I cannot doubt that such a system of *leges* which until now does not exist, nevertheless could be brought to perfect fulfillment. But the common man thinks the opposite, because he believes that there are infinite legal matters and that to grasp them all is beyond human force. I concede that it would be so if our goal were to calculate all cases; but he who knows [*novi*] universal concepts can divide into classes the abundance of innumerable things, so that nothing can escape from him.[3]

The science of *ius* cannot aim to enumerate the entire range of possible cases. As we saw in chapter 2, such a combinatorial exercise falls prey to the common man's assertion of the "innumerable abundance of things." Instead, the system of *ius* seeks to unite the multiplicity of *leges* through "the formation of categories, of classes under one another in concepts that are ever more categorically dependent."[4] The system of *ius* is an architectural rather than a mathematical construction, one in which the *leges* are known from their real unity and thus can fit together in a single construct.

The drafts, notes, and proposals from Leibniz's unfinished codification projects comprise many thousands of pages. Though much of this material remains unedited and unpublished, Gaston Grua has published parts of two untitled systematic projects—the so-called Tables of Law (*Tabula Iuris,* 1690, 1695–1696) and the System of Law (*Systema Iuris,* 1695–1697)—which represent the culmination of Leibniz's lifelong attempt to complete a full system of *ius.*[5] Grua's edition of these drafts ignores some of Leibniz's original handwritten emphases and often elides Leibniz's textual divisions; nevertheless, these two difficult texts, still untranslated and—with one noteworthy exception—largely unremarked on in the literature[6]—represent Leibniz's most concerted effort to bring to fruition nearly thirty years of work on the *Codex Leopoldus.*

This chapter offers an initial attempt to unravel the complicated system that structures what appear to be the first ever drafts for a systematic legal code. The first section addresses the framework of the code, which is thought to consist of an introduction and two main parts. Against this reading, the entirety of the *Systema Iuris* is better understood as a "General Part" of law, what in the nineteenth century came to be called in Germany the *Allgemeiner Teil*. The *Systema Iuris* is in fact a system of *ius*, one that unifies the entirety of legal rules under a single scientifically certain system and that proceeds from a single idea of the good as it is willed by God.

The second section pays special attention to two distinct definitions of *ius* that appear in the *Systema Iuris*. While *ius* is sometimes understood within Leibniz's system as a right derived from a legal cause of action, the *Systema Iuris* begins with a different definition: namely, *ius* is jurisprudence. It is this idea of *ius* as the science or knowing of *ius* that is Leibniz's overriding contribution to legal science. *Ius*, in other words, is to be known as a product of the science of justice.

Finally, the third section shows that the force of justice is the wellwilling (benevolence) of God, what Leibniz expresses in the formula *caritas sapientis*, or the charity of the wise: *ius* has its ground in the will of God. While Leibniz is careful to emphasize that *ius* remains essentially rational, the subordination of *ius* to the will of God is the philosophical foundation of the advent of positive law.

Leibniz's Legal System: The *Allgemeiner Teil* of *Ius*

Both the *Tabula Iuris* and the *Systema Iuris* begin with the heading *Generalia*. The *Generalia*, or, as Leibniz sometimes refers to them, *Praecognita*,[7] contain the knowledge of *ius* that is necessary prior to the understanding of *ius* as a right that operates in the two main parts of the *Systema Iuris*. The *Generalia* is divided into three parts: *Leges*, or the kinds of laws; *Verborum Significatio*, or the interpretation of laws; and *Regulae Iuris*, the legal rules (§1–3). The *Generalia* is followed by two main parts, the first titled *Factum* (§4–20); the second, *Iura* (§21–72). The divisions are highlighted in Leibniz's handwritten manuscript both by the double underlining of the main concepts (e.g., Generalia, Factum, Iura) and sometimes by textual breaks that emphasize the beginning of a new section.[8] Both parts, *Factum* and *Iura*, contain further *generalia* that precede tripartite divisions of the particular subject matter. The *Systema Iuris* concludes with two short sections titled *Semipublica* (§76–82) and *Jus Publicum* (§83–85).

Within the section *Factum* comes first another *generalia*, an account of the different ways in which a fact can be given a determinate meaning. Facts in general can be proven *(probationes)*, presumed *(praesumtiones)*, or fictionalized *(fictiones juris generales)*. The question of proof concerns the determination of whether something actually occurred, and this section includes the procedural rules conditioning the use of witnesses, torture, and other methods of proof. In cases where proof is legally or factually indeterminable, the determination of facts proceed according to presumptions, which indeed "in reality are fictions."[9] Presumptions and fictions provide a means for the incontestable legal determination of a fact that is to be accepted as valid, even when it cannot be proven. The general rule for presumptions and fictions comes from Ulpian: "In matters that are obscure we always follow the least difficult view."[10] There are four kinds of fictions, taken from Aristotle's discussion on rhetorical substitutions: namely, the ellipsis (when something is taken for nothing) or pleonasm (when nothing is taken as something), the metonymy, the metaphor, and the synecdoche (when something is combined with another).[11] The *generalia* that introduce the section on facts, therefore, concern interpretation—not interpretation in general, but specifically the interpretation of facts that is necessary for the consideration of the three main categories of facts that follow, *persona, res,* and *actus.*[12]

Following the discussion of facts, the section "Concepts of Law" *(Iura)* contains the presentation of the actions and comprises by far the largest part of Leibniz's code. The method for systematically listing the available *iura* begins again with a *generalia* (§21–32): The most general concept of law *(ius generalissime)*, Leibniz writes, "is what is common to law as well as to the modifications and dissolutions of law."[13] Every right, as well as every exception or modification of a right and also every dissolution of a right, brings some *ius* into existence and grants to some person a moral power to execute his or her will; at the same time, every right imposes on another the moral necessity to forebear some right. What all *iura* share is a *causa*, the ground for *ius* coming into being; *exceptio* or *modificatio*, grounds for the limitation or modification of *ius*; and *dissolutio*, grounds for the fulfillment and thus extinction of *ius*. *Causa* (§23–27), *modificatio* (§28–29), and *dissolutio* (§30), therefore, are the three general ways that *ius* in the sense of a right or an obligation can come into being. In addition, statutes of limitations and adverse possession are included within the *Generalia Iura*, since the passing of time and extended use can engender rights as well (§22). Finally, there are two kinds of actions, one private *(jus propriae autoritatis)* and the other semipublic *(jus actionis popularis)*, by which private rights can be affirmed or denied (§31–32).

Following the *Generalia Iura* are the three main divisions of *ius*. *Ius* in respect to persons *(ius personalissimum)* (§34–36) and *ius* in respect to things *(ius realissimum)* (§37–40) are today called *ius ad rem* and *ius ad personam*; *ius personale* (§41–72) addresses remedies in situations where the rights of two persons are in conflict. Since *ius* is a moral power or a *libertas* to act as one wills, the division of *iura* reflects the need to distinguish between the power and liberty one has over different kinds of objects. *Ius personalissimum* and *realissimum* are expressed in the superlative to reflect the complete subjection of the legal object under the right of a legal subject.[14] *Ius realissimum* expresses the essence of ownership rights, the complete right over a thing, including the right to exclude others from its use.[15] *Ius personalissimum* concerns the rights over persons insofar as those persons are treated as things.[16] The *ius personalissimum* is primarily concerned with family law—for example, the right of the father over his children—but also includes semipublic rights and obligations proceeding from one's status or official duty. Both *ius personalissimum* and *realissimum* are labeled "precise" in that as complete *iura* they represent a total subjection of the legal object and thus allow the owners, when deprived of their rights, to claim the full return of their property.[17]

Against these precise *iura*, the *ius personale* does not grant control over an object but instead regulates relations among legal persons. Whereas the *ius personalissimum* and *realissimum* concern a full subjection of the *res* under the right of the legal subject, the *ius personale*, since it involves otherwise equally positioned legal persons, cannot be a precise right for the recovery of the performance or thing in question. Since contractual partners cannot relinquish the free will that is the core of their personality, the *ius personale* grants only a right to the approximate cost of replacement of the object. The *ius personale*, because it governs all *iura* arising out of contract and compact, from cause *(causae)* and even from wrong *(dolus)*, is equated with the law of obligations.[18]

More than two thirds of the *Systema Iuris* is dedicated to the discussion of *iura*, within which all three kinds of *ius* are considered according to their cause or ground, limitation, and extinction. The presentation of the *iura* is dominated by a discussion of the *ius personale*. Not only does this section include the widest range of possible causes, limitations, and extinctions that can be the origination of a *ius* (Leibniz considers transfer, wrong, accident, labor, and probity), but it also incorporates an extra discussion of the effects of the *ius personale*, that is, the remedial effects that arise from the various legal causes. Whereas the effects of the *ius personalissimum* and the *ius realissimum* demand the clear disposition of complete ownership of some thing, the remedies awarded in *ius personale* are rarely the tidy return of the object itself but rather a replacement for its monetary value.[19]

What is immediately apparent in considering the *Systema Iuris* is that it is a *Systema "Iuris."* If Leibniz conceives of the whole *Codex Leopoldus* as a *systema legum*, the *Systema Iuris*, although it is an integral preliminary part of the *systema legum*, limits its material to the *iura*. The *iura* in the *Systema Iuris* precede and order the *leges;* the systematic coherence of *ius* is what makes the entire *systema legum* possible. The *ius* or *iura* are the systematic building blocks of the system.

At the same time, the *Systema Iuris* is also a *"Systema" Iuris*. The structure of Leibniz's system is simple. Sandwiched between an introductory *Generalia* and a conclusory expansion into public *ius* are the four basic elements of private *ius:* person, thing, action, and *ius*. What Leibniz adds to the classical Roman law division into person, thing, and action is the systematic distinction between fact and law. By applying the *generalia* of interpretive methods to the three factual categories of *ius*, Leibniz believes that the short treatment of legal facts can comprehend the entirety of the legal material. No legal matter can arise in which the factual elements cannot be understood as a person, thing, or act interpreted in some way. Humankind, for example, as a species includes not only factual or provable persons but also presumed and fictional persons, including elliptical persons (e.g., when a person, such as a slave or child, is taken as not a person), metaphorical persons (where in actions for injury animals are considered to be persons), metonymical persons (e.g., a guardian or succession where one person represents another), and synecdochal or corporate persons. The factual elements of *ius* contribute to the system, therefore, as that part of the totality of juridical causes that can be ordered.[20]

In attempting to understand the structure and place of the *Systema Iuris* within Leibniz's codification, it is worth recalling that the title of the *Systema Iuris* is not Leibniz's but is supplied by the editor, Grua. While it is not incorrect to highlight the systematic aspect of Leibniz's codification project, it is important to understand how precisely the text published as the *Systema Iuris* relates to the systematic project as a whole. For the *Systema Iuris* and the *Tabula Iuris*, though they are clearly important parts of the system, are only partial editions of a much larger body of legal writing that Leibniz composed in the late 1680s and early 1690s.

If one thinks back to Leibniz's early distinction between the *Elementa Iuris Civilis* and the *Nucleum Legum*, where the latter contains the words of the law that adds flesh to the skeleton of the elements, then it is clear that what Leibniz sets out in the *Systema Iuris* is the naked skeleton of *ius*. To cover the skeleton of juridical principles with flesh, Leibniz also compiles a "synopsis of singular materials of law, suiting a new system."[21] The synopsis of laws is the successor to the *nucleus legum*; it includes the text of the *leges* with descriptions of the rules, along with references to the Roman *Corpus Iuris Civilis*, all fitting within the structural form of the system. Without the *nucleus legum*, what Hans-Peter Schneider calls the "proper core of the new code,"[22] the *Systema Iuris* is pure bones, a scaffolding that encompasses the whole of the civil law.

While Schneider is certainly correct to see that Leibniz is not content with a purely formal legal system, one ought not to place too much importance on the *Nucleus Legum* as the kernel of the code. Not only does Leibniz set far greater worth on the monadic elements of *ius* than on the nucleus, but he also concentrates the force of his work on the derivation of the *Systema Iuris*. While Schneider writes of numerous "unpublished overviews" of particular legal institutes, it appears that at least a large part of the 153 handwritten pages he refers to in his footnotes are the *Systema Iuris* itself and other studies that cannot be correctly identified with the *Nucleus Legum*.[23] If the code is to be a system of *leges*, the difficult work of bringing the *leges* into a coherent system does not involve the writing of the *Nucleus Legum*, but rather the discovery of the organizational structure of the juridical principles that is at once the source and the framework for the *leges*.

Precisely in the organization of *ius* as a universal system of knowledge rather than as a collection of cases and *leges*, Leibniz's *Systema Iuris* represents the first in a series of modern technical codes. The technique of codification is that of formally constructing a coherent system in which not only each legal principle fits together with every other, but also the whole represents a full and complete presentation of *ius*. As a formal system and categorization of juridical principles, the *Systema Iuris* is, as a whole, prior to those parts of the proposed *Codex Leopoldus* that contain the *leges* themselves. The rules of *ius*, therefore, have a systematic function, one that does not simply organize the *leges* under various headings, but also brings the entirety of legal material into a coherent and unified system.

With this in mind, it is clear that the division of the *Systema Iuris* into *Generalia*, *Factum*, and *Jura* is not, as one otherwise perceptive commentator has argued, a division between an *Allgemeiner Teil* and two particular parts,[24] but rather is in its entirety an *Allgemeiner Teil* of *ius*, a presentation of the bare skeleton of *ius* that organizes and also founds the words of the *leges* that are to be presented in the *Nucleus Legum* and code itself. The *Systema Iuris*, as a part of the code, is less a collection of the *leges* than a system "designed for the education of jurists and lawgivers."[25] Since singular positive *leges* are always subject to interpretation and argumentation concerning their meaning, the *Systema Iuris* is set before the singular *leges* and instructs legislators and judges how to issue just *leges* and how to resolve disputes among the existing *leges*.

In considering the ordering of the system of *ius*, Leibniz elsewhere discusses three methods, each with its own end and advantages.[26] The action for ingratitude *(revocatio in servitutem)*, for example, by which a patron can revoke the manumission of his slave on account of the latter's ingratitude, can be ordered in the system according to its factual categories, its effects, or its reasons. The factual ordering of a system of laws, as in the *Corpus Iuris Civilis*, is appropriate for a system directed toward the private man or the legal advocate who wishes to know his rights and obligations as well as the legal remedies available to him in case of injury. The patron or the slave could, given access to such a code, easily determine his mutual rights and obligations. A second possible ordering of the legal system proceeds not by facts but rather according to legal means—by the actions and exceptions as well as their conditions and effects. The action *revocatio in servitutem* would, consequently, be ordered under the section on freedom and slavery, since freedom and enslavement are the effects demanded by the suit. The ordering according to legal actions and exceptions is appropriate for a system intended for use by judges who are assigned to interpret and apply the particular legal conflicts.

Both of these orderings of the main parts of the *Systema Iuris* share a common shortcoming—namely, that the number of legal facts as well as the number of reasons for legal actions and exceptions is indefinitely large.[27] Leibniz routinely collapses both the order according to facts and the order according to effects into a single category that he contrasts with a true system of *ius* that proceeds from out of the grounds and reasons *(causae rationesve)* of *ius*.[28] If the system of *ius* is to be directed at the legislator and is intended to instruct the lawgiver regarding the giving of the best *iura*, then the system should proceed not according to the convenience of application or to the empirically determined calculation of legal effects, but rather according to highest science of *ius*. *Ius* must be derived, Leibniz suggests, from the "reasons of will" *(ratione voluntatis)* as opposed to the "reasons of effects" *(ratione effectus)*.[29] "Since when the rational will is maintained, the effect, which is the power of the will, follows on its own accord," writes Leibniz, reasoning that the scientific system of *ius* can best be determined from out of an inquiry into rational will alone.[30] Only those effects, or valid actions that are willed by the most rational, most wise, and most loving mind—namely, God—should be recommended to the legislator.

Leibniz argues that a systematic code must proceed from a single principle, the rational will of God, or the definition of justice. There is a first cause *(initia causa)* that founds the "System of Civil Laws" *(Systema Legum Civitatis)*:

> *Civil* Ius is the system of law of a commonwealth.
>
> *Society* is the initial cause of the happiness of the commonwealth.
>
> *Lex* is the proposition concerning a doing or forebearing backed by violence.
>
> *System* is the collection of legal propositions designed for education.[31]

The system of *ius* has an initial cause, a force or ground, that weaves the collection of positive law into an organic system and fits into a scientific teaching. As a comprehensible and knowable system, the system of *ius* is a doctrine built on a presupposed idea of the good that informs the *Generalia iuris*. However, there must also be something prior to the *Sys-*

tema Iuris itself. The division of *ius* into facts and *jura*—the entire presentation of the skeleton of *ius* in the *Systema Iuris*—must also be derived from a prior principle.

Generalia Iuris: The Double Meaning of *Ius* Within the *Systema Iuris*

At the beginning of the *Systema Iuris* is a science of justice—namely, jurisprudence.[32] The *Systema Iuris* announces that *ius* itself is a science of *ius*: "Taken most generally *ius* in its genus signifies jurisprudence [the science of *ius*], not ... that which brings forward actions or exceptions."[33] Defined most broadly, *ius*, in its genus (i.e., in its coming to be), is the science of *ius*—the scientific knowing of *ius*. Since the science of *ius* seeks the force of justice, *ius* is the scientific determination of a rational will—God's will and also, to the extent that man is a "little God," man's will. It is the redefinition of *ius* as the science of the force of justice that is the true innovation at the heart of Leibniz's systematic jurisprudence.

Leibniz's initial definition of *ius* as having its genesis in jurisprudence—that is, the science of rational will—is contrasted with his later definition, one that governs *ius* as it is employed throughout most of the *Systema Iuris*. *Ius* is defined at the beginning of the section *Iura* as that which has its origin in an "abstraction that gives rise to legal actions and legal change."[34] The *iura*, as they are presented within the section *Iura*, are abstractions of *ius*, not *ius* itself. The list of obligations that make up the bulk of the section are not rules of *ius* but categorical headings of the available actions and modifications related to causes, modifications, and dissolutions. These headings include obligations arising from a disposition without acceptance (i.e., *conventio*) (§45), obligations arising from a mutual agreement based on a cause (§48), obligations from a naked pact (§47), and obligations from crime (§50) and injury (§51). These *iura* have their origin either in posited *leges*, and therefore are abstractions from legal rules, or, more properly, in prior general rules and principles of *ius*. In either instance, however, the rules of *ius*, as abstractions, are neither the *leges* nor precisely *ius* themselves.

In this abstract sense, *ius* is understood in relation to the existence of an action or exception, a claim or a rejoinder, that can be validated through a court. Thus, *ius* is simply the right one has. The section on *ius*, therefore, is where the actual rights persons have to make claims over things are listed. It is "thus a setting together and accumulation of actions."[35]

Caritas Sapientis and the Principle of Justice in the *Systema Iuris*

Whereas within the body of the system of *ius* the meaning of *ius* is an abstract right or moral power *(potentia moralis)* to demand an action or an exception, the *generalia* or *praecognita* address *ius* from a more universal perspective—that of its genesis in the force *(vis)* of justice. The discovery of the force of justice, therefore, is the secret motive force *(arcanus motus)* of jurisprudence. The definition of justice is the real and substantive formal definition from which all abstract rules of *ius* can be known in advance with scientific certainty. "I have found the secret source," Leibniz reports to Herzog Johann Friedrich in a letter from May 1677: It is "a demonstration of natural jurisprudence from this single principle: the fact that justice is charity of the wise."[36] From this single principle of the charity of the wise, Leibniz seeks to know the entirety of *ius*.

The relation between *caritas sapientis* as the force of justice and the abstract *leges* is made clear in the preface to Leibniz's only published account of his mature legal thinking, the *Codex Iuris Gentium* of 1693.[37] The *Codex Iuris Gentium* represents Leibniz's collection of medieval treatises and statutes that will, "above all, help to understand the law of peoples."[38] This *codex* includes documents from the pope, ecumenical councils, and the treaties of nations; however, the foundation of international *ius*, Leibniz writes, lies in the principles of natural law.[39] Specifically, the highest principle of natural law, what Leibniz names the "*charity* of the wise man, that is, charity which follows the dictates of wisdom,"[40] is the source and limit of *ius*.

The definition of justice as the charity of the wise shows that for Leibniz, justice is not a particular rule or *lex* but is, in its essence, the formal force that has its manifestation in the will of a wise being, most explicitly in the will of God.[41] Charity, Leibniz writes, is understood as *benevolentia universalis* or a universal well-willing.[42] Justice is a charity or love that is rightly determined, above all, as the love of God, or by God's eminently wise will.⁴³ The wisdom of God, not an abstract proposition but the judicious wisdom of an all-knowing, loving, and virtuous being, is the source of justice, and it is this wisdom that Leibniz believes can be scientifically comprehended through a *scientia felicitatis*—a science of happiness.⁴⁴

The natural law that flows out of the science of happiness is, Leibniz writes, divided into three degrees or levels, each governed by its own rule. The lowest degree of natural law is *ius strictum*, or commutative justice. Strict justice regulates the relations among persons according to the rule *neminem laedere:* injure no one. It is according to this lowest level of justice that legal persons confront each other as formally equal bearers of rights. The second and higher degree of natural law is *aequitas*, or distributive justice, which governs the political relations among citizens of the state according to the rule *suum cuique tribuere:* to give to each his own. Along with the *ius strictum*, the equitable demand of justice comprises the *forum externum*, the sphere of society that governs external actions according to principles of justice. Finally, the highest degree of natural law is *pietas*, or universal justice, which governs the *forum internum* according to the rule *honeste vivere:* to live honestly (or piously).⁴⁵

It is important to recognize that Leibniz's tripartite division is a division of natural law. All three levels are part of the natural law. The *ius strictum*, therefore, even as much as *pietas*, has its source in the original force of justice, the charity of the wise. It would be wrong, therefore, to see in the *ius strictum* an endorsement of the rule of *lex* or the arbitrary command of a sovereign power.⁴⁶ While the *ius strictum* is enforced in the *forum externum* in a way that neither equity nor piety are, it is nevertheless held to the demand of justice, albeit within the limitations of uneducated men in the public sphere. For those men not "accustomed to the thought of virtue or to the appreciation of the goods of the mind, whether through a liberal education or a noble way of living,"⁴⁷ the *ius strictum* is demanded by equity itself, "except when an important consideration of a greater good makes us depart from it."⁴⁸ The *ius strictum* is born, Leibniz writes, from the "principle of the conservation of peace," and it seeks not the attainment of the best but merely the avoidance of misery.⁴⁹ Leibniz's overriding tendency, however, is to exclude what is naturally unjust from the *ius strictum*.⁵⁰ Even the *ius strictum*, in other words, remains limited by the principles of justice.

Although he cannot be accused of privileging *lex* over *ius*, it nevertheless is not wrong to see in Leibniz's development of the three grades of natural law from the principle of charity regulated by wisdom the first stirrings of positive law. Because he understands the highest principle of justice to be *caritas sapientis*—God's benevolence, or a well-willing—that is a formal force directing every rational being, Leibniz is the first jurist to set the question of *ius* within the province of will. *Ius*, in other words, is transformed into something knowable, measurable, and calculable as the well-willing of God. And legal science becomes the discovering and calculating of that willful force of law. Over the next 300 years, legal science would come to raise the scientific law code over custom and statute as the central way laws would be understood in modernity.

PART **II**

The *Allgemeines Landrecht:* From *Recht* to *Gesetz*

> The emerging Christian Church objectified the religious spirit that filled it in dogma; the 18th century found the highest form of the objectification of its spirit in the giving of *Gesetz*.
>
> —Wilhelm Dilthey, *Das Allgemeine Landrecht*

Leibniz died on November 14, 1716, his lifelong dream of a new imperial legal code never fulfilled. The world would have to wait nearly a century before the Prussian *Allgemeines Landrecht* of 1794 (ALR) was adopted as the first scientific and systematic legal code. As if the floodgates then swung open, three new scientifically inspired legal codes followed the ALR within a space of seventeen years. The French *Code Napoleon* (also known as the *Code Civil*) in 1804 and the *Austrian Bürgerliches Gesetzbuch* (ABGB) of 1811 were both successfully implemented. A similarly influenced code in Bavaria was commissioned and proposed in 1811, but never adopted. Collectively labeled the natural law *(Recht)* codes, the Prussian, French, Austrian, and Bavarian codes are correctly understood by legal historians to mark a transition from old to new and from pre-modern to modern; specifically, the natural law codes are said to import enlightenment values and norms into the teetering fundament of scholastic legal practice.

The ALR, as the first and arguably the most philosophically consistent natural law code, inaugurates the golden age of modern legal codification. In the 106 years from the coming into power of the ALR in 1794 to the implementation of the German *Bürgerliches Gesetzbuch* (BGB) in 1900, the legal community in Europe and throughout the world engaged in one of the greatest and most ambitious scientific projects of the modern era: namely the scientific and systematic reformulation of the old laws and their formal manifestation in published legal codes. The incorporation of *Recht* in written language as posited *Recht*—that is, as *Gesetz*—was no longer merely "an old wish," as Kant had written; instead, as Hegel would soon write, codification had come to be regarded as the right of every advanced society.[1] As the first modern law code, the Prussian ALR stands at the threshold between the classic natural law thinking characterized by Leibniz and the approaching historical positivism of Friedrich Carl von Savigny, the founder of the nineteenth-century German school of legal history.

As a transitional code, the ALR differs from prior efforts at codification, such as the *Codex Maximilianeus Bavaricus civilis* (1756). Such pre-modern codes are correctly understood as attempts to order and reform scholastic law. Instead, the natural law codes were infused with a new and fresh systematic and scientific spirit.[2] *Recht,* which had for centuries been found in the ancient books and formulations of jurists, in the fitting ways of custom, and in the individual statutes of princes and kings, was now to be given and known as an object of will and objective scientific knowledge.

The novelty of the ALR is a truism of legal scholarship. Franz Wieacker, in his classic history of German law, *Privatrechtsgeschichte der Neuzeit,* concurs with the common characterization of the ALR, the *Code Civil,* and the Austrian ABGB as codes that break with the past of legal thinking and practice. The ALR, Wieacker writes, shares with the other natural law codes a "common intellectual profile" that distinguishes it from all prior codes.[3] Namely, the natural law codes are essentially willful creations that seek to subjugate the actual world to "the spiritual and powerful will of a free system, albeit one obligated ethically and methodologically to the logos."[4] They are distinguished from earlier legal codifications by their common drive to willfully posit a comprehensive and total plan for society.[5]

As much as the ALR and its progeny reflect a break with the past, there is nevertheless an important connection between Leibniz's natural scientific approach and the natural law codes that followed more than 100 years later.[6] While Leibniz's central role in the development of modern legal history has been largely ignored in Anglo-American legal histories,[7] his youthful calls for legal reform, if not his lesser known later attempts to develop a system of *Recht,* has been recognized more commonly in Germany and the rest of Europe. Indeed, Leibniz is the force behind the German field of legal science and the related drive toward legal codifications that swept through Europe (and much of Asia and Latin America) throughout the nineteenth century.[8]

From a historical point of view, Adolf Trendelenburg has shown that Leibniz undoubtedly wrote an anonymous proposal that sparked the ninety-four-year movement culminating in the Prussian ALR.[9] The proposal, couched in the form of an essay, was found in the files of the Prussian minister of state, Paul von Fuchs. It was Fuchs who, on November 6, 1700, initiated the Prussian movement for a legal code when he ordered the juridical faculty in Frankfurt to bring together certain constitutions regarding dubious cases, with an eye toward bettering the judicial process. Leibniz was in Berlin in May of that year, and it is likely, Trendelenburg speculates, that in or around that time he wrote the essay that instigated the century-long effort at Prussian legal reform.[10]

More important than Leibniz's historical patrimony of modern codifications is his intellectual articulation of the basic philosophy and metaphysical tendencies that constitute the kernel of the scientific idea of *Recht* and thus of the eventual transformation of law from *Recht* to *Gesetz*. What the ALR most manifestly shares with Leibniz's codification is the scientific demand—founded upon the principle of sufficient reason—for a total and universal expression of *Recht*. The ALR sought a "complete codification" *(Gesamtkodifikation)* that would scientifically and rationally order the entirety of legal life.[11] As did Leibniz's *Systema Iuris*, the ALR aimed toward a system of *Recht* within which each of the code's positive laws would have its corresponding ground and justification.[12] Governed by the simple principle of the common good understood as the common happiness *(gemeinschaftlichen Glückseligkeit)*,[13] *Recht* was to be, as it was already for Leibniz, knowable as an object of science—that is, the science of happiness.

As it was for Leibniz 100 years earlier, the impetus behind the ALR was the furtherance of happiness through a scientific knowing of *Recht*. The erection of the modern codes as willfully posited systems of law was a concrete response to a pressing need of the times, namely the increasing sense of the loss of the authority of law. Just as Leibniz responded to the erosion of spiritual and political authority by appealing to the certainty of rational and scientific truth, so did the natural law jurists of the late eighteenth century respond to an increasing skepticism toward the rationality of scientific authority itself. The naïve hope that science could provide access to unquestionable truths that might stem the swelling tide of uncertainty and doubt fell victim to the same disagreements and doubts that toppled the religious truths they had striven to replace. The result was not a repudiation of the science of *Recht* itself, but rather an effort to transform it and to set it on firmer ground.

While the ALR did embrace the scientific approach to natural law developed by Leibniz and his followers, it did so in a particular and significantly different way, one that has shaped, and that continues to influence, the understanding of *Recht*. Unlike the French *Code Civil*, which, swept up in the needs of revolution and politics, ignored the emerging imperative to set the new laws on a scientific foundation,[14] the ALR was firmly rooted in the scientific spirit of the age. As the next two chapters show, the code's scientific presuppositions, combined with its enlightenment rejection of Leibniz's universal theological jurisprudence, made the ALR the world's first positivist legal system. The ALR, therefore, marks the moment of the ascendency of *Gesetz* over *Recht* that characterizes the modern legal tradition.

CHAPTER 4

From the *Gesetzbuch* to the *Landrecht:* The ALR and the Triumph of Legality

> Such a book of laws as that of the Manu arises as does every good lawbook: It gives anew the experience, the wisdom and the experimental-morality from long centuries, it concludes, it creates nothing more. The presupposition of a codification of its kind is the insight that the means to create the authority of a slowly and expensively acquired truth are different in their ground from those means by which the authority of that truth would be proven. A lawbook never explains the needs, the grounds, the casuistry in the pre-history of a law: For with that explanation the lawbook would lose its imperative tone, the "You Shall," the pre-condition for that it would be obeyed.
>
> —Friedrich Nietzsche, *Twilight of the Idols*

What we know of today as *Das Allgemeine Landrecht für die Preußischen Staaten* of 1794 (ALR) was originally titled *Das Allgemeine Gesetzbuch für die Preußischen Staaten* (AGB). The seemingly innocuous semantic substitution of *Landrecht* (in English, "provincial law") for *Gesetzbuch* (in English, "lawbook") has typically been ignored or downplayed by historians. This is true despite the fact that the title of the Prussian code was at the center of a two-year battle that very nearly resulted in its wholesale rejection.

The stakes in the fight over the title of the *Allgemeines Landrecht* become clear only when one takes seriously the fierce opposition to the *Gesetzbuch* appellation on the part of the Prussian nobility. If the AGB were simply an example of collecting laws in an accessible and understandable lawbook *(Gesetzgebung)*, it would hardly have engendered the intense opposition that it did. Conceived as a book of laws, the *Allgemeines Gesetzbuch* would have been seen as yet another codex in a tradition stretching back to antiquity.

72   The *Allgemeines Landrecht:* From *Recht* to *Gesetz*

What made the Prussian code controversial at the time and important now as a historical event is its ambition to ground the Prussian laws in a scientific system. Against the nobility's repulsion at the need to justify *Gesetz* within a *Gesetzbuch,* the writers of the *Allgemeines Gesetzbuch* took pride in their efforts to educate and inform the citizens of the state about the sources and justifications for the laws it imposed upon them. "I cannot see such propositions as extraneous," wrote Carl Gottlieb Svarez, the main author of the ALR, for these justifications

> seek to educate the subjects of the state about the true ends of the state and to make them aware of the beneficent rules and maxims according to which it is governed, and to show them the rational grounds of their duty of obedience to the *Gesetz* and their rulers, and to make visible the tight bond of this duty with the conservation of public and private happiness.[1]

The idea that the authority of *Recht* is not taken for granted but depends upon its justification was clear to Svarez and the ALR's many supporters. Positive laws, they argued, need to be explained and justified if they are not to seem arbitrary and willful. The elaboration of the rational connection between the duties imposed by the legal rules and the public and private well-being of the citizens was necessary, the codifiers argued, if the laws of the state were not to appear an imposition by a despot.[2]

The nobility, on the other hand, insisted that if the Prussian code were to include justifications for laws, it be called a *Landrecht,* and not a *Gesetzbuch.*[3] Laws *(Gesetze),* the nobility argued, were general rules issued as direct commands from the king to his citizens, irrefutable and absolute. Justifications, elucidations, and explanations for the laws, on the contrary, were only suited to guide judgments of trained professionals rather than to manifest the king's will and command. To the extent that the draft AGB included not simply a statement of the existing laws *(Gesetz)* but also the reasons, explanations, and justifications of the laws necessitated by its scientific and systematic method, the code could not legitimately be labeled a *Gesetzbuch.*

A good *Gesetzbuch,* as Nietzsche writes, expresses an aristocratic spirit. It does so first and foremost by making manifest those laws *(Gesetze)* that already exist. The *Gesetzbuch* does not create new *Gesetz* but gives anew the already existing law of a people. Further, the laws within a *Gesetzbuch* are not to be debated or justified, for there is no reliable measure for the *Gesetz;* the *Gesetze* command, and their authority proceeds from their existence itself, buttressed by the "holy lie" that attributes them to divine provenance and to the presupposed reasonableness of one's ancestors. The *Gesetzbuch* simply manifests the already existing ancestral and traditional law as an imperative.[4]

The debate between a *Gesetzbuch* and a *Landrecht*, therefore, went to the very heart of the code as a positing of the law of the land. The question was whether the code, insofar as it included justifications and grounds for the *Gesetze*, could legitimately be called a *Gesetzbuch*, or whether it was more properly to be seen as a guidebook written for judges to assist them in discovering and finding *Recht*. While the nobility may have won the battle over the actual name of the code, it has long since been clear that they lost the war over law.

The History of the ALR and the Fight over the Naming of the Prussian Code

The fight over the ultimate title of the Prussian code caps a long and tempestuous history that spans nearly the entire eighteenth century and is divided into roughly four stages. The first, beginning on November 6, 1700, encompasses Leibniz's proposal for a codification, which Prussian Elector Friedrich III forwarded to the Brandenburg *Kammergericht* and the law faculties of the Frankfurt and Halle universities. The faculties, most notably that at Halle under the influence of Christian Thomasius, were given six months to scrutinize their collected decisions *(Urtels-Bücher, Responsa und Consilia)* and to purge them of all doubtful cases. They were given a further six months to set out a collection of purified laws and to report their conclusions back to the ministry of justice.[5] Whether the legal faculties complied with the elector's order remains unclear; in any event, once the elector became King Friedrich III, he took no further action toward a legal code.

The movement toward a Prussian code accelerated with the ascension of King Wilhelm I. In 1713, Wilhelm issued a "general order concerning the improvement of justice" *(allgemeine Verordnung die Verbesserung des Justizwesens betreffend),* an order calling for the creation of an *allgemeines Landrecht.* Wilhelm repeated his predecessor's demand for a "general book of *Recht*" that would for once and for all resolve all dubious and unclear cases; the effort centered around the attempt to reform, homogenize, and clarify conflicting and difficult laws. In 1714, Wilhelm directed the new minister of justice, Samuel von Cocceji, to distill from the Roman laws and from the Prussian statutes of 1685 a principled code based on natural fairness (in German, *Billigkeit*). Cocceji was elevated to *Chef de Justice* in 1738 and instructed, once again, to produce a "lasting and eternal provincial code" *(bestandigen ewigen Landrechts)*, a code that would abolish the confusing and unfitting parts of the Roman laws in Prussia.[6]

The third stage of Prussian codification began with the coronation of Friedrich the Great in 1740. In a royal edict issued on December 31, 1746, Friedrich directed Cocceji to complete a German legal code *(deutsches allgemeines Landrecht)* that would be founded completely on natural reason and existing provincial laws.[7] Despite Friedrich's demand for a code that reflected his enlightenment conviction that laws should be grounded in reason, the code Cocceji published between 1749 and 1751 was infused with a scholastic spirit.[8] Rather than using a systematic method, Cocceji sought to reform the Roman law through a selected compilation of its still-valid rules. In language, style, and breadth, the code remained a product of the past.[9] Cocceji's *Project Fridericiani* was never adopted, and Friedrich's interest in a legal code waned as his attention turned to pressing matters of foreign conquest.

More than thirty years would pass before Friedrich would reinitiate his plan for a new legal code. The extended abandonment of his youthful codification project has encouraged the belief that Friedrich had little interest in or influence upon the ALR.[10] Hans Hattenhauer has further suggested that one ground for Friedrich's reluctance was his acquired conviction "that perfection lies outside the sphere of man."[11] While Friedrich may have nurtured a lifelong suspicion regarding the potential for mortal man to know a thing as sublime as the law, he also, as a son of the Enlightenment, believed firmly that human reason must at least strive for such perfection. Friedrich's *Dissertation sur les raisons d'établir ou d'abroger les lois*, finished in 1749 and read in the Prussian Academy of Sciences in 1750, called for the production of "a perfect book of laws," an accomplishment that "would be the master stroke of human understanding in the realm of the art of governing."[12]

Friedrich the Great's foray into the question of positive legislation was not some arbitrary intellectual query to be quickly abandoned; rather, it was an attempt by a wise king to think through one of the great questions of his realm. Friedrich carried out his research into the grounds of legislation just as his minister of justice, Cocceji, was publishing the *Corpus Fridericiani*—the fruit of thirty-five years of work on a Prussian legal code with which Friedrich was wholly dissatisfied. When at the end of his dissertation Friedrich characterizes his own words as "short observations to which the laws *(lois)* have driven him" and adds that though he has "limited himself to a sketch rather than a painting," he fears still that he "has said too much," we see his words for what they were: an attempt to think through the grounds of laws to be issued in his name.[13]

Friedrich the Great's fear that the grounds of *Gesetz* ought not to be made known reveals an innate and aristocratic sense that the *Gesetz* should confront those for whom they are made as sovereign commands and not as reasoned entreaties. Nevertheless, Friedrich saw the need to write down his thoughts on the grounds for the establishment of *Gesetz* and to share those thoughts with the scientific public at the Academy of Science. Friedrich's compulsion to rationalize and justify the *Gesetz*, even as he recognizes that *Gesetz qua Gesetz* needs no justification, reflects the basic scientific spirit that underlies the entirety of the movement for modern codifications. While Friedrich understood that a modern code of laws could not be simply a collection of ungrounded *Gesetze*, he also felt the danger lurking in the necessity of a scientific transformation of law.

Although Friedrich developed his rationale and justification for a new code as early as 1750, work on what would become the ALR would not actually begin until late in his life. The fourth and final stage of the ALR's composition began with "The Highest Royal Cabinet Order in Consideration of the Betterment of Justice from April 14, 1780."[14] The cabinet order was written by Carl Gottlieb Svarez, a Silesian jurist who was brought to Berlin by Johann Heinrich Casimir Graf von Carmer, Friedrich's new minister of justice. The king's selection of von Carmer and the hiring of Svarez had little to do initially with a desire for a new private law code and much to do with Friedrich's demand for concrete legal reforms arising out of the controversial case of a miller named Arnold.

Arnold had repeatedly sought damages arising from the diversion of a stream that had rendered his mill worthless. Unfortunately for Arnold, the culprit was a local nobleman, and Arnold's claim was repeatedly rejected in patrimonial courts during four years of legal battles; moreover, he was held liable for the rent he owed for his land. Once he was made aware of the case, the king became convinced that his judicial ministers were conspiring to assist a fellow nobleman at the expense of a common miller. Arguing that his name, which stood behind every judgment, had been "cruelly misused," Friedrich dismissed the minister of justice and imprisoned a host of other judicial officials.[15] Von Carmer was selected as the new minister of justice largely on the strength of his earlier efforts to reform criminal procedures in cases between nobles and peasants.[16] By allowing judges to question parties directly and by eliminating the influence of highly paid advocates, von Carmer's reform had made the criminal process shorter and fairer.

Despite the king's limited aim of improving legal procedure, von Carmer and his team of reformers gradually convinced him to exploit this opportunity to legislate a new code of private law. It was likely Svarez who was responsible both for extending this task to include the composition of a new code and for the vision that gave rise to the ALR.[17] Svarez, however, did not work alone. During the fourteen years of intense work on the ALR, Svarez, von Carmer, and a series of other assistants—the most important of whom was Ernst Ferdinand Klein—lived and worked together in von Carmer's rented palace just before the king's gate. Svarez reportedly worked daily from five in the morning, then met with von Carmer and Klein from nine until one to present the day's work. The afternoons were spent walking together through the palace gardens.

So completely did the three principal authors of the ALR collaborate on the project that little is known about any of them outside of the code they produced.[18] In the 200 years since the ALR was written, one book each has been dedicated to Svarez and Klein, and none to von Carmer.[19] Not one picture or portrait, outside of a silhouette, exists of Svarez, who is remembered chiefly for his diligence and for assiduously avoiding social gatherings.[20] Von Carmer was a well-traveled nobleman who rose up through the ranks of the Prussian government.[21] Little of interest is known of him other than that he studied law.

Ernst Ferdinand Klein is perhaps the best known of the codifiers,

The ALR and the Triumph of Legality   77

largely because of his *System des Preußischen Civilrechts*, a work that appeared in 1801 and was designed to present and explicate the ALR for the Prussian legal world. He joined the team of editors late and has often been considered little more than an assistant to von Carmer and Svarez. Recently, however, studies of the unpublished drafts of the ALR have led to speculation that his influence on the ALR was greater than previously believed.[22] Klein had the temperament of a publicist and was the founder and editor in 1788 of the *Annalen der Gesetzgebung und Rechtsgelehrsamkeit in den Preussischen Staaten*, a journal largely dedicated to articles defending and propagating the arguments for the ALR. His principal scholarly work, *Grundsätze der natürlichen Rechtswissenschaft nebst einer Geschichte derselben*, published in 1797 while he was a professor in Halle, is a solid but undistinguished work of the Enlightenment genre of natural law scholarship.

Finally, Carl Gottlieb Svarez, whom every commentator acknowledges as the animating force behind the ALR,[23] lived anything but an extraordinary intellectual life. After studying law, he entered the Prussian governmental service where he was taken under von Carmer's wing. Svarez never fully emerged from his protector's shadow. Even his nomination to the Berlin Academy of Sciences was rejected by King Wilhelm II.[24] The single revealing contemporary description of Svarez—by Christoph Goßler, a jurist and short-lived collaborator on a nontechnical introduction to the code for laypeople—characterizes Svarez as a man of small stature, lacking in worldliness; shy, thoughtful, and careful, he was someone whose strenuous work left him no time for society. Goßler praises Svarez for his honesty, dutifulness, and orderliness before adding that Svarez also possessed a deep knowledge of his subject and a sharp sense.[25] The German legal historian and philosopher Erik Wolf writes of Svarez, that he showed "what a sense of *Recht* could accomplish when it is directed by a strong moral will grounded in natural reason."[26] It seems that it was Svarez's sense of duty and his readiness to sacrifice himself for his single-minded goal of a new Prussian legal code that— more than any overriding philosophical system—framed the fifteen-year odyssey of composition and acceptance of the ALR.

The intimate communal work of von Carmer, Svarez, and Klein led, with the initially ambivalent but later strong support of the king, to the publication of a first draft of the new code, which was published in parts between 1784 and 1788. An extensive period of public comment followed, spurred by a competition Svarez administered for the best commentary on the first draft of the *Allgemeines Gesetzbuch* (AGB). Even after Friedrich II's death in 1786 and his succession by Friedrich Wilhelm II, a new version of the AGB was printed and submitted to the public in 1791. On March 20, 1791, King Friedrich Wilhelm II issued a patent for the publication of the new *Gesetzbuch* and announced that it would go into effect on June 1, 1792.

On April 18, 1792, just over one month before the AGB was to be officially adopted, King Friedrich Wilhelm suspended the project indefinitely. The reasons for the king's sudden change of heart were various. The nephew of Friedrich II, he had never been as friendly either to the Enlightenment or to the reform efforts so prized by his uncle. Unlike the more independent Friedrich II, Friedrich Wilhelm depended heavily on the support of his landed nobility. It was the Prussian nobility, already on edge as a result of the French revolution, who became increasingly wary of the AGB as an Enlightenment code.

The Prussian aristocrats rebelled against what they perceived to be the ignoble spirit of the AGB. Friedrich August Ludwig von der Marwitz, a nobleman from Brandenburg, set the tone for much of the protest against the AGB when he labeled it a *Gleichheitskodex* or "code of equality."[27] Published reviews of the AGB pointed out similarities between the Prussian code and parts of the French *Déclaration des droits de l'homme et du citoyen* of 1789.[28] Reports circulated among the landed aristocracy that peasants were buying and reading draft versions of the AGB, fanning fears that the new code could lead either to a violent uprising as in France or to a "revolution from above," as Carl August von Struensee would later characterize the ALR.[29] In spite of detailed protections of aristocratic privileges and rights within the AGB, the nobility came to fear the code's guarantee of equality before the law as a dire threat to its historic privileges. Faced with increasing opposition and lingering doubts, Friedrich Wilhelm took advantage of a request from the Silesian minister of justice to suspend the AGB and deal it what seemed to be its death blow.

And yet, the AGB did not disappear. In spite of its suspension, printed copies of the code found their way into the hands of Prussian jurists and judges who began using the code in their decisions.[30] At the same time,

The ALR and the Triumph of Legality   79

the code's supporters launched an all-out defense, arguing that the AGB was not only not revolutionary but also fully accepting of the rights of the aristocracy. In fact, the AGB incorporated and confirmed customary aristocratic privileges, and, as its framers argued, merely set out the existing Prussian laws in a clear, useful, and systematic way. Finally, Prussia's annexation of parts of southern Poland raised the question of what law should be imposed on the newly acquired territories. In the end, largely as a result of the de facto acceptance of the code as the uniform Prussian law, Friedrich Wilhelm reversed himself and reauthorized the adoption of the code—but not before it underwent certain necessary changes. Certain "offensive" paragraphs of the AGB were removed, including the prohibition on royal *Machtsprüche* by which the king could overturn legal decisions.[31] More importantly, the paragraphs expressing the "General Principles of *Recht*" were largely excised. And finally, the opponents of the code prevailed in their ultimate demand: the changing of the name from *Das Allgemeine Gesetzbuch* to *Das Allgemeine Landrecht*. With only these few alterations, the new code, virtually unchanged, was finally adopted on June 1, 1794.

Positive *Recht (Gesetz)* as the Ground of Natural *Recht* in the *Landrecht*

Most commentators on the ALR have either ignored the change in name from *Gesetzbuch* to *Landrecht* or dismissed it as inconsequential. Ferdinand Klein does not even mention the name change in his historical account of the code.[32] Adolf Stölzel, Svarez's biographer, continues to speak of the ALR as *Das Allgemeine Gesetzbuch* and notes that so few changes were made to the original draft of the *Allgemeines Gesetzbuch* that the very same copy that had been submitted for review to the Prussian committee on legislation was used for the printing of the *Allgemeines Landrecht;* only a few pages had to be retyped to reflect the changes.[33]

This attitude of indifference seems justified, especially since the ALR itself continues to speak of itself as a *Gesetzbuch* and of its rules as *Gesetze*.[34] Even in the first paragraph of the introduction to the ALR, in a section titled "On Laws in General, *Von den Gesetzen überhaupt*," the original language of the AGB is retained: the section states that *"Das allgemeine Gesetzbuch* contains the prescriptions according to which the rights *(Rechte)* and obligations of the inhabitants of the state are to be judged."[35] The pitched battle in which prominent members of the nobility successfully opposed the passage of the *Allgemeines Gesetzbuch* over the strenuous objections of the law book's proponents seems, if one believes the traditional account of the ALR, to have been, in the end, a semantic dispute of little import.

As inconsequential as the name change has been thought to be, the stubborn fact remains that it was fought fiercely by Svarez, Klein, and their team of reformers. Similarly, the nobility clearly saw the change from a *Gesetzbuch* to a *Landrecht* as crucially important. For both sides, the fight over the name of the code was not simply a dispute over words but a struggle that went to the very idea of law that would reside in the code itself.

The opposition to the *Allgemeines Gesetzbuch* was led, in large measure, by Adolf Albrecht Heinrich Leopold von Danckelmann, the minister of justice from Silesia. In a letter to von Carmer in 1793, von Danckelmann argued that the AGB wrongly included statements of *Recht*—that is, statements of justification and elucidation that did not belong in a true *Gesetzbuch*. A *Gesetzbuch*, he argued, must contain nothing beyond the civil laws that citizens need to know. These mere *Gesetze* are limited to "short expressions of command, prohibition or determination of the consequences" of an act.[36] More than this, von Danckelmann argued, is unnecessary: "For the inhabitant of a state," he wrote,

> it is generally sufficient, that he knows that, for example, for doing this or that act, the death penalty is legislated. The citizen, thereby, would [know] the danger, into which he sets himself through his action, and it would certainly be unnecessary to make known to him the doctrines and teachings of imputation [*mens rea*] and every mitigation and aggravation.[37]

Von Danckelmann's defense of mere *Gesetz* against the justification of *Gesetz* by *Recht* is an expression of a positivism of nobility in its truest form. His radical positivism asserts that *Gesetze*, once posited by a nobleman—in this case King Friedrich II—require no justification.[38] The positing of the law carries its authority in itself, and any rationalization is not only unnecessary but also risks diluting the posited command's natural authority. All that goes beyond the *Gesetz* itself—the "brief expression of a command *(kurze Ausdruck eines Geboths)*, a prohibition, or a determination of the consequences," of an action—von Danckelmann argues, is part of jurisprudence and does not belong in a civil code.[39]

What von Danckelmann and other critics objected to in the proposed AGB was the very ambition of the code, the replacement of a mere codex of simple laws with a scientifically coherent and complete system derived from and unified by fundamental principles. The *Allgemeines Gesetzbuch* sought to posit rules that aspired to the claim of legality as a result of their scientific derivation from fundamental principles. Denying this need to justify *Gesetze* by conformity to higher principles, von Danckelmann argues that a code of positive laws cannot and need not be scientifically coherent; even the most complete *Gesetzbuch* would fail to resolve many cases and would require constant reform and updating.[40] Von Danckelmann argues that the scientific grounding of *Gesetz* by *Recht* in the proposed AGB has its proper place in the teaching of natural law. Such a natural law teaching might assist judges in discovering the correct natural law in every instance in which there is no direct positive law that decides the case. Although legal decisions would be subject to the varying talents, insights, and capacities of particular judges, von Danckelmann accepts this incompleteness of the code as the "lot of all human order."[41]

Opposing the importation of the scientific study of natural law in a civil code, von Danckelmann argues that legislation must not be made a part of jurisprudence. Rather, legislation is a work of politics: "Legislation is, in my eyes, just as little a piece of jurisprudence as an attribute of the department of justice; rather, it is a work of politics that is demanded by the competition of all departments, if the *Gesetze* are to find trust and willing compliance."[42] A decidedly nonscientific politics—namely, the negotiation and determination of *Gesetze* by different departments and divisions of the state ruled by the king—should be the source of all *Gesetz*, and these positive laws should be posited in the code.

Svarez answers von Danckelmann's argument that the code should avoid the justificatory exercise of jurisprudence, *Rechtswissenschaft*, in a letter he writes for von Carmer. The science of natural law, he writes, is of importance for the lawgiver just as much as for the judge: "I also am fully convinced of the great value of a true philosophical natural law as much for the lawgiver as for the judge."[43] As important as the natural law is, however, Svarez remains unconvinced that a truly philosophical natural law, on its own, can constrict and direct judges with enough precision in their decisions and judgments. The fact remains, he writes in another letter, that there is no agreed upon and certain way of knowing the natural law: Since "there is no universally recognized *codex* of natural law upon which the lawgiver can rely, so must he make the effort also to lay out the positive sanction of such propositions that already appear to be contained in natural law, in order to preclude all doubts over what is or is not *iuris naturalis*."[44] The darkness and uncertainty that plague natural law can only be solved by the clarity afforded by positive law. Instead of positive law depending on natural law, therefore, the grounding relation between natural and positive law must be inverted.

Prior to a science of natural law that would guide the decisions of judges, there is needed, Svarez argues, a posited *Gesetz* that the science of natural *Recht* presupposes. "Natural *Recht* presupposes in advance something given, something positive."[45] In order for legal science to deduce the correct decisions from general concepts and rules, it is first necessary that the concepts be posited.[46] The edifice of legal science presupposes, and requires, the determining of concepts upon which the science of *Recht* depends, and nothing is so appropriate for the setting of legal concepts as a *Gesetzbuch* that announces the will of the sovereign lawgiver: "For if correct conclusions are to be derived from out of concepts, then the concepts must themselves first be set fast; and this cannot better be done in the matter of *Recht* in civil society than through the declared will of the lawgiver."[47] Only once the sovereign authority has determined what the basic legal concepts and principles are (e.g., what a contract is, or what the overriding principle of justice is) is it possible to make judgments on the basis of those concepts and principles. *Gesetzgebung*, the giving of *Gesetz*, precedes legal science to the extent that the very principles and concepts on which a science of *Recht* is built can be recognized and agreed upon only once they are posited.

And yet, the positing of *Gesetz*, though prior to legal science, must also be in some way guided by legal science. The *Gesetz* must itself justify its *Gesetzlichkeit*—its status as valid and legitimate *Gesetz*. Against von Danckelmann, Svarez argues that the positing of the basic concepts of *Recht* through *Gesetz* can occur only through a scientifically guided positing of

Gesetze; Gesetzgebung, the giving of positive laws, cannot exclude the scientific philosophy of *Recht*, which is an important and necessary aspect of the activity of legislating.[48]

The apparent difficulty in Svarez's argument is that of circularity: *Recht* presupposes *Gesetz*, which in turn is necessarily guided by *Recht*. Whether this circularity is indeed a problem—that is, whether circularity is a meaningful rebuttal to an argument about the source of law—must remain an open question; it may indeed be the case that the recognition of the circularity of the attempt to justify legal rules is a necessary though hardly sufficient first step toward a truer insight into the original spring of *Recht*.[49] What is important here, however, is that Svarez's commitment to the code as a *Gesetzbuch*, as a book of laws, rather than as a more theoretical statement of *Recht*, must ultimately be understood to reflect one of the central characteristics of the ALR: namely, a certain priority of positive *Recht (Gesetz)* over natural *Recht*.

Legality *(Gesetzmäßigkeit)* and the "Reign of *Gesetz*"

The subordination of *Recht* to *Gesetz*—so that the former exists only when it accords with what is posited as the latter—is called in English "legality." Legality, from the Latin *legalitas* (itself derived from the Latin *lex, legis, legere*), is not—as typically assumed—etymologically related to the English word "law." Rather, it is, by virtue of its Latin root, associated with *lex*, which in the tradition of Roman law stands opposed to *ius* in much the same way that German jurists distinguish *Gesetz* from *Recht*. Legality thus names the idea of law that gains its authority and validity in its being posited (from *legere*—itself derived from the Greek *legein*, meaning to say, and *setzen*). As that which accords with *lex* or *Gesetz*, legality is, in German, *Gesetzmäßigkeit*—that which is measured by what has been posited or set out by the lawgiver (that is, by the *Gesetzgeber*).[50]

The principle of legality *(Gesetzmäßigkeit)*—itself founded upon Leibniz's principle of sufficient reason—says that all concepts of *Recht* must have a reason: specifically, legality requires that the reason of *Recht* accord with and be measurable by a posited and knowable proposition of *Gesetz*. This principle of legality was given its definitive modern form in 1789, one year after the publication of the draft of the AGB. Article 8 of the French *Déclaration des droits de l'homme et du citoyen* guarantees that "no one shall suffer punishment except that it be legally inflicted in virtue of a law passed and promulgated before the commission of the offense."[51] Legality, in other words, grounds obligation and punishment on the necessary existence of a valid rule.

Another understanding of legality *(Gesetzmäßigkeit)* was given form in the writing of Immanuel Kant just three years after the ALR came into power. In *Die Metaphysik der Sitten*, Kant employs the Latin word *legalität* in place of the German *Gesetzmäßigkeit* to name the essentially "pathological" juridical relation—that is, "the mere agreement or disagreement of an action with the *Gesetz*, without consideration of the action's driving motive."[52] For Kant, legality refers not to the morality or immorality of legal obligations themselves; rather, legality names the driving force motivating one's action in obedience to *Gesetz*. One acts legally, therefore, when one conforms to *Gesetz*, but does so without the proper will required for moral action.

The perversity of legality for Kant results from an action's complete separation from the "idea of duty" *(Idee der Pflicht)*. Instead of acting from moral obligation, the actor who seeks merely to conform his behavior to positive laws submits to external laws, whatever they may be. Legality, in this sense, characterizes the objective conformity or nonconformity to *Gesetz;* it is not that legal or juridical actions are opposed to moral actions, but that they are amoral. The opposite of Kant's legality *(Gesetzmäßigkeit)* is not morality but nonconformity to *Gesetz (Gesetzwidrigkeit)*—what might be called illegality.[53] Since legality justifies actions not on ethical grounds but simply on the fact of their conformity to *Gesetz*, Kant calls legality a "pathological determination of the will *(Willkür)* by inclinations and disinclinations."[54]

While the Kantian idea of legality has largely faded into obscurity, the ideal of legality introduced by the ALR forms the essence of what is known today as the "rule of law" and, in German, somewhat misleadingly, as *Der Rechtsstaat*. For the first time in the ALR, the principle of legality embraced in the rule of law is made equivalent to the "positive law of the state." The ALR is, as a consequence, the first embodiment of a Hobbesian conception of the posited will of the sovereign as the source of *Recht*. Law, traditionally identified as what is right *(Recht)*, is now determined first and foremost by its having been posited *(gesetzt)*. In embracing the principle of legality as the grounding principle of the code, the ALR inaugurates the coming era of legality and the reign of *Gesetz* over *Recht* as the supreme source of law.[55]

The superiority of *Gesetz* over *Recht* announced in the ALR—what Max Weber almost 100 years later would term *"Die legale Herrschaft*, the reign of legality"[56]—says that morality and *Recht* have no claim to be followed unless and except when they are posited as *Gesetz*. On their own, moral rules of *Recht* remain incomplete and powerless, precisely because they are not posited as *Gesetz*. On the contrary, it is only *Gesetz*, what is posited *(gesetzt)*, that establishes itself as *Recht*. Specifically, "any law *(beliebiges Recht)*" can be set out as *Recht* so that "any *Recht* can be *posited* through rational pacts or imposition . . . with the claim of being respected."[57] Within the realm of legality, *Recht* as positive *Recht* becomes nothing more than what is enacted by a sovereign power, an expression of legislative will in pursuit of its version of the common good.

Recht in accordance with willful *Gesetz* was, Weber saw, an inescapable consequence of the ascent of rationalism and science to the throne of political and legal reason. It should not be surprising, therefore, that Weber calls the Prussian *Allgemeines Landrecht* Europe's greatest monument to the "modern welfare state."[58] Its governing quality and highest characteristic, he writes, is that *Gesetz* declares war on all *Recht* that deviates from the posited laws themselves: for example, customary law or ethical claims of natural law.[59] In the realm of governmental administration, it is the willful desire of the administrator and the lawgiver that is the "guiding star" of the specifically modern subsumption of the individual to the "reason of state." What is more, the rationally determined end of the state can be "any" reason; the reason of state is limited by nothing other than the legislator's assertion of the common good.[60]

The common good, however, turns out to be not much of a limitation. Indeed, the common good comes to include even the need to obey positive laws—any positive laws—in order to justify and legitimate the impersonal and bureaucratic rule of law. Like bureaucratic rationalism that is distinguished by its capacity to dispose of the matters of governance "without consideration of the person" but rather according to "calculable rules," the legality that governs the ALR insists that *Gesetze* must at all costs be posited and obeyed lest the rationality, calculability, and security of society suffer.[61] As Weber puts it, only calculable norms of comportment and activity permit the "dominance and rational balancing of 'material' ends"; it is precisely the mastery of a rational and technical "weighing of ends and means" that Weber calls the decisive mark of modern legality.[62] The ability to decide on the valid rules in the pursuit of broad societal interests is indispensable for the progress of modern society, and this *Berechenbarkeit der Erfolge*—the calculation of the ends—is increasingly successful as the "dehumanization" of man is permitted to proceed.[63]

To say that the ALR gives priority to *Gesetz* over *Recht* is not to say that it endorses the arbitrary will of the lawgiver. On the contary, the ALR insists that its posited laws be justified and rationalized according to a science of natural law. Since Svarez and Klein reject both transcendental and rational grounds for *Gesetz*, they seek to develop a new justification for *Gesetz* grounded in a science of rationalized social and political ends. These ends, however, are ultimately determined by nothing other than the will of the legislator—the Prussian king. What prevents the ALR from the descent into the arbitrary rule of will is the lingering conviction that the king's sovereign will follows calculable and therefore rationalizable ends. The ALR's rule of legality, therefore, justifies the authority of its posited laws through a belief in the natural rationality of the king's will. Only thus can the ALR remain a natural law code. What must be asked, however, is what understanding of natural law operative in the ALR can give precedence to positive *Recht*, that is, *Gesetz*?

CHAPTER 5

The Rule of Law: The Crown Prince Lectures and the Grounding of Legality in Order and Security

> The easiest of all literary works, bulk for bulk, is a code of law stark naked: a code, altogether bare of reasons in any shape: next to the easiest, a code with no other habiliment, than a separate tissue of vague and common place generalities, with a gloss of reason on the surface of it. Not only the most important but the most difficult of all human works may be safely pronounced, a uniformly apt and all-comprehensive code of law, accompanied with a perpetually interwoven rationale, drawn from the *greatest happiness principle*, as above.
>
> —Jeremy Bentham, *Codification Proposal*

From sometime in the winter of 1791 to the spring of 1792, shortly after the death of Friedrich II and the coronation of Friedrich Wilhelm II, Svarez was given the honor and duty of lecturing the twenty-one-year-old Prussian crown prince, later Friedrich Wilhelm III, on the science of *Recht*. The lectures began in the fall of 1791 as Svarez was basking in the success of the publication patent of March 20, 1791, which announced the publication and coming implementation of the *Allgemeines Gesetzbuch* (AGB); the lectures ended before the royal order suspending the AGB in April 1792. Therefore, Svarez could proceed on the assumption that the AGB, scheduled to become law in June 1792, was the valid law of the land. At once a presentation of the *Recht* in the AGB and a course designed to educate the future king regarding the grounds of *Recht* and the duties and rights of a just king, the *Crown Prince Lectures* offer the best window into the thinking and legal theory of the most influential writer of the ALR and into the principles underlying the first modern code.[1]

Svarez begins his *Crown Prince Lectures* with an inquiry into the nature of happiness. The "Principles of the Natural and General *Recht* of States," the first section of the lectures, announces a science whose object is the determination of the ends of the state for which men sacrifice their natural freedoms.[2] The end of the state, and of legislation as well, is for Svarez, as for Leibniz, happiness, though the meaning of happiness has changed in the century separating the two.

Since man in the state of nature pursues his natural drive for happiness,[3] the first question of what Svarez calls "practical philosophy" is the following: what is happiness for man in the state of nature? Happiness translates the German word *Glückseligkeit* (literally "blessedness"), which itself is a translation of Aristotle's Greek word *eudaimonia*, which is usually translated as happiness. Etymologically, it retains the sense of the original Greek, "what is smiled upon by the gods," which Leibniz renders as *felicitas*. For Svarez, however, the meaning of *Glückseligkeit* is decidedly double-edged. While the pursuit of happiness in the state of nature continues to name the good, the good comes to be identified overwhelmingly with the material security granted by the certainty of *Gesetz* as opposed to the blessedness of *Recht*.

Following the rationalist tradition of natural law, Svarez writes that the drive for human happiness, planted in our breast by God, is learned from reason. The brighter a man's reason and understanding shine, the more closely he approaches the "great end of his being."[4] The inborn "drive to *Glückseligkeit*" underlies the natural right man has in the state of nature to do all that is necessary to advance his happiness, and also the natural duty to forego all actions that interfere with the happiness of others.

The science of happiness that is to justify the authority of the ALR's positive laws is a principle of external freedom. In accordance with the natural law of happiness, "we have the right from nature to do everything that serves our happiness," so long as there are no positive laws against it.[5] Happiness, in other words, is limited to the pursuit of public and social interests. As a result, Svarez insists that the ethical goods of human life—the moral sense that "honorable, generous and beneficient attunement to the nature and worth of our immortal soul," and the natural moral feeling that binds the "well-being of every individual man with the good and the happiness of his neighbors"[6]—are utterly distinct from the concerns of natural law. Svarez's separation of the realm of *Recht* from the realm of morality reflects a corresponding and explicit shift in the nature of *Recht* away from justice and toward an exclusive concern of action in the external sphere.

Svarez's division of *Recht* from justice might be thought to be simply a modern version of the traditional identification of *Recht* and external justice that stretches from Aristotle to Kant. Aristotle distinguished justice *simpliciter (to haplos dikaion)* from political justice *(to politikon dikaion)*, just as Kant differentiated virtue *(Tugend)* from law *(Recht)*.[7] According to Aristotle and Kant, justice is split into two realms. Simple justice *(to haplos dikaion)* or virtue *(Tugend)* inhabits a *forum internum*, whereas political justice *(to politikon dikaion)* or *Recht* governs in the world of affairs, the *forum externum*. Within the *forum externum*, justice is, as Aristotle writes, "as it appears to others" *(pros heteron)*.[8] The *forum externum* regulates justice between free and equal persons living a common life in order to attain their self-sufficiency.[9]

Similarly, Kant adapts Aristotle's distinction between simple justice and political justice in his division of virtue and *Recht* as the two realms of ethics *(Sittlichkeit)*. Duties of *Recht* concern only "the external and even the practical relation of one person against another, insofar as their actions as facts can have influence upon each other."[10] In addressing only the external and political duties, the duties of *Recht* are "pathological" because the incentive to do one's juridical duty comes not from one's own free decision, thus denying man's moral freedom. And yet, despite the pathology of the laws of *Recht (Rechtsgesetz)*, Kant insists—however problematically—that juridical duties are nevertheless obligatory, necessitating obedience by a bond that is grounded not in a moral will but rather in a "consciousness [*Bewußtsein*] of the obligation of each according to *Gesetz*."[11]

Although Aristotle and Kant distinguish political justice from justice *simpliciter*, they still comprehend political justice as essentially rational and moral. Aristotle's political justice—a product of legislation—is never reducible to mere will but instead has its source in some nonhuman and noncontingent realm. The laws *(nomos)*, command or forbid rightly *(orthos)* when they have been rightly laid down, but not well when they have been set down at random *(apeschediasmenos)*.[12] Even justice displayed to others within the *forum externum* remains governed by a final end *(arete men esti teleia)*.¹³ Political justice *(to politikon dikaion)*, therefore, is not merely a subspecies of justice but is one way in which all justice appears—namely, the way justice itself *(to haplos dikaion)* appears to others in the *forum externum*. Justice always has another way of appearing: in the *forum internum* one knows the truth regarding the justice or injustice of what he has done and therefore need not appeal to public laws. For Aristotle, both the internal and external manifestations of justice are thought together and reflect different ways in which justice is active in the world.

Kant, too, is clear that the moral duty of *Tugend* and the juridical duty of *Recht* are two ways of speaking about the same activity of justice. The posited laws are, in Kant's terminology, *Rechtsgesetze*. As such, they are positive expressions of *Recht*. As a positing of *Recht*, the positive laws must include that one obey the posited *Recht*.¹⁴ The Kantian legal doctrine, despite its strict separation of ethical from juridical duty, still imagines that the obligations imposed through legislation of *Gesetz* are necessarily rational and universal.

While Svarez participates in the natural law tradition of Aristotle and Kant, he also limits the pursuit of happiness in a manner utterly novel to the natural law tradition. Svarez's science of natural law asks after the rights and duties of man to pursue happiness only insofar as those rights are enforceable by the state. "The object of this science [of natural law] is simply the natural rights of man against others and under these only those that he, if necessary, is empowered to exercise with violence and force."¹⁵ This limitation of the science of natural law so that it takes as its object only those rights and obligations that are enforceable by the state is one of the key shifts in the natural law doctrine of the late eighteenth century.¹⁶ By strictly separating justice from the enforceable rules of law, Svarez jettisons the traditional connection between *Recht* and the moral realm of piety and virtue. He reflects, therefore, the absolute differentiation of *Recht* from transcendent justice that gives rise to legal science as the modern way of knowing positive law.

In contrast to the natural law tradition, Svarez radically limits natural law to the enforceable rights of the *forum externum*. In doing so, he relies upon his reconceptualization of happiness from justice to security. Since the highest principle of happiness and thus the first goal of law is the preservation of social, political, and legal order, justice abandons its traditional connection with a transcendent ethical world and comes, instead, to be concerned with order.

Svarez's intention is clear: to establish the power to legislate and the corollary authority of posited laws firmly on natural law grounds. In the pursuit of order, justice demands that *Recht* be limited to those rules that can be known and agreed on by everyone. The need for posited written laws is not simply an arbitrary desire; on the contrary, the absolute authority of *Gesetz* is a necessary demand of justice when justice is understood as the overriding ambition for security. Since only clear, knowable, and written laws can yield the kind of security that justice demands, the ALR grounds its submission of *Recht* to legality *(Gesetzmäßigkeit)* in a requirement of *Recht* itself.

The order and security granted by the certainty of *Gesetz* is of such importance, Svarez argues, that any legally issued *Gesetz* has the power to obligate simply by virtue of its having been posited. While citizens may disagree with the state's laws and may debate the relations between the laws and the goal of security, they may not disobey. Having lawfully entrusted to the sovereign the making and application of *Gesetz*, the people now owe obedience; the positive *Gesetz* of states can limit the natural freedom of man to such an extent that they can even extinguish it.[17] In the name of order and security, the social contract establishes *Gesetz* and not *Recht* as the essential characteristic of law in the ALR.

The Social Contract: Security through *Gesetz*

The good of the state entails, above all, "that each member of the state ought to enjoy for his person and his property the greatest possible security against all forceful attacks and intrusions by others."[18] It is to escape the war of all against all, a state that, Svarez writes, corresponds all too well with the teachings of human history, that men sign the social contract and enter into civil society.[19] Security of person and property within an ordered social whole is that end toward which the participants in the social contract aspire, and it is the driving force of what Svarez calls "the system" of the science of natural *Recht*.[20] In the name of order and security, the ultimate principle of *Recht* is the need to contract for positive laws that then become the criteria of the validity of existing *Recht*.

Since Svarez's natural law theory begins with the presupposition that men enter civil society to evade the destructive war of all against all, it follows that the ultimate end of the state is that every member should enjoy the highest possible level of security for his person and property.[21] Security against the outward threats to our person and property, Svarez writes, is "the highest end of all state-ties, and that towards which all institutions and organizations must aim."[22] The need for order engendered by the chaos of the state of nature is the highest end of Svarez's natural law thinking.

The principal source of insecurity in the state of nature is simply that men can and do disagree over the actual content of natural law and its application to particular cases. Transferring the enforcement of enforceable rights to the state, however, does not in itself solve the problem of insecurity, for there is no guarantee the state will be better at recognizing or applying the natural law than individuals were in the state of nature. And yet, Svarez writes, the state can remedy this potentially dangerous shortcoming in a way that persons in the state of nature cannot: namely, the state can set out the rules of *Recht* in positive *Gesetz*.

The state, once it has assumed responsibility for enforcing the natural law in the name of its subjects, "must necessarily know these *Rechte*; it must be in the position to know and to judge what actually belongs to the *Rechte* and duties of each and every citizen."[23] While sometimes the question of mine and thine is clearly discernible from out of the nature of the matter, as when I know that the apple I pick from my tree and hold in my hand is my own, there are many cases, Svarez believes, in which the questions of ownership, possession, and *Recht* are subject to debilitating doubts.[24] It is to address these uncertain and potentially chaotic situations that the state must issue positive, accessible, and knowable *Gesetze* that serve as outwardly visible marks *(äußere Merkmale und Kennzeichen)* of the valid legal rules. Only such a "concretizing of the characteristics of property and of rights" can provide the "general and concrete determinations"—namely, *Gesetze*—that make clear "whether one actually has a *Recht* that he claims to have as his own."[25]

The authority to issue positive rules is not simply a power the state holds, but a justifiable and necessary demand of natural law. In accordance with the highest end of natural law—namely, the security of person and property—the state is empowered to secure the material content of *Recht* in *Gesetz;* it can do so, Svarez reasons, in two ways. First, it can interpret the rules of natural law through "clear and determinate statements and thereby overcome all doubts and contradictions" that typically plague natural law.[26] Second, it can "alter some parts of the natural laws and [natural] obligations and determine them differently."[27] In either case, once the state has posited what it takes to be the valid rules governing the outward conduct of its citizens, these concrete markings become the contractually binding law of the land. Just as a written contract voids any and all provisions agreed upon orally, so does properly issued *Gesetz* supersede any divergent natural laws. Only when *Gesetz* replaces *Recht* as the arbiter of permissible and impermissible conduct, Svarez argues, can "there be, among men who live in civil society under *Gesetze,* no more questions [regarding] what powers and obligations exist among them according to natural law." In the interest of order and security, natural law loses its claim to authority. Instead, "it all depends upon what the *Gesetze* of the state say about their *Rechte* and duties."[28]

The securing of *Recht* in *Gesetz* is for Svarez neither arbitrary nor dangerous, but on the contrary, it is a need of natural law itself. The binding of naturally free subjects into a state does not simply happen but is directed toward an end *(Zweck),* namely, the advancement of the common happiness.[29] According to Svarez, the communal happiness or the common good requires, as shown above, the pursuit of order and security that itself makes necessary the reign of *Gesetz.* The rise of *Gesetz* is not, therefore, something to be feared, but a necessary step toward the achievement of happiness understood as the "common good." Happiness, it seems, is no longer a state of blessedness; instead, the product of the science of natural law—happiness—is reduced to the preservation of social order.

However, the ALR's attempt to ground its legislative project in natural law is plagued by the same question that haunts John Locke's theory of the social contract: why is positive law needed if legislators themselves must govern according to natural law? Locke's answer, that positive law solves the problem of uncertainty and self-interest in the application of natural law, is notoriously problematic. Why is it that legislators are thought to have a better or surer knowledge of natural law than others? And if they have no privileged insight and may posit unjust laws, there is no reason for individuals to submit to positive laws that run counter to natural law. The one reason typically offered in Locke's defense—the need for certainty in the application of law—runs afoul of Locke's own recognition that no rational being can contract away that which he does not have *(Nemo dat quod non habet)*.[30] In other words, since every rational person is obligated to obey natural law, he may not contractually abandon his obligation to act in accord with natural law. Positive laws, therefore, cannot provide the added security that they promise.

What remains an unaddressed question for Locke becomes an enabling confusion within the ALR. Svarez argues that obedience to clear and knowable positive laws is itself a demand of natural law. In an ideal world, Svarez writes, all men have an equal natural right to the freedom to do everything demanded by their pursuit of happiness; thus, no state of civil society and no legal code would be necessary.[31] In reality, however, such a condition where each is a judge in his own case would lack the basic security of property needed for true happiness and would lead to a world where might makes right. To avoid the original state of natural law from degenerating into a Hobbesian war of all against all, Svarez imagines that the natural law commands men in the state of nature to enter civil society grounded on the "rule of law."

The rule of law is a foundational idea underlying the ALR. No less a thinker than Wilhelm Dilthey, the most perceptive critic of the ALR, asserts that "the *Landrecht* signifies an important moment on the way to the realization of the *Rechtsstaat*."[32] And yet, what Dilthey refers to as the rule of law—the *Rechtsstaat*—is, arguably, more accurately identified as a *Gesetzstaat*, or a "state of *Gesetz*."

The ambiguity within the rule of law comes from the same confusion regarding the relation of *Recht* and *Gesetz* explored in this book. On the one hand, the rule of law is the rule of *Recht*. The English expression "the rule of law" is actually a translation of the German *Rechtsstaat*, which literally means a state of *Recht*. The *Rechtsstaat*, in this sense of the rule of law, moves beyond mere conformity to *Gesetz* as the principle of justice. Instead, the *Rechtsstaat* expresses what Lon Fuller has called an "inner morality" of law: namely, "the enterprise of subjecting human conduct to the governance of rules."[33] As a moral principle of the justice of fair and equal rules, the rule of law is thought to embody eight formal features, ranging from the clear and coherent promulgation of legal rules to the applicability of these rules to "those people with the authority to make, administer and apply the rules in an official capacity."[34] The obeying of rules and laws is not accepted blindly but is thought to serve a higher moral end.

Against this view, the rule of law can also be understood as the rule of *Gesetz*. Of Fuller's eight formal criteria for the "rule of law," the most fundamental is the equal application of laws that have been validly established according to "open and relatively stable general rules."[35] As long as laws are promulgated in accordance with rules of validity—that is, a rule of recognition that determines which rules are to be recognized as a law—then the posited rule is thought to be both valid and just. The measure of a law's justice, therefore, is simply its having been validly posited. The fact of *Gesetz*, in other words, is what determines *Recht*.

Happiness, Security, and the Common Good

In spite of the undeniable reduction of happiness to an ideal of security based in the rule of law *(Gesetzmäßigkeit)*, there are, nevertheless, hints that Svarez understands the relation between happiness and security to be more complicated than the simple hierarchy of the latter over the former. In fact, it sometimes seems as if happiness and security are intricately, if confusedly, related to the higher ideal of the common good. "The legislative power," Svarez writes, "has no other rule that binds it than the end of the state, i.e. the preservation and securing of the common peace and security." In the same sentence, however, he writes that the pursuit of social order and personal security are the means "through which each and every individual can be given the opportunity to advance his private happiness without interference or injury by others."[36] Happiness, as the end of the state, at times aims pointedly at the security offered by knowable *Gesetze;* at other times, however, it seems to reach higher, toward an ideal of happiness beyond security if, admittedly, below the blessedness of *eudaimonia*.

Svarez most directly addresses the ambiguity in the composition of happiness—and with it the final end *(Zweck)* of civil society—in his speech "Concerning the Ends of the State" ("Über den Zweck des Staats"). Svarez begins by asking, "What is the end that must be presupposed toward whose attainment this civil contract is agreed upon?"[37] After considering the answer that he might be expected to give, that "the end of the state is only the security of persons and their property against external attacks," he rejects it. Security alone is too narrow and confining an end to guarantee civil happiness. Instead, Svarez continues,

> we find in every well-ordered state a number of arrangements and applications of the highest power which we joyfully submit to without any grumbling, without regard to the fact that they aim to transform imperfect duties into perfect [duties], merely moral rights *(Befügnisse)* into enforceable rights *(Zwangsrechte)*, not for the best of the totality, but rather for the best of certain individual members of the state.[38]

The end of the state is broader than mere security and order. Instead, the end of the state includes the individual fulfillment of its citizens. In order to further individual fulfillment, the state must demand that moral duties—duties normally excluded from a legal code because of their unknowability and unenforceability—be "transformed" into enforceable duties.

Svarez offers little guidance on the question of which moral duties are so important to the general happiness of the state and the individual fulfillment of its citizens that the state should abandon its general restraint regarding moral duties and incorporate them into the legal code. Certain social policies are, he assumes, enforceable beyond question. Thus, *Gesetze* requiring parents to care for children and those forcing children to care for helpless parents, as well as those forcing citizens to contribute to welfare institutions for the poor, all belong to enforceable moral duties. More to the point, the ALR is stuffed full of rules and policies that import matters of morality and policy normally thought to be internal matters into the *forum externum*. Among these, the rules of family law—beginning with section one of the chapter on marriage, which reads, "the principal end of marriage is the production and education of children"—have drawn the most critical comment.[39] But the code also prohibits the storing of loaded rifles in one's house, especially in places where children might find them. Forests capable of producing lumber may be used by their owners only for this purpose, "so that no clearing of the forest occurs that contradicts the principles of forestry."[40] And villagers must contribute time and money to support the "neighborly duties" of the village, including the support of village shepherds.⁴¹ Although Svarez concedes that these *Gesetze* impose limitations on the natural freedom of citizens and that they are "limitations not grounded in the end of the state"—namely, security of person and property—he nevertheless insists that they "contribute uncommonly much to the well-being of the state," and "augment the sum of civil happiness."⁴²

Svarez concludes that where the failure to enforce otherwise moral duties would "hinder the attainment of the main end of the state or would have as a consequence the dissolution of the bond of the civil society," the state should not hesitate to act. In circumstances when the common good—however loosely defined that may be—requires it, certain personal, private, and traditionally moral activities typically considered part of the *forum internum* can be incorporated into the *forum externum* regulated by public *Gesetze*. The legislation of morals, Svarez writes, contains an internal contradiction in that virtuous acts, by definition, are done regardless of the threat of enforceable laws. Too great a reliance on moral legislation risks devaluing virtues, and, more importantly, a despotism of *Legislation à la Chinoise*.⁴³ That does not mean, however, that *Gesetze* that advance the common good should be abandoned.

Svarez's openness to legislation in the name of the common good differs, however, from the ideal of happiness expressed by Leibniz's *caritas sapientis*. The inclusion of positive *Gesetze* regulating policy and morals is not a recognition of an intimate connection between positive law and a transcendent justice; rather, it is a further expansion of the demand for security based on the power and authority of *Gesetz*. Indeed, the importing of private moral ends into the ALR's system of positive laws actually expands the reign of *Gesetz*; insofar as what were once personal ends have come to be regulated by the state's decision concerning the legitimate ends of personal life, the ALR's incorporation of morality into positive law increases the power of *Gesetz* and expands the realm of activity subject to legislative regulation in a welfare state. Not only external actions but also increasingly private choices and social duties are set under the ultimate authority of *Gesetz*. By endorsing the pursuit of traditionally moral and social ends by legislative means, therefore, Svarez advances his ultimate aim—to bolster the security of persons and property by concretizing *Recht* in positive *Gesetz*.

The Universal Principle of *Recht* in the ALR

The foundation of *Gesetz* on the firm ground of natural *Recht* is not simply a theoretical exercise, but is also adopted within the Prussian *Allgemeines Landrecht* itself. The ALR, like Leibniz's *Systema Iuris*, is composed of an introduction *(Einleitung)* and two main parts. Each part is divided into twenty titles, the first covering the "*Recht* of Things" *(Sachenrecht)*, and the second the "*Recht* of Persons" *(Personenrecht)*. Three introductory titles, "Of Persons and Their *Rechte* in General," "Of Things and Their *Rechte* in General," and "Of Actions and the *Rechte* That Proceed From Them," preface the first part of the code. It is in the introduction to the code, and specifically the second part of the introduction dealing with the "General Principles of *Recht*," that the ALR reveals its natural law foundations.

The "General Principles of *Recht*" begins with a solitary paragraph, set off from the others, that reads:

> §.73. Each and every member of the state is obligated to support the well-being and security of the commonwealth in accord with his estate and capacity [*vermögen*].[44]

Such a statement of the "General Principle of *Recht*" must seem anticlimactic; it must especially disappoint if it is to be read, as has been argued, as a principle of proportional taxation.[45] But even if the German word *vermögen* (in English, usually translated as money or property, but also meaning capacity or faculty) is held to mean more than property and the paragraph consequently is read more generally than as a principle of taxation, it still does not appear to encompass anything so broad and inspiring as befits the general first principle of *Recht*.

To understand the significance of paragraph 73 as a foundational legal principle, it is helpful to follow its evolution. Paragraph 73 is all that remains from a series of paragraphs from the *Allgemeines Gesetzbuch* that more fully express the code's core ideals. These provisions were stricken from the code in a last-minute political compromise; yet, they illuminate the animating vision of the ALR:

§.50. The general well being is the ground of the *Gesetze*.

§.51. The state is obligated to care for the inner and outer peace and security of its members.

§.52. It has the right to regulate the external actions of all who enjoy its protection according to this end.

§.53. Every citizen of the state is obligated to contribute his own to the attainment of this end.

§.54. Every single *Recht* of a citizen of the state must be subordinated to the end of general peace and security.[46]

Through its many formulations, the original section of the published draft of the *Allgemeines Gesetzbuch* on the "General Principles of *Recht*" firmly established the "general well being" as the source and end of all positive laws.[47] As paragraph 50 of the AGB reads, "The general well being is the ground of the *Gesetze*." Paragraph 54 characterizes the general well being, explaining that the rights of every citizen must be subordinated to the "ultimate end" of the state. In accordance with the sacrifice of the citizen to the good of the whole, paragraph 53 obligates every citizen to "contribute his own" *(das Seinige)* to the general end of the state. That paragraph is, likely, the precursor to paragraph 73 of the ALR. If *Vermögen* is a replacement for *das Seinige*, then paragraph 73 of the ALR states the obligation of every citizen to support the "well-being and security of the state" in respect to one's estate. The word *Vermögen* in paragraph 73, therefore, should be read broadly as encompassing the obligation to set oneself and one's capacities under the overriding end of the good of the state.

Despite their condensed form in the published version of Prussian *Allgemeines Landrecht*, the *Allgemeine Grundsätze des Rechts* from the draft code express the grounding principles on which the ALR is based. First, every *Gesetz* must have a ground without which it cannot exist as a *Gesetz*. The writers of the ALR insist that posited laws must have reasons underlying their existence. Second, the *Gesetze* exist for and must be measured against the ultimate end of the good of the state—here the enlightened monarchy of Friedrich II. The *Gesetze*, therefore, only exist as *Gesetze* insofar as they support the universal well-being of the Prussian state.

A third principle of the *Allgemeine Grundsätze des Rechts*, that the state can regulate only the external actions of its subjects, serves, as discussed above, as a liberal limitation of the justification of *Gesetze* by the good of the state (§52). Accordingly, citizens are secured an internal forum of conscience that the laws must tolerate. The freedom of religion and speech is largely protected. It is in the distinction between the *forum externum* and the *forum internum* that the ALR finds its distinctive voice. Only those *Rechte* and duties that are publicly enforceable are considered *Gesetze* according to the code. Finally, the fourth general principle of *Recht* is security. The state is obligated to care for both the external and internal "peace and security of its members" (§51). All individual rights must "be subordinated to the final end of general peace and security" (§54).

Together, these four general principles of *Recht* manifest the tensions that animate the ALR. It is a code that sets *Gesetz* above *Recht* even as it insists that *Gesetz* is grounded on the common good. The focus on the general well-being of the state hearkens back to a traditional formula of the common good—*salus publica suprema lex esto* (the good of the republic is the highest *lex*). This does not mean that the individual is to be routinely sacrificed to the will of the state or the king. On the contrary, the good of the state includes the good of its inhabitants. As the AGB expresses this thought in a later version of paragraph 51, "The well-being of the state and its inhabitants is the end of the civil union *(bürgerlichen Vereinigung)* and the universal aim of the *Gesetze*."[48]

The view that the common good incorporates a bond between the king and his people reflects a core tenet of Friedrich II's Enlightenment thinking, that there is "only one good for the prince and his subjects."[49] While the king does incur obligations to his subjects through his giving of *Gesetz*, his duties as well as his rights come together in the pursuit of the common good. It is for that end that the king and his state maintain order and peace. And it is to that end that citizens are obligated to subordinate their own interests and even their own rights to the end of the state. The common good of the state is, therefore, the guiding principle of the ALR, according to which the entirety of the code must be interpreted and understood: namely, the dependence of the individual upon the state to such an extent that the individual good must at times be legally sacrificed to the good of the state.

Yet, even as the ALR seeks to set the common good above the interests of individual citizens, it denies the possibility of rational knowledge of what makes up the common good. Whereas Leibniz sought to ground *Recht* in the rational and just will of God, Svarez and his colleagues abandoned the attempt to gain certain scientific knowledge of a divinely guaranteed natural *Recht*. Because they nevertheless continue to insist that *Recht* be scientifically knowable, the authors of the ALR are forced to exclude the moral sphere from the legal inquiry. In doing so, however, the ALR is forced to give up on justice as the ultimate ground for *Recht*. The foundational principle that animates the ALR is not justice, at least as Leibniz understood it; instead, it is merely the secular demands for security and certainty.

While Leibniz sought the security granted by clear and certain knowledge of the laws, this certainty was just one of the diverse ends of justice included within his expansive definition, "charity of the wise." At times, Svarez seems to reach for such an all-encompassing idea of justice as well, and his desire to ground the authority of *Gesetz* in a theory of natural law reflects his sense that the scope of justice surpasses the mere demand for order.[50] Nevertheless, the overwhelming concern for the order and security offered by the rule of *Gesetz* marks the ALR as an important departure from Leibniz's codification attempts. If Leibniz sought a code guided by principles of justice and designed to manifest the natural law, Svarez instead finds in natural law a means for the justification of the mastery of *Gesetz* over *Recht* as the essential character of law.

For the jurists behind the ALR, therefore, it is in the name of happiness understood as order and security—or in the language of John Locke, "the enjoyment of their Properties in Peace and Safety"[51]—that men in a society join together to establish a legislator with the power to posit law. The ALR's replacement of *Recht* by *Gesetz* as the pith of the idea of law is not a result of a rejection of natural law and of legal science. On the contrary, the rise of *Gesetz* and thus of legality as the core of legal inquiry results from the very demands of the scientific project itself: namely, that law—as *Recht* or *Gesetz*—must have a ground. It is the distinction of the ALR's legal science that the ground of law is, in the end, the will of the legislator, King Friedrich the Great.

PART **III**

From Science to Technique: Friedrich Carl von Savigny, the BGB, and the Self-Overcoming of Legal Science

> One says that scientific knowledge is compelling. Certainly. But in what does its compelling consist? In our case, the compulsion to give up the jug filled with wine and to set in its place a hollow-space in which a fluid spreads itself. Science makes the jug-thing into something null, insofar as it does not admit things as the measure-giving actuality. Scientific knowledge, compelling in its domain, that of objects-standing-against, has already annihilated things as things, and did so long before the atom-bomb exploded. The explosion of the bomb is only the grossest of all gross corroborations of the long since already accomplished annihilation of the thing.
>
> —Martin Heidegger, *The Thing*

The *Allgemeines Landrecht* remained the valid law, at least in some parts of Prussia, until the adoption of the *Bürgerliches Gesetzbuch* (BGB) on January 1, 1900. A few sections of the ALR addressing administrative and public law even remained in effect until the 1930s. Nevertheless, the code's 106-year reign should not fuel fantasies of either its success or influence. On the contrary, the ALR was an unmitigated failure. It began to unravel almost as soon as it was adopted. As Hans Hattenhauer, a leading scholar of the code has written, "the history of the ALR after [its adoption in] 1794 is that of its progressive evacuation."[1]

There are many reasons why the ALR, nearly a century in the making, arrived stillborn. Even before the Prussian defeat at the hands of Napoleon and the introduction of the French *Code Civil* throughout much of Prussia, the ALR was succumbing to its fateful status as a political compromise. Because the ALR combined the institutional structure of the social and economic estates and feudal serfdom with the modern ideas of egalitarianism and liberal legalism, it came to be seen as what Alexis de Tocqueville called a paradoxical code that attached a "modern head" to a "gothic body."[2]

In addition to its political problems, the code also suffered from its failed attempt to found legal authority on the rule of law and the promise of certainty. As with all attempts to legislate legal certainty, the ALR proved incapable of delivering. The code's heralded claims to universality and scientific completeness crumbled in the face of actual cases that could not be decided simply by applying one of the code's provisions. By 1803, the ALR already required an appendix with over 200 revisions and new laws.

In spite of the failure of the ALR, nineteenth-century German jurists remained obsessed with the ideal of scientific codification. Literally dozens of proposals for and drafts of new codes were published between 1800 and 1850.[3] On March 28, 1849, in the wake of the revolution of 1848, the revolutionary drafters of the *Paulskirche* Constitution called for the "passage of a general codification for civil law, securities law, commercial law, criminal law, and legal procedure in order to ground the legal unity of the German people."[4] Two years before, nineteen German states had adopted the General German Securities Code. And just a few years later, the adoption in 1861 of the General German Commercial Code gave important momentum to the cultural and legal interests advocating for a new German civil code. Finally, in 1873, the *Bundestag*, the newly formed German legislature, won authority over legal matters for all of Germany. In short order, the *Bundestag* named a five-man committee to begin drafting a new German civil code. The work of that preliminary committee and its two successors eventually became the German Civil Code—the BGB—which was officially adopted in 1896 and came into power on January 1, 1900.

For Michael John, the author of the only book-length treatment of nineteenth-century German codification published in English, the drive to codification found its energy in the liberal and nationalist politics that spanned the entire century. The codification movement, he argues, saw legal uniformity and legal certainty throughout German society as essential to the creation of a German state. The "campaign for a national legal system" is, in John's telling, part of a "political debate in nineteenth-century Germany." Indeed, John is an able and insightful guide to the political history of German codification.

John's account, however, pays scant attention to the specifically legal trends that contributed to the adoption of the BGB. While he acknowledges that the eventual passage of the German Civil Code (BGB) in 1900 was "essentially the product of developments in politics and jurisprudence before 1867," his treatment puts much greater emphasis on the political at the expense of the jurisprudential.[5] Indeed, his book, *Politics and the Law in Late Nineteenth-Century Germany*, focuses the bulk of its pages and nearly all of its energy on the political debates around the adoption of the BGB after 1867.

James Whitman, a legal historian, has also argued that nineteenth-century German jurisprudence is dominated by political motivations. In his book, *The Legacy of Roman Law in the German Romantic Era*, Whitman persuasively argues that German law professors "claim[ed] for themselves a new role as national leaders."[6] German legal scholars, faced with the fearful example of the French Revolution, sought to advance a liberalizing political program in the guise of conservation. They embraced the rule of law but balanced their reformist liberalism with a conservative rhetoric that discovered the sources of the emergent liberal legalism in ancient customs and longstanding traditions. Specifically, German jurists argued that the developing liberal order was fully consistent and even required by the ancient system of Roman law. German legal culture through the first six decades of the nineteenth century, Whitman writes, was a "visionary political activity"[7] that can best be described as the revival of the Roman legal order as the model of political impartiality and social peace.[8] These legal politicians blended a liberal political program with a romantically tinged legal conservatism that would allow for stable constitutional change.

Given Whitman's presentation of German legal scholars as romantics more obsessed with the law of the past than with the law of the future, it is not surprising that he sees the passage of the German BGB as evidence of the "failure" of nineteenth-century German jurisprudence. Whitman's study ends in 1861, the year of the passage of the General German Commercial Code and the year of the death of Friedrich Carl von Savigny. Whitman calls the year 1861 a milestone because the turn to legal codification and the rationalization of law in the latter half of the nineteenth century marks the end of an era "of unrealized hopes and miscalculated programs."[9] The move to codify German law, Whitman argues, represents a distinct break with the original drives and desires of German legal science.

Both John and Whitman share an approach to the history of nineteenth-century German law that is dominated by politics, albeit in different ways and with different goals. For John, the BGB is largely a result of politics understood in the traditional sense of interests, power, and advantage. For Whitman, the BGB is a result of the failure of a visionary politics of romantic restoration. Although both Whitman and John bring great insights to the understanding of nineteenth-century German law, their decidedly political emphases overlook an even more important transformation in law itself.

The German BGB, the next two chapters argue, grew out of an approach to law as a science as it was developed and popularized by the founder of the historical school of legal science, Friedrich Carl von Savigny. The German code, therefore, stands squarely within the tradition of modern legal science initiated by Leibniz. Without denying that the BGB or Savigny also had political motivations, these chapters argue that the transformation of law and legislation into a science was the real force behind the rise of nineteenth-century scientific legal positivism, which has its culmination in the German BGB.

For anyone with a cursory knowledge of nineteenth-century German legal history, the claim that Savigny was the forerunner of the German Civil Code's scientific positivism must appear as a provocation. In his now-famous essay, "Vom Beruf Unsrer Zeit für Gesetzgebung und Rechtswissenschaft" ("On the Vocation of Our Age for Codification and Legal Science"), Savigny responded to a proposal by Anton F. J. Thibaut calling for a modern legal code for all of Germany based on the model of the ALR.[10] The legendary *Kodifikationstreit* (in English, "codification dispute") between Savigny and Thibaut has long been understood to have been won decisively by Savigny. Indeed, Savigny's "Beruf" essay quickly established itself as the most important legal text of the nineteenth century, and it became, in hindsight, the founding document of the German historical school of legal science. So powerful was Savigny's

Savigny, the BGB, and Legal Science 107

opposition to legal codes, that the "Beruf" has been seen as a successful "excommunication" of codification from German legal science.[11]

While not wrong, such a one-sided view has tended to obscure Savigny's crucial contribution to the historical development of modern legal science and to scientific codification. Especially relevant in this regard is Savigny's eight-volume *System des Heutigen Römischen Recht (System of Modern Roman Law)*. A few scholars have noted that Savigny's *System*, along with the systematic work of his disciples, especially Bernhard Windscheid and Rudolf von Jhering, worked out the "intellectual framework for the German Civil Code and exerted a demonstrable impact on basic notions of modern American law."[12] As Joachim Rückert, perhaps the most insightful German authority on Savigny's thinking, has suggested, Savigny "prepared the way for the modern codification of private law."[13]

While Savigny's "Beruf" essay was, on one level, a polemic against codification, its influence extends much further. Savigny's greatest contribution to modern law is his influence on the scientific legal system brought to fruition seventy-five years later in the BGB. Only after Savigny succeeds in legitimating a specifically historical and social legal science as a new and important source of law is it possible for the BGB to elevate social science to the ultimate source of law. There is no denying that the social scientific system in the BGB differs fundamentally from Savigny's understanding of a historical science of law. Yet as the founder of the historical school of legal science, Savigny paved the way for the eventual shift from science to social science as the source of law.

The two chapters in this section explore the emergence of the social scientific approach to law in the course of the nineteenth century. Chapter 6 traces Savigny's opposition to codification to Leibniz's fundamental scientific effort to make *Recht* knowable. It argues that both Leibniz and Savigny saw themselves as saviors of law whose destiny was to reinvigorate a moribund jurisprudence. While they deny the possibility of a return to an original "naive" or transcendent insight into the natural law, Leibniz and Savigny insist that the lost natural insight into law must be replaced with an artificial—yet nevertheless highly potent—scientific knowing of law.

For Savigny, as for Leibniz, the scientific approach to law is imagined as a remedy for the loss of insight into the ethical unity of law. Just as Leibniz's proposed cure worked, against his intentions, to further the separation of law from justice, so too does Savigny's legal science lead, unintentionally, to the amoral social–scientific positivism of the BGB. If Leibniz was the unwitting father of modern positive law, Savigny was positive law's most influential and equally unwitting midwife—and the BGB, Chapter 7 argues, is their most significant progeny.

In the name of scientific neutrality, the BGB claims to avoid all metaphysical principles. Whereas previous efforts at scientific codification set their technique of judicial construction in the service of a substantive principal of justice, the BGB is the first code that seeks to free its technical system from the guidance of a substantive ethical principle. It is no accident that while the Nazi jurists of the 1930s severely criticized the BGB for its abstraction and value neutrality, they nevertheless found the code malleable to their own purposes. Because the BGB offers a pure technique of law in the service of external social and political ends, it proves amenable to a multitude of potential and actual ends that come to govern its application. The BGB, therefore, is the culmination of a pure scientific metaphysics that subordinates law itself to whatever ends are put into the system. As a system for and toward any end, the BGB shows itself to be a pure technical code in which *Recht*, once an expression of mankind's highest ethical ideals, has been reduced to a mere means to social and political ends. *Recht*, in other words, comes to be a product of science.

CHAPTER 6

From Reason to History: Savigny's *System* and the Rise of Social Legal Science

> When one first learns that he has tread the wrong path, then he takes care to turn back; and where a great destruction has brought things to an end, there he takes care to build anew. The abstract direction in the philosophy of law had abandoned all holy bonds of the will, beginning with those invisible and secretive bonds that alone announce themselves with certainty to belief—the immediate relations of man to god . . . As now the feeling for the emptiness and baseness of such a state has become lively, so also the insight into the untruth of the way of thinking that leads to it.
>
> —Friedrich Julius Stahl, *The Philosophy of Law*

In 1790, Gustav Hugo introduced the first volume of his new legal journal, *Civilistisches Magazin*, with an article titled simply "Leibniz." Hugo, Savigny's predecessor in the development of the historical school of legal science, observes that while most of his legally trained readers are aware that Leibniz had published the *New Methods on Learning and Teaching Jurisprudence*, few have read it. If they had, he surmises, they might have had the same experience of "surprise and joy" Hugo himself felt when he found that "some of my propositions and proofs were [the same as] Leibniz's."[1] He then proceeds to provide German translations of those sections of the *Nova Methodus* that he most wishes all jurists would consider.

The bulk of Hugo's translation concentrates on Leibniz's comparison of jurisprudence and theology. Theology is a model for Leibniz's jurisprudence because, according to Hugo, both have a "double source of knowledge, at once in reason—manifested in natural religion and natural law—and then again in writing and sovereign will."[2] Hugo wrongly understands Leibniz to express a complete disconnect between the rational laws of nature and positive law. As a result, he argues that Leibniz's insistence on law's double nature serves to justify Hugo's own evolving claims for historical legal science. Since Hugo believes that positive written laws have a source that is fully distinct from natural laws of reason, he concludes that these positive laws are historically given and can be empirically known.

Hugo's interpretation of Leibniz's "double source" thesis is clearly mistaken. As was shown in Part I, Leibniz believed that the principle of sufficient reason made impossible any rift between the two worlds of reason and will. Leibniz's legal science presumes that the two sources of law share a common wellspring in the rational thinking of God. Because Leibniz sought the source of *Gesetz* in scientifically knowable rational *Recht*, his jurisprudence at once frees positive law to be a separate source of law and yokes positive law to the conclusions of a universal legal science.

Regardless of his error, Hugo's embrace of the double source thesis had a profound influence on the future course of German legal science. This thesis became the battle cry of the German school of legal history initiated by Hugo and given its most lasting and effective form in the writings and persona of Savigny, the "brightest star produced by German jurisprudence"[3] and arguably the greatest jurist of the last 200 years.[4] Law, Savigny wrote, originates not in reason but in the existing social and legal relations that develop over time. Against both Leibniz and Svarez, who sought law in the rational will of God and king, Savigny follows Hugo's (mis)appropriation of Leibniz, concluding that *Recht*, like theology, has its source in positive laws.

Savigny's insistence that *Gesetz* and *Recht* have their common source in historically existing positive laws may appear to sanction a positivist reduction of *Recht* to *Gesetz*. Savigny, however, does not fall prey to the simple positivism that infects modern theories of positive law. Far from locating the source of law in the arbitrary will of a sovereign, Savigny develops a new double source thesis grounded in his science of history.

The two sources of law, Savigny argues, reflect the external and the internal historical existence of law. Just as Leibniz builds a scientific bridge between legal fact and its ground in reason, so too does Savigny construct a scientific tunnel connecting visible historical laws *(Gesetze)* to their hidden yet controlling inner historical law *(Recht)*. In Savigny's retelling of Leibniz's double source thesis, the inner laws of history replace the laws of reason as the guiding force of positive *Recht*. Because the external historical laws are scientifically derived from the internal laws of history, they are necessary laws and not solely the expressions of sovereign will. What connects these two sources of law is science. Law, in other words, has a double existence that is revealed, authorized, and constructed by a science of history.

In setting the inner laws of history above the external manifestation of positive *Recht,* Savigny, knowingly or not, established himself as Leibniz's heir. Like Leibniz 140 years earlier, Savigny saw himself as a savior of law who must return law to its ethical roots and protect it from the threat of positivism. If Leibniz perceived the positivist threat in the voluntarism of Hobbes and Pufendorf, Savigny saw the danger in the willful positivism animating the supporters of natural law codification. Most importantly, however, Savigny shared with Leibniz the belief that the only possible way to reenliven *Recht* was through science. Just as Leibniz's turn to science as a way of knowing *Recht* emerges from his sense that insight can no longer provide a certain knowing of *Recht,* so too does Savigny embrace legal science only once *Recht* has ceased to be knowable, either through reason or through a common insight into the culture and tradition of a people. The very *raison d'être* behind Savigny's call for a legal science is his insight into the loss of the traditional idea of *Recht,* the existence and authority of which would be immediately recognized and accepted.

Any effort to understand the importance of Savigny's legal thinking requires that one see how Savigny separates law from Leibniz's rational legal science even as he connects law to the rationality of history. Near the end of his life, Savigny gathered together all of his published writings—excepting his major works, the *Recht des Besitzes, Die Geschichte des Römischen Rechts im Mittelalter* (6 volumes), *Vom Beruf Unserer Zeit für Gesetzgebung und Rechtswissenschaft,* and *System des Heutigen Römischen Rechts* (8 volumes)—and reprinted them in a five-volume collection entitled *Vermischte Schriften* or *Collected Writings.* In a new introduction to the sixth essay reprinted in volume 1 of the *Collected Writings,* "Ueber den Zweck der Zeitschrift für geschichtliche Rechtswissenschaft" ("On the Goal of the Journal for Historical Legal Science"), Savigny writes that this essay "stands in relation to the many other works of the author in which he, as he does here, lays down his convictions regarding the true essence of legal science and the correct procedures for the solution of its task."[5] He then proceeds to name the pamphlet *On the Vocation of Our Time for Codification and Legal Science* and volume 1 of *The System of Modern Roman Law* ("mainly the preface and the second chapter of Book One, especially section 15") as the other two of his published works that address the central question of the task of legal science. The *Beruf*, especially, was "above all a presentation of my views on our science."[6] Not included in Savigny's account—but undeniably relevant to the task of legal science—are his unpublished lectures on legal methodology.[7]

This chapter turns to these highlighted works in order to discover the hidden land of Savigny's legal science. Savigny attempts to return law to its transcendent roots in "the mythical, prehuman time" that is the fertile origin of law.[8] And yet, just as Leibniz was forced to turn to science to reconnect law with the whole and the universal in the face of the loss of insight, so too is Savigny's return to insight mediated through science. Savigny calls for a historically oriented legal science that aims to make manifest "the common conviction of the *Volk*" *(die gemeinsame Ueberzeugung des Volkes)*.[9] In place of Leibniz's divine will and the ALR's sovereign will, Savigny substitutes the will of the folk *(Volkswille)*.

Savigny, however, introduces a radical shift in the relation between law and science. The legal scientist does not simply discover the *Volksrecht*, the original law of a historical people. Instead he sets the *Volksrecht* into concepts and formulas that eventually come to supersede the original content of the *Volksrecht*. Science, in other words, is not simply a way of knowing the material *Volksrecht;* science also gradually comes to be a second and formative source of the material law itself. Law, as a result, comes to be, essentially, a product of social and historical science.

The *Volksgeist* and Law's Social Existence

It is one of the truisms of legal history that Friedrich Carl von Savigny was a steadfast opponent of codification. Savigny's argument in the *Beruf* against the desirability of codification was deceptively simple. The English jurist and scientist Francis Bacon had demanded that codes be written in times of advanced legal insight.[10] Unfortunately, Savigny lamented, the "entire eighteenth century in Germany had been miserably short of great jurists."[11] While Germany produced many diligent lawyers, few were distinguished in the philosophical sense necessary for great legal insight. On the contrary, eighteenth- and early nineteenth-century jurists were castrated by a weak and flat philosophical spirit. Given the impoverished state of legal thought, Savigny argued that the undeniable advantages of codification—legal certainty and uniformity throughout Germany—were beyond the capacity of German jurists. "We do not," he concluded, "in fact have what it takes to create a good Code."[12]

In spite of his reputation as one of the great opponents of codification, Savigny did not actually reject codification outright. Instead, he disputed the belief, endorsed by Thibaut and other proponents of codification since the ALR, that "all *Recht* comes to be from out of *Gesetz*."[13] Against this "reigning opinion," Savigny argued that *Recht* has its origin not in the will of a legislator but in the *Volksgeist*—the spirit of a people or a nation.

The idea that law originates in the *Volksgeist* names the core thought of Savigny's jurisprudence: the source of law is located in the historical spirit of a nation and not in the rationally deduced laws posited by a legislator. Whereas the concept of the state includes citizens united by abstractions like a social contract, the German word *Volk*—much like the English word "folk," which shares the same root—identifies a group of men and women bound together as a people; the *Volk* is united by its inner relatedness, its spirit, and its common consciousness.[14] Whether Savigny speaks of the *Volksgeist*, the *Volksbewußtsein* (the consciousness of a people), or, most helpfully and consistently, the *gemeinsame Überzeugung des Volkes* (the common conviction of a people), each of these ideas points to an inner and necessary unifying "spiritual existence" of a national people.[15]

The *Volksgeist* is marked by this natural necessity, as Savigny shows through the analogy of law to language. Language, he argues, arises "independently from accident and the free will of individuals." We do not decide to learn our native language; rather, every member of a linguistically defined people or nation grows into their tongue "from out of an activity of the *Volksgeist* that works uniformly on all individuals."[16] Individuals do not freely choose the words and language they speak; in the same way, individual members of a *Volk* do not choose their laws.

Just as every people has its language, it also has its constitution and its law. It is an "incontrovertible fact," Savigny writes, that whenever and wherever people become conscious of a legal question or a problem of law, "legal rules for that problem have long been present, and thus, it is neither necessary nor possible to first now discover them."[17] When one looks at the actual history of nations and peoples, the law of that people is always already there: "civil law already has a defined character, appropriate to the *Volk*."[18] Law, in other words, evolves with the nation, unconsciously; it is presupposed by and precedes the legal consciousness of a nation.

Savigny's claim that law originates not in a willful positing *(Gesetz)* but in the *Volksgeist* is, on one level, a lawyer's argument about the source of positive law. A lawyer or a jurist who wants to know the law cannot simply rely on the written laws issued by a legislator. Since positive law has its original source in the *Volksgeist*, any true and meaningful knowledge of positive law requires an engagement with the spirit of the people. The epistemological demand to know positive law requires an insight into the spiritual life of a people.

On another level, however, the argument that all positive law originates in the *Volksgeist* is a claim not just about the source of law but also about the philosophical question,[19] what is *Recht?* Savigny's argument is more than simply a methodological innovation. It speaks to the nature of law.[20] *Recht*, for Savigny, is not something that can be made or given by human command. It is not a product of reason that can be known and set down in a code. In other words, *Recht* is not a thing that is, but a living and changing consciousness that is forever in the state of becoming.

Law *(Recht)* exists in its rootedness in the history of a people; in an important sense, therefore, law does not exist. This is in fact what Savigny argues when he writes that "*Recht* has no existence in itself, but rather its essence is the life of man itself, seen from one particular side."[21] This is a claim about the nature of *law*. Instead of existing in itself, "*Recht* has its existence in the common *Volksgeist*, thus in the general will *(Gesammtwille)* that is, to that extent, also the will of each individual."[22] Law is indistinguishable from the legal consciousness of a people *(Volksrecht)*. Law's existence and its being are situated in life. And the life of man is, in turn, situated in the historical existence of the *Volksgeist*.

Savigny's *System* and the Rise of Social Legal Science   115

The claim that law does not exist separate from life has been called "the timeless inner kernel of [Savigny's] new teaching."[23] It means that *Recht* cannot be separated from the social and historical locus of its development. Against Svarez and Thibaut's belief that law is a product of legislative wisdom, Savigny argues that all *Recht* exists first and foremost as customary law *(Gewohnheitsrecht)*.[24] *Rechte*, as Rudolf von Jhering writes of Savigny's theory, "are not made, but become, they come forth like language and customs from out of the innermost of the life of the *Volk* and the life of thought, without the mediation of calculation and consciousness, [so] that not legislation, but rather customary law, is the original source of law."[25]

By situating law in the *Volksgeist*, Savigny is able to thread a needle between the reduction of law to positive law *(Gesetz)* and the rationalist assumption of a universal *Recht*. Since law *(Recht)* exists in history, it is actual and empirically knowable, at least in principle. And yet, since *Recht* originates naturally in the *Volk*, it is neither arbitrary nor willful. As an attribute of a people, the *Volksrecht* is necessary and true.

From *Volksgeist* to Legal Science

Despite the significance of Savigny's identification of law with the social actuality of the *Volksgeist*, it is important to recall that he qualifies his statement of law's social existence. The claim that law has no independent existence is true only when law is viewed from one side.[26] Since the inner consciousness or spirit of the people is invisible and difficult to discern, we most easily recognize the spiritual source of law as it manifests itself in external actions. The true law, as it exists in the *Volksgeist*, must be made manifest if it is to exist as a binding law.

It is a logical consequence of Savigny's identification of law with the *Volksgeist* that law must have, in addition to its necessary and, invisible core, an actual, visible, and to some extent, arbitrary external existence. The nature of law must be double: it must, as Joachim Rückert argues, "presuppose a doubling in its concept."[27] The true and necessary origin of *Recht* is in the life of the *Volk*. Viewed externally, however, and from the perspective of persons who are empowered by legal rights, the "existence of law" must be "self-sufficient."[28]

The question that drives Savigny's work is, how can these two competing aspects of law be reconciled? The traditional response to this dilemma—that natural law is given a positive existence through written laws—is, Savigny argues, inadequate. Indeed, while legislative codification has the advantage of tangibility, the posited existence of law in written rules suffers under an incredible burden. Written laws necessarily take the form of general rules, and no matter how much care goes into the writing of the rules, the rules themselves are separated from the original conviction of the *Volksgeist*. As a result, a divide grows between positive laws that must convey their rules in abstract formulas and "organic nature that cannot be exhausted *(erschöpft)* in abstract form."[29] The form of positive laws is not adequate to its content, which must be the "already existing *Volksrecht*."[30]

Savigny's legislator is faced with a seemingly insurmountable paradox. On the one hand, he must accord *Recht* its due and provide it with a real and self-sufficient existence. Indeed, a perceptive legislator can perform a great service by changing the written laws to reflect the altered consciousness of the *Volk* more swiftly than would naturally occur. Thus, the establishment of positive written laws belongs to the "noblest right of the sovereign."[31]

On the other hand, the legislator who attempts to manifest the *Volksrecht* in written law must take serious risks. The attempt to derive rules that would govern all future cases is an impossible task. Such an undertaking must—as Leibniz eventually concluded—remain "fruitless," Savigny writes, "because there is ultimately no limit for the proliferation of actual cases."[32] The fatal flaw in legislation is that the supposed advantage of codification—a set of rules that encompasses the totality of law—is an impossibility. Further, since the positive laws rendered in a code would have a claim to be the highest and only valid source of law, they "divert all attention to themselves and away from the true source of law," in the *Volksgeist*.[33] Positive laws run the risk not only of not achieving their purpose, but of actively obscuring the original law that lives in the folk.

If it is impossible to create a complete code out of abstract laws, it is possible, Savigny argues, to seek the perfection of the laws somewhere else. Although *Gesetz* can never completely express the entirety of *Recht*, it ought to be possible to develop a science of *Gesetz* that traces positive laws back to their necessary and true roots. Just as every triangle has definite principles from which all its other characteristics necessarily follow, "so in a similar way does every part of our *Recht* have such parts through which the rest is given: we can name these the guiding principles [of *Recht*]."[34] To discover these principles, "to feel them out" *(Diese heraus zu fühlen)*, as Savigny revealingly puts it, "belongs to the most difficult task of our science; more, it is what gives our work its scientific character." So it is that the art of feeling out principles becomes a science of distilling them. And it is through the difficult but essential work of legal science that it becomes possible "to discover the inner unity and the manner of relating of all juridical concepts and propositions."[35]

Savigny enlisted science as the way to reinvigorate law's fading connection to its spiritual and political force. It is in this sense that James Whitman has rightly seen that Savigny sought to revive and build on Europe's Roman law traditions. Legal science, in other words, offered the "hope that that seemed real: the hope that an ancient constitution could be revived."[36] Jurists, by whom Savigny means legal scientists, emerge as the last bastion defending the living and spiritual law from its descent into the deadening existence of abstract legal rules.

The science of law is not a universal phenomenon but is instead a sign of mature legal systems. In "a nation's youth," Savigny writes, there is an "organic unity" *(organische Zusammenhang)* between law on the one hand, and "the essence and character of the Volk," on the other. At first, a people's law emerges naturally, free from concepts. The members of a national community "enjoy a clear consciousness of their conditions and their relations." As the nation grows and matures, however, the natural unity between law and the *Volk* is "overpowered" by its own advances.[37] It is part of the natural development of nations that their progress is accompanied by ever more complicated relations that result in a division of labor among social and economic classes. Similarly, the creation of law increasingly comes to be the property of a special class of jurists.

From Legal Science to Scientific Law
(Wissenschaftliche Recht)

The role of jurists trained in legal science is paramount in Savigny's thinking about the sources of *Recht*. The ultimate ground and reason of *Recht* comes to be—at least in advanced legal societies—the will of the jurists. Legal scientists, through the activity of building conceptual understandings of *Recht*, become a second and increasingly dominant source of *Recht*, what Savigny calls scientific *Recht (wissenschaftliches Recht)*.

It appears, Savigny writes, "that jurists exert a many-layered influence on positive *Recht*." There is, therefore, the danger that jurists will use this influence toward an "unauthorized usurpation" of the power to posit *Recht*. This is only possible because "anyone who makes . . . *Recht* his vocation, will have more influence on *Recht* than others."[38] In spite of Savigny's never-abandoned insistence that the source of *Recht* lies outside of human will in the living spirit of a people, his embrace of legal science leads him to the conclusion that *Recht* is ultimately posited through the will of jurists.

In creating law, jurists are, on one level, constrained by the law as it exists in the *Volksrecht*. As Savigny insists, "*Recht*, in the particular consciousness of [the jurists], is only a carrying forward and proper development of the *Volksrecht*."[39] In this sense, the law of the jurists *(Juristenrecht)* is analogous to both custom and legislation, insofar as these serve to illuminate and support the original *Volksrecht*. The jurist, like the legislator, "represents the totality *(Gesammtheit)*" of the *Volk* in the sphere of law and assumes responsibility for the "more specific reformulation and application [of the *Volksrecht*] in its specifics."[40] At least in regards to the historical matter of law, the activity of the jurists remains tied to the *Volksgeist*. Unlike Svarez, who held that the ultimate source of law *(Recht)* was the rational will of the legislator set down in positive laws *(Gesetz)*, Savigny insists that positive laws are merely the "organ of the *Volksrecht*," the tool by which the *Volksrecht* gives itself its actual presence in the world.

On another level, however, the scientific activity of the jurist has a transformative effect on the law. Savigny's legal science does not just reflect the *Recht* living in the *Volksrecht*, but gradually comes to replace it.[41] As legal science conceives the *Volksrecht*, it sets the *Volksrecht* into concepts and formulas; these easily knowable and applicable concepts and formulas herald the rise of conceptual jurisprudence *(Begriffsjurisprudenz)* that eventually comes to supersede the original material content of the *Volksrecht*. Science, in other words, is not only a way of knowing the material *Volksrecht*, but also comes to be a second and complementary and formal source of the material *Recht* itself. *Recht*, as a result, increasingly comes to be a product of science.

Savigny's *System* and the Rise of Social Legal Science 119

The scientific form of *Recht* soon takes on a life of its own. As Savigny writes, "A new organic life originates through the scientific formalization of the given stuff, a form that strives to uncover and complete its innermost unity, and which itself constructively works back upon the matter, so that a new way of creating laws emerges irresistibly from out of science as such."[42] The scientific creation of law is both an organ of the *Volksrecht* and a new, organic, and living form of the law itself. Science, therefore, joins the *Volksgeist* as one of the two original sources of law.

Against the reigning vision of the age that subordinates *Recht* to *Gesetz*, Savigny counters that *Recht* is, originally, *Volksrecht*, and thereafter scientific law: "this special way of producing *Recht*" that emerges in advanced societies, is what Savigny names "*scientific* law."[43] Savigny calls the "scientific life of *Recht*" law's "*technical* element." In doing so, he distinguishes the scientific nature of *Recht* from its "*political* element," by which he clearly recalls the classic conception of politics as expressed in the Greek polis.[44] While the political element of law originates in the event of a multitude of people uniting around a common conviction and common vision of the good, the technical element of law originates in the distinctiveness of the scientific method. Whereas *Recht*, viewed from the perspective of its political element, is nothing other than the common consciousness of the *Volk*, the technical side of *Recht* is expressed in self-sufficient general rules.

Savigny's hope, and his belief, is that the technical element active in scientific law *(wissenschaftliche Recht)* will remain connected to and inspired by the political spirit of the *Volk*. The aim of legal science is to develop an artificial and technical form for the positive expression of *Recht* that is still shot through with life-inspired insight.

Ideally, legal science would marry the technical and political sides of law into a harmonious whole. But realistically, the scientific approach is fraught with dangers. Its philosophical and technical qualities could lead to a stale and formalist law of abstract rules, where nuances of specific cases could be lost and individual human concerns would be overridden by rational concepts. If legal science becomes too powerful, it could, like positive law *(Gesetz)*, forget and neglect the original source of law in the *Volksgeist*.[45]

Savigny holds out the example of Roman law as evidence that legal science need not fall prey to its overly technical and rule-bound nature. More than any other civilization in history, Rome in the republican era was blessed with jurists who serve as a model for Savigny's revival of legal science. Even the Romans saw the potential pitfalls of legal science *(Omnis definitio in jure civili periculosa est)* and that all efforts to define law and to set it into technical rules risk the gravest danger—neglecting to represent the *Volksgeist*. Yet what distinguished these jurists is that they saw the actual case and the living dispute even when they thought and decided according to abstract principles. Blessed with a vibrant and animated insight into the living spirit of Rome, they developed a precise legal language so they could move "with unmistakable mastery . . . from universal to particular and from particular to universal."[46] The Romans, in other words, succeeded in developing an artificial science of law "without sacrificing insightfulness and life."[47]

Indeed, it is in the spirit of Roman jurists that a true legal science must connect law's technical side with its political and spiritual unity in the *Volksgeist*. Law, as a creation of legal science, is a free creation of jurists. Scientific law, however, must infuse the technical element that distinguishes it with the breath of the organic and political element of law's ultimate origin in the *Volksgeist*. Only insofar as scientific law grounds its technical mastery in the depth of its political insight can law, as Savigny insists, find its origin outside the arbitrary will of a sovereign. The law, in other words, is to be at once free and necessary.

For Savigny, as for Leibniz, the scientific approach to law is both a symptom of law's divorce from an original insight into justice and a proffered cure. Just as Leibniz's turn to science as a way of knowing *Recht* emerges from his sense that insight can no longer provide a certain knowing of a rational law, so too does Savigny embrace legal science only once law has ceased to be knowable through a common insight into the culture and tradition of a people. Science is, Savigny imagines, a cure for the loss of insight as the source of law.

Savigny's response to the promise and the danger of legal science is to insist that science can and must be attentive to the question of history. If science aims to rejuvenate the civil law and invigorate a legal world dulled by the abstract universalism of natural law philosophizing, the solution is to enliven the technical science of law through history. Only history can infuse the technical aspect of legal rules with the living soul

Savigny's *System* and the Rise of Social Legal Science 121

of the national spirit. And since law originates in a historically existing *Volk*, every rule of law must be seen as a necessary product of a long history of development. The scientific effort to know the guiding principles of the law, therefore, cannot hope to succeed without a finely tuned historical sensibility. Legal science, Savigny insists, is necessarily a historical science.

Savigny's Legal Science: From History to Insight

In 1815, the same year that he published *Vom Beruf Unserer Zeit für Gesetzgebung und Rechtswissenschaft*, Savigny cofounded the *Journal for Historical Legal Science (Die Zeitschrift für Geschichtliche Rechtswissenschaft)*.[48] In his introductory essay, Savigny endeavors to explain what he calls "the true essence of legal science."[49] The journal is designed, Savigny writes, to reflect his strongly held view regarding "the way in which legal science must be seen and practiced."[50] To that end, he divides legal science into two main schools. The preferred method is represented by the historical school. The other, he writes, encompasses a wide range of different positions united only by their opposition to the historical school. For this reason, Savigny names it simply the "unhistorical school." What divides these two schools "cannot fundamentally be understood, however, as long as one limits one's glance to [legal] science."[51] The legal historical school has its roots in a larger and deeper dispute about science itself.

The "universal question" within which Savigny situates his theory of the historical existence of law is the relationship between being and becoming.[52] On the one hand, Savigny writes, rationalist and Enlightenment thinkers teach that every age freely and willfully creates itself according to its own insight and power. For these philosophically minded thinkers, the past can be useful as a "moral-political collection of examples" that can help the present age avoid history's mistakes and emulate its greatest achievements.[53] Yet, as a product of rational and legislative will, law exists apart from and beyond its history. Law, for the unhistorical rationalist legislator, is a personal creation that demands only a clear scientific understanding of the present.

On the other hand, historical thinkers see that there is no such thing as a "completely singular and divided human existence, but rather, what can be seen as singular is, considered from another side, a member of a higher whole."⁵⁴ Every individual is necessarily also a part of a family, a *Volk*, a state, just as every historical age must be understood as the present stage of a historically developing nation. A person, a family, and a people—in short, any living and thinking being—only is and only lives in the unfolding of its history. What Savigny means is that man lives historically. "The life-space *(Lebensraum)* of this *Volksgeist,*" as one legal historian has noted, "is 'history.'"⁵⁵

However, if the present is essentially only a part of history, the historical approach to law is distinguished by its unifying understanding of law as existing through and even beyond historically measurable time. Law, as Savigny often repeats, has no definable point of origin. It always precedes the origin of even the nation whose law it is.⁵⁶ The science of history, therefore, is no mere collection of examples; rather, history comes to be seen as "the only way to true knowledge of our own condition."⁵⁷

The historical entirety of law, inclusive of its prenational existence, is difficult to determine; nevertheless, the scientific penetration into the prehistoric "Ur" laws of nature—what the anthropologist Pierre Clastres has called the mythical "time before men"—is of the highest importance and cannot be abandoned.⁵⁸ This is true despite the fact that the invisible origin of law in the historical *Volksgeist* cannot be definitively and empirically proven.

Fortunately, Savigny writes, there are other kinds of proofs that show that law's existence is always a historical existence. For example, the fact—Savigny asserts it is a fact—that all historical peoples recognize the authority of law demonstrates that law must have its existence prior to the existence of distinct nations or states.⁵⁹ Law's universality, combined with its apparent necessity, proves that law *(Recht)* emerges before the creation of the state. Further proof of the historical existence of law is found in the already discussed analogy between law and language. Since the law has its true existence in an invisible, indeterminate, and prehistoric origin, Savigny concludes that "the matter of law is given through the entire history of a nation, and thus not through willfulness . . . but from out of the innermost essence of the nation itself and its history."⁶⁰

Given Savigny's assertion that law emerges in the shadowy realm before both the creation of states and the rise of written histories, how can

Savigny's *System* and the Rise of Social Legal Science 123

a legal scientist hope to win knowledge of such a legal object? If law is invisible, undiscoverable through conventional means, and diffused through the entire historical existence of a nation, how can it possibly be the knowable object of a historical legal science?

Savigny's answer is that law can only be known through insight. He writes:

> The form, however, in which *Recht* lives in the common consciousness of the *Volk* is not that of the abstract rule, but the *living insight* into the legal institute in its organic unity, so that where the need arises to come to know the rule in its logical form, that form must first be formed through an artificial process from out of that *total insight*.[61]

The form *(Gestalt)* in which law comes to be known is insight *(Anschauung)*. The knowledge of law through science must aim not at a philosophical understanding of universal and rational legal principles, but rather at insight into the historically grounded legal principles active in the national consciousness. "The illuminating [*besonnen*] activity of every epoch," Savigny concludes, "must be directed towards the seeing through into the inner necessity of the given matter, [in order to] rejuvenate it, and to maintain its freshness."[62] Law, for Savigny, is seen in the scientifically generated insightful vision into the formal historical core of a nation.

The connection between law's historical existence and the scientific knowing of law through insight helps to explain one of the paradoxes of Savigny's historical approach to law. While "Savigny has long been securely ensconced . . . in his own particular niche in the history of European thought as the founder of the Historical School of Law," it is equally true that Savigny's main works are not overtly historical."[63] The paradox of Savigny's nonhistorical legal history dissolves, however, once it becomes clear that the emphasis on history as a way to an organic and necessary truth must be distinguished from what is typically understood as historical research. The rigorous historical method, Savigny argues,

> does not consist, as a few recent opponents have unfathomably maintained, in the exclusive valuation of Roman law: also not in demanding the unconditional preservation of the given [legal] material . . . Its effort is rather to analyze the given material down to its roots so as to discover

its organic principle, by which what is still living will automatically separate itself from what is dead and belongs only to history.⁶⁴

The historical approach to law does not argue that ancient laws should serve as a model for the present. This historical method must be distinguished from the obsessive involvement with the facts and laws of the past, something that is poorly understood even today.⁶⁵

Instead, Savigny's legal history seeks to find "the living unity that binds the present to the past."⁶⁶ To take Savigny's favorite example of historical legal inquiry, the value of Roman law lies not in the laws of Rome themselves, nor even in the principles used by Roman jurists, but in the method through which the Romans combined a mastery of legal principles with an unparalleled insight into the historical life of the Roman *Volk*.⁶⁷ Above all else, the Roman jurists excelled at the melding of legal knowledge with insight into the historical unity of the people. Without this insight, "we can only perceive the outer appearance of the legal condition of the present, and cannot reach into its inner essence."⁶⁸ Blessed with a vibrant insight into the Roman *Volksgeist*, the jurists of the republican period proved themselves masters at the scientific creation of new laws that seemed to spring directly and seamlessly from out of the old. "What made Rome great," Savigny writes, was this "active, living, political sense with which this people was always ready to rejuvenate its constitution in such a way that the new served merely the development of the old."⁶⁹ The great talent of the Roman lawyers was their "living insight" into the unity of the needs of present law with its roots in the past.⁷⁰

By focusing on an insight into the seeds of the present that lies concealed in the fields of history, Savigny does not abandon the historian's traditional concern with what has been. Instead, his historical method demands that given laws be understood in accord with the historically developing *Volksgeist*. The laws, in other words, must be rationalized as the institutional expression of a historical consciousness. "According to the method that I hold correct," Savigny writes, "the higher unity, the life-principle, from out of which individual appearances are to be explained, is sought out in the manifold that history offers, and thus the materially given [laws] have always been more spiritualized."⁷¹ In the truly historical approach, the manifold of history is not made rigid, but,

Savigny's *System* and the Rise of Social Legal Science 125

on the contrary, "the original given [things] are transformed and spiritualized [*vergeistigt*], so that what first appeared as dead and material matter now is seen as the living force and activity of a people."[72]

The spiritualization of nature Savigny claims for his historical science is a common trope animating much of German idealist philosophy around the time of Savigny's intellectual maturation. German scholars have delighted in exploring Savigny's intellectual and philosophical roots. Influences have been sought in Schelling's objective idealism,[73] Friedrich Schlegel's "natural philosophy,"[74] Kant's idea of autonomy,[75] and Hölderlin's idea of immanent laws of nature.[76] This scholarship has successfully and helpfully showed that Savigny read widely if not profoundly across a broad spectrum of German romantic and idealist philosophy. In the end, however, it must be recalled that Savigny was not a philosopher. What he took from his "philosophical education,"[77] was, above all, a sense that law's historical ground does not mean that law is reducible to a thoughtless and oppressive force of habit. Instead, Savigny's philosophical and literary influences taught him that law is profoundly and irrevocably connected to poetic insight.

Insight and Poetry

Savigny's insightful approach to law has particular resonance with the idea of insight expressed in Hölderlin's *Hyperion*. Sometime after 1812 and around the time of his work on what would become the *Beruf* essay, Savigny copied down the following text from Hölderlin's prose poem and filed it with other materials marked *Politik und Neuere Legislationen* ("Politics and Newer Legislations")—materials that have been shown to be Savigny's source for the *Beruf*.[78] The quotation from Hölderlin reads:

> Men began and grew from a plant-like happiness, grew until they ripened; from then on they have been in ceaseless ferment, inwardly and outwardly, until now mankind lies there like a chaos, utterly disintegrated, so that all who can still feel and see are dizzied; but Beauty forsakes the life of men, flees upward into spirit; the Ideal becomes what Nature was, and even though the tree is dried out and weatherworn below, a fresh crown has still sprung from it and flourishes green in the sunlight as the trunk did once in its days of youth; the Ideal is what

Nature was. By this, by this Ideal, this rejuvenated divinity, the few recognize one another and are one, for one thing is in them; and from them, these few, the world's second age begins.⁷⁹

There are at least two points of intersection between Hölderlin's text and Savigny's conception of historical legal science. First, Hölderlin's image of human progression from an innocent beginning in nature through corruption by thought and, finally, rejuvenation in the second age of the world is clearly recalled by Savigny's own account of the development of law. In both the *Beruf* essay and the *System of Modern Roman Law*, Savigny writes of how nations progress from a natural law in their youth—albeit a natural law understood differently from how lawyers typically understand it—to a learned law in their maturity. The spoiled and corrupted natural law of a people's youth must be rejuvenated and reborn by an artlike science of law. Just as Hölderlin imagines that the "dried out and weatherworn" copy of nature can be given new life, so too does Savigny believe that a true science of law can breathe new life into the otherwise abstract legal rules that characterize advanced legal systems. The science of *Recht* is needed, Savigny writes, to elevate a primitive and undifferentiated experience of law to its truth.⁸⁰

The second and more important connection concerns Savigny's adaptation of Hölderlin's faith that "the few" enlightened men will recognize one another by their perception of the "rejuvenated divinity" of idealized nature returned to its second beginning in nature. As Hans Kiefner suggests, Savigny alludes to the last sentence of the Hölderlin quotation in the section of the *Beruf* essay entitled "What We Should Do Where There are No Codes."⁸¹ If law is to have a future, he writes, it will depend on the insight of a few great jurists: "A living school must emerge, just as in fact the entirety of the Roman jurists . . . formed one great school. For only from out of such living work broadly diffused across the entirety of jurists can the few themselves come forth who are called through their spirit [*Geist*] to authentic discovery."⁸²

It is the few among Savigny's legal scientists, just as it is the few to whom Hölderlin entrusts the rejuvenated ideal of nature, who possess "the capacity to *make* true experiences."⁸³ The idealization of nature requires that a denuded nature be returned to its former glory, and that can only happen through a mastery of the technical arts, which necessitates a broadly diffused cultivation of legal science throughout the entirety of the lawyerly population. What distinguishes the great jurists, however, is that they combine technical mastery with penetrating artistic insight. For only one who has "the clear, living consciousness of the whole present" before him will be able to fully comprehend and decide the individual case.[84] The vision into the true is manifest only to those few who, "having investigated all kinds of truth in poetry, history and science with true and loving eyes" are in the end able to see the world with "the simplicity of a child's sensibility."[85] The poetic capacity to see with a child's eye into the truth that inheres in the law is the highest hope of Savigny's historical approach to legal science.

The Science of History and the Art of Seeing

Nowhere is the tension between Savigny's poetic striving for an original insight into law and his scientific historical approach to law more apparent than in his university lecture courses. First in 1802–1803 and again in 1803–1804, 1808, and 1809, Savigny wrote down his thoughts in the form of lectures on the methodology of law.[86] There are, Savigny argues in the *Lectures on Methodology*, three basic approaches to law, which he names the philological, the systematic, and the historical. He writes:

> The completed presentation of our science rests on 3 operations, following three different views of codification:
>
> 1. Philological view—the laws *(Gesetze)* considered in and as singularities *(einzelnen)*—*Interpretation*.
> 2. Systematic view—the content of the laws considered as a simultaneous whole, following the inner unity of concepts and principles—*system*.
> 3. Historical view—the content of the laws considered as a successive whole, following the law of historical development, thus following the necessary unity of different epochs of the same *Volk*—inner legal history *(Innere Rechtsgeschichte)*.
>
> None of these 3 operations can stand on its own . . . Each is only *one element* of the perfected science in its entirety—this itself is nothing other than the *system* created in its historical *development* and out of more immediate [and] more perfect *insight into the sources*."[87]

This fragment contains the entirety of Savigny's scientific approach to law. It addresses "the perfected science in its entirety," by which he means, first, the system or the technical mastery of law as a unified whole according to general principles; second, the system created by jurists who are capable of constructing the system not only in accord with its present inner unity, but, more importantly, in sympathy with its necessary inner laws of historical development; and third, that both the first and the second activities presuppose and also make possible an "immediate [and] more perfect *insight into the sources*." The historical approach to law does not replace the systematic and interpretive approaches. All three are necessary "elements or activities from out of which the entire activity of our science consists and must consist."[88] And yet it is the historical approach to law that Savigny sees as his novel contribution to jurisprudence.

History is the name that Savigny claims for his legal science. History presupposes an insight both into the meaning of individual laws (philology) and into the principled unity of the entirety of the present laws (system).[89] The historical approach seeks "to know the present state of law itself, since the past lives forth *in* her [the present] as an integrated part."[90] As a creative and productive science, historical legal science strives to give birth to new law that is knowable only through an insight into the living historical spirit of a people. It is only through "insight into the sources" of law that the system of law can be known in its historical development.[91]

Savigny's greatest achievement was to introduce a new way of seeing into the law through an insight into its historical unity.[92] In a letter written to the Brothers Grimm in 1812 about the goal and meaning of historical legal science, he says:

> It is quite beautiful what you say about the very one-sided and deficient truth of new documentary history. But the essential difference between the goal and meaning of history for the ancients and for ourselves must be better appreciated. Then history had a clearer goal, a wiser insight and teaching, for us history ought to prove our affinity with the divine origin of our people, through whose forgetting we must descend into a hollow stupor, an affinity that for the ancients lay much closer in immediate feelings. Thus does history have for us a holy office.[93]

Savigny's *System* and the Rise of Social Legal Science 129

There is a deep and undeniably romantic connection between Savigny's understanding of poetry, "scientific activity, and religiosity."[94] What historical science offers is a method for poetic insight into the divine—or at least, the prehuman—origin that is, at all times, the "inner essence" of the present.

It is precisely the "recognition of the living divine reign in history" that Friedrich Julius Stahl calls the philosophical foundation of Savigny's historical school. From out of the vision of the divine in history, Stahl writes, "comes the reverence before what persists, the human shyness in changing what is, the looking out upon a higher power from which one must expect the most essential and best."[95] Touched by the "great destruction" that positivism has brought to the world of law, Savigny saw an insightful reverence for the unceasing presence of the truth of the past as a way to build the law anew.[96] Savigny spent his entire adult life working toward the publication of his historical system of law. "Every [learned jurist] has a method," Savigny announced in a lecture in the fall of 1802, "but only with a few scientists does that method come to consciousness and system. The method is brought into a system so that we can think a science to its completion according to its own laws of its nature, or that we can think an ideal of science. The insight into the ideal alone leads us to the correct method."[97] Savigny knew himself to be one of those few, blessed not only with technical mastery but also with an insight into the beating heart of the law's ideal. Savigny's historical legal science, therefore, must be seen as an attempt to think legal science to its completion from a fundamental and guiding insight into an idealization of the preconceptual organic law of nature.

From Insight to the Science of Justice: Savigny's Legal System and Christian Equality

From 1840 to 1849, Savigny published the eight volumes of his *System des Heutigen Römischen Rechts* or the *System of Modern Roman Law*. Savigny's *System* is actually two systems.[98] There is a system of logically coherent legal rules *(Rechtsregeln)*, and there is the organic system of legal institutes *(Rechtsinstitute)*. The first system of legal rules emerges out of an insight into the system of legal institutes. As a scientific work, Savigny's *System* grounds law on a single insight that manifests the living spirit of a *Volk*.

In accord with the demand of the principle of sufficient reason, Savigny does in fact set a single reason atop his *System of Modern Roman Law*. In section 15 of the *System*—a section that he himself recommends as particularly important to his understanding of the "true essence of legal science"[99]—Savigny writes: "The universal task of all *Recht* simply lets itself be led back to the ethical determination of human nature."[100] Law *(Recht)* serves the ultimate ends of an ethical world.[101] Law exists and has force only insofar as it furthers a scientifically knowable ethical ideal. Specifically, law is subordinate to that particular ethical world embodied "in the Christian approach to life."[102] All law, Savigny argues, must promote and conform to the ethical goal of a Christian world.

Just as Leibniz sought to derive his *Systema Iuris* from a first principle of Christian justice understood as the charity of the wise, so too does Savigny set a Christian ethics atop his system. Against Leibniz, however, Savigny denies that the highest end of law is to be found in rational and logical norms that float high above the real world. Instead, the highest end of law is its contribution to an historical task, one that unites a particular historical people to its higher calling. Christianity, he argues, is not simply recognized as a rule of life. The Christian ethos is not an abstract idea or a theological opinion; on the contrary, it is an actual and active force in the world.

Christianity has "in fact, transformed the world," Savigny argues, "so that all of our thoughts, no matter how strange or even antagonistic they might seem to Christianity, are nevertheless governed by it and infused by it."[103] Christianity is less a theology than an anthropology. The Christian ethos that Savigny reveres as the ultimate source of law is found not in religious texts or doctrines but rather in the actually existing social conditions of Christian life.

Savigny's Christianity is an ethical comportment based on "the recognition of the overall equal ethical worth and freedom of man."[104] As a doctrine of the equality of souls, Christianity infuses its institutions with the spirit of equality. At the center of the Christian world, Savigny argues, is the ethical imperative that every man advance the free flourishing of his potential. Equality and freedom, the two pillars of Christian and liberal ethics, combine in Savigny's jurisprudence to require that every man be guaranteed a free realm for the development of his own capacities and talents.

In the service of the Christian world, the ultimate task of law is to secure for man a space for his free development. "This is only possible," Savigny writes, "through the recognition of an invisible boundary within which the existence and effectivity of each individual is granted a secure and free space. The rule through which this boundary and free space is determined, is law *(Recht)*."[105] While Savigny's ideal of law as a boundary protecting free and equal persons appears similar to liberal theories of law, it differs insofar as liberal jurists sever law from its roots in an ethical system. Law's securing of a personal legal realm is necessary, Savigny argues, only because of the grounding ethical commitment to a good Christian life. Law, in other words, is that rule which makes the free pursuit of a Christian ethic a possibility.

Law *(Recht)* must "serve ethics."[106] *Recht* is set under the overriding task of ethical freedom. Christian ethics itself requires that law retains its "self-sufficient existence"[107] and that it not be "dissolved into a broader realm" of social and economic interests.[108] Law serves Christian ethics, Savigny writes, but it does not do so by carrying out specific ethical commands of a Christian *Volk*. Instead, law secures for Christians the free and equal space for them to develop their powers. The ethical command of Christianity is that man must make his world, whether for better or for worse. Man is free to stand and free to fall, and law is that boundary marker that guarantees him the space to act.

Out of this single task of law emerges the whole logical system of legal rules. The system of private law protects the free and independent wills of otherwise equal individuals. Accordingly, there are two kinds of objects over which a willing subject can exert his independent mastery. Man can exert his will over objects, and he can will to master other willing subjects, at least insofar as concerns their activities. The legal protection of the subject's mastery of unfree things is called the law of things, or property law. And the legal protection of a subject's control over the actions of other free beings is called the law of obligations. There are certain persons, however, with whom a legal subject cannot freely contract as equal willing beings; family members, for example, are not simply willing subjects, but must be considered also as members of a larger whole, so that willful relations within the family follow special rules that "only partially belong in the realm of [private] law" and are to be treated within the system under the heading of family law.[109] Finally, the extension of a subject's will over both free and unfree things lasts only so long as he himself lives and possesses a will. The law of inheritance, therefore, comprises the fourth and final division of Savigny's system of private law. The four-part division of civil law into property, obligation, family, and inheritance law is, Savigny argues, complete; more importantly, it is "grounded in the innermost essence of the legal institutes, namely their organic unity with the essence of man himself, in which they inhere."[110]

If the four areas of private law all emerge from a single scientific insight into the essence of law, then it is to be expected that the entirety of law is founded on common legal concepts. It ought to be possible, and fruitful, Savigny writes, to abstract from the different substantive legal realms the most general legal concepts. Precisely in order to gain greater clarity regarding "the living unity of their parts," Savigny insists that a system of law needs a "general part of not insignificant dimensions."[111] The general part of law *(allgemeiner Teil)* seeks a fundamental knowledge of what is truly common in the various parts of the system.

When he published volume 1 of the *System* in 1842, Savigny envisioned that the general part would consume the first three volumes of the work, to be followed by single volumes on the various substantive areas of law. By the publication of volume 8 in 1850, however, the general part had come to overwhelm the system itself. The entire eight volumes of Savigny's *System of Modern Roman law* are dedicated to nothing but the general part, which addresses the conceptual structure and rational framework for the entirety of legal relations. As Savigny writes, the general part explores not only "the nature of legal subjects and in particular their legal capacity," but also the creation and voiding of legal relations and the legal actions available for the protection of one's rights against injury.[112] As with the *Generalia Iuris* that introduces Leibniz's *Systema Iuris*, Savigny's general part aims to discover the fundamental legal principles that govern the systematic edifice of law.

The Doctrine of Mistake in Savigny's General Part of the *System*

To understand Savigny's general part and his system of *Recht*, it is helpful to consider the example of contracts based on errors and mistakes. Savigny considers the question of whether obligations based on mistakes can be enforced both in chapter 3 of the general part of his system that concerns the creation and voiding of legal rights and in a special appendix at the end of volume 3. The appendix, itself nearly 150 pages, shows the importance Savigny attached to this problem. What is most interesting here, however, is the careful way in which Savigny systematically sets about to resolve the question of mistake in declarations of will.[113]

The problem of mistake in questions of contract arises because the system of private law is grounded on free will. As shown above, every law addresses a relation either between a person and a thing (property law) or between a person and another (law of obligations). The question of the creation of legal relations depends on what are called "juridical facts" *(juristische Tatsachen)*, which are divided into facts that arise from the free negotiation of the parties and those that come into being accidentally. The freely created legal facts are in turn divisible into actions that are immediately taken to create a new legal relation and those that while aimed at nonlegal goals have the effect of creating legal relations. The former of these legal activities, those taken between the relevant parties acting intentionally to bring about a new legal obligation, are called "declarations of will" *(Willenserklärungen)*.[114] Of the various obligations that arise from a mutual declaration of wills, the most important and most frequent is contract, which Savigny defines as the coming together of more than one person in an agreement of declared wills that determine their legal relations.[115]

The question raised by the possibility of a mistaken declaration of will is the following: Under what conditions should a contract be voided because the will declared was in error as the result of a mistake? Savigny's answer is that, as a rule, a mere mistake (as opposed to fraud or coercion) has no effect on a contract.[116] When a person willfully contracts with another to buy the latter's Jaguar, but as a result of an innocent mistake does not know that the jaguar in question is a ferocious cat and not a British roadster, Savigny's rule would prevent the unhappy new owner of the cat from voiding the transaction.

Such a rule—that a contract made in error remains valid[117]—seems to contradict Savigny's basic understanding of contract, that all obligations are grounded on will. As Savigny himself argues, an erroneous will is an important consideration "insofar as we recognize from it that the will, which must be accepted after the declaration, is, in fact, not present, for which reasons the legal consequences of the will cannot ensue."[118] Further, Savigny's defense of erroneous contracts contradicts numerous statements of Roman law that hold that those who are in error are not regarded as agreeing *(non videntur, qui errant, consentire)*.[119] Why then does Savigny deny the effect of error?

In an insightful article on Savigny's doctrine of legal error, the German legal historian Klaus Luig has argued that Savigny's decision to reject the importance of legal error has a "material ground."[120] What Luig means is that the need to consider errors as irrelevant comes not from the idealistic framework of Savigny's legal system, but from the social and economic needs of commercial society. To make this point, Luig cites Savigny's statement that "in this regular ineffectivity of error lies . . . the only salvation of commerce against infinite insecurity and arbitrariness."[121] If every time someone made a mistake—or claimed they had made a mistake—an otherwise valid contract could be nullified, and commerce would come to a standstill. It is because of these utilitarian considerations, Luig suggests, that Savigny departs from what would otherwise be his expected position.

However, there is another explanation for Savigny's rejection of error as an invalidating condition of contracts. Shortly after mentioning the interests of commerce, Savigny writes that the rule regarding the ineffectivity of error "follows first of all from out of the nature of the free will itself, whose existence and effect are fully independent of the true or mistaken motive: and moreover from the general consideration of freedom."[122] Free will, Savigny argues, is not affected by error. Since the legal actor is at all times the one who has the choice among competing courses of action, it is the willing and acting subject who gives error its force: "the freedom of this choice between opposing resolutions was unlimited."[123] It may be true that, insofar as the will is thought to exist in the soul separate from the declaration of will, an error negates the existence of the will. For Savigny, however, the "will is a self-sufficient fact that is of sole importance for the formation of the legal relation."[124] Because Savigny abstracts and separates the declared will from its apparent foundation in the mind of the willing subject, he can and does argue that the will is nothing other than its momentary expression in the context of the contractual relation.[125] Outside of its positive existence in the expression of the willing subject, the will, for Savigny, is without substance.

It might be thought that Savigny's positivist reduction of the will to the fact of its declaration is a result, as Luig suggests, of his consideration of material and social interests. Savigny, however, continuously rejects such an explanation. Since *Recht* serves "the higher truth through its bond with the whole" of the ethos, Savigny is clear that this "one end is fully sufficient, and it is in no way necessary to set an entirely different and second end next to it under the name of the public good."[126] The consideration of the social and economic interests of the commonweal as grounds for law is, Savigny argues, unnecessary. Since these interests go toward the "expansion of our mastery over nature," they only increase the means through which the ethical end of human nature seeks to enrich itself. What is useful for the common good is, in the end, encompassed by the needs of Christian ethics and the demand that man develop his capabilities to the fullest. Freedom, and not commerce, is the ultimate end that Savigny's system of law aspires to promote.

Savigny's Unintentional Positivism and the Rise of Social Science

It is important to understand why Savigny's scientific system of *Recht* could not be a code. He saw a code as an absolute statement of the law that immediately upon its introduction established itself as the highest and exclusive source of law. Once it is admitted that codes can only be complete when they transform themselves into scientific codes, the very idea of codification shatters. Since science necessarily strives for an integration of particular legal relations into the entirety of a historically existing ethical world, even a scientifically complete code must admit that there are sources of law beyond the legal rules themselves. To say that *Recht* is a construction of science means, as Leibniz saw 150 years earlier, that *Recht* is in need of reasons and grounds that must necessarily be above the law.

Like Leibniz, Savigny's legal science was inspired by a felt need to reconnect law to its ethical ground. We have seen that the need to rejuvenate law is a consequence of the loss of insight as a source of law.

If Leibniz sought to cure the loss of insight with the promise of certain knowledge of justice, Savigny no longer took seriously the Enlightenment faith in reason. What was needed was not the replacement of insight with knowledge, but the resurrection of insight through science. By bringing the scientific approach to bear on law as it actually exists in historical nations, Savigny thought that he could lend his insights a scientific authority that Leibniz's more ethereal conclusions could not bear. And yet, just as Leibniz's insistence that law provide reasons for its being had unintended and unwanted consequences, so too has Savigny's insistence that law originates in the social life of a people helped advance the positivization of law that he sought to prevent. Even as Savigny distinguished law's transcendent existence in the social life of a people from law's more mundane existence in social and economic norms, his followers questioned that distinction—and not without justification. By bringing the grounds and reasons of law down to earth, Savigny opened the door to the rise of new sciences of law—sociology and economics—that sought to locate the principles of justice in decidedly earthly and positive norms.

CHAPTER 7

The *Bürgerliches Gesetzbuch* (BGB) of 1900: Positive Legal Science and the End of Justice

> The question considered here is a pure question of instrumentality, ... how ought *Recht,* regardless of its content, be instituted and formed so that through its mechanism the application of legal rules to concrete cases can be done most simply, more easily, and more surely?
>
> —Rudolf von Jhering, *The Spirit of Roman Law*

Friedrich Carl von Savigny died in 1861. His death, as James Whitman has suggested, marked a caesura in German legal history. With Savigny died the last great attempt to call science to the rescue of law. Like Leibniz, Savigny sought to enlist science in rejuvenating law as an ethical activity. Faced with the loss of the natural insight into the connection between the legal and ethical worlds, Leibniz and Savigny called on science to save law from the omnipresent threat of its descent into the ordinary. After Savigny, the science of law in Germany (and beyond) gradually aligned itself with the positivist social sciences. For social scientists, law is to be found in empirically discoverable norms and conventions. With only a small risk of overstatement, it can be said that with Savigny's passing, Germany—and the Western world more generally—lost its last great defender of the spiritual sanctuary of the law.

Upon hearing of the death of the man "in whom, as in no other, the history of jurisprudence has been embodied since the beginning of our century," Rudolf von Jhering—one of Savigny's greatest disciples—sat down to write his obituary.[1] As befits a man of science and ideas, Jhering moved quickly from eulogy to engagement. He compared Savigny's towering stature in jurisprudence to Goethe's in letters; then, after proclaiming that Savigny's unmatched brilliance would continue to shine brightly for centuries, Jhering attacked the very core of Savigny's historical legal science.

The heart of Savigny's teaching, Jhering writes, is that "laws are not *made*, but rather *become*, that they come forth like language and custom from the innermost life and thinking of a nation unmediated by calculation and consciousness."[2] In setting the essence of law in the invisible activity of national history, Savigny, Jhering insists, concedes too much to the past and underestimates "the worth and the significance of human activity and human force."[3] To elevate history to the highest source of law is to devalue "the role that free resolve, reflection, and intention play in history" and in law.[4] Savigny's fatal error is that he imagines law to "become" without the active participation of human force. Against Savigny, Jhering advances his own thesis that the original essence of law is not a historical becoming but a human act.

Jhering's insistence that law is a product of human activity challenges Savigny's double source thesis, which imagines a true and necessary law existing beyond human will in the *Volksgeist*. Just as Savigny denied the accessibility and reality of Leibniz's situating the second source of law in divine reason, so now does Jhering deride Savigny's faith in a second and true source of law in history as a "flight from historical fact."[5] For Jhering, Savigny's conviction that historical science can uncover the invisible laws behind the creation of *Recht* partakes of the basic natural law fantasy that the true scientist must expose. By invoking science, Jhering makes clear that his criticism of Savigny's double source thesis is anything but an abandonment of the scientific approach to *Recht*. On the contrary, Jhering seeks to replace Savigny's "lazy" science with his own rigorous and courageous science that stays true to the facts of life.[6]

Jurisprudence, Jhering argues, must remain a science. As such, it must come clean with the facts and admit that *Recht*—in addition to *Gesetz*—is a creation of man. Against thinkers like Savigny and Leibniz who insist that *Recht* has a more-than-human source in history or reason, Jhering flatly asserts that the first and original source of law lies in the human breast.[7] For Jhering, "the entire human world inclusive of *Recht* and morality is the creation of men."[8]

That man makes *Recht*, however, does not mean that Jhering endorses a brute positivism that subordinates *Recht* to arbitrary *Gesetz*. On the contrary, Jhering curses simple nonscientific positivism as the "deadly enemy of jurisprudence" against which jurisprudence must constantly defend itself.[9] Beyond the mere facts of *Gesetz*, the science of *Recht* must see through the apparent willfulness of human action and thereby raise *Gesetz* to a higher idea of *Recht*.

Above the mere formality of judicial logic, Jhering continues to believe in a scientifically knowable "substantial idea of justice and ethics" that must be actualized in particular legal institutes and rules.[10] He insists, however, that the substance of justice is contained in humanly posited ends and interests. Since *Recht* is first a product of human action, its higher second source cannot exist outside of the man-made world. The higher "justice" of *Recht*, therefore, must be a creation of man that follows the ultimate law of all social development: the law of ends.[11] "The end"—as Jhering writes in the epigraph to his most famous book, *The End in Recht* (or, alternatively, *Recht as a Means to an End*)—"is the creator of the entirety of *Recht*."[12] That law is essentially a means to an end, Jhering asserts, is the "motto" governing his legal thought.

Jhering's focus on ends is, on one level, reminiscent of the scientific drive to justify *Recht* through jurisprudence that this book has traced to its most forceful beginning in Leibniz's legal thinking. It should not be surprising, therefore, that Jhering names Leibniz as a precursor to his own project and that the opening sentence of *Der Zweck in Recht (Law as a Means to an End)* announces Leibniz's principle of sufficient reason as the guiding idea of Jhering's legal thinking. For Jhering, as for Leibniz, Svarez, and Savigny, the principle of *Recht* is that *Recht* must have a reason—what Jhering renames an "end."

On another level, however, Jhering's scientific grounding of *Recht* differs fundamentally from the legal science that came before him. Whereas Savigny and Leibniz imagine that *Recht* has its organizing principle in a transcendent unity that connects the individual to a more-than-human whole, Jhering answers emphatically: "NO! My friends, the truth does not lie outside of the world, she lies in the world, and that is the great advance jurisprudence has made in our present century."[13] Jhering gives up on the dream of a transcendent *Recht*.

Jhering's originality is to argue that legal science, in the name of science, must abandon the search for an unknowable ethical ground of justice. The attempt to justify *Recht* according to ends, Jhering argues, is a political rather than a metaphysical project. The search for ends is destined to lead not to a single rational or historical truth, but to the conclusion that all ends in *Recht* are interested ends.[14]

For Jhering—and here he is the precursor of both the German BGB and almost all of twentieth- and twenty-first-century Western legal thought—the science of *Recht* is divided into two fully separate yet dependent sciences. On the one hand, the science of *Recht* is a technical and formal science of legal rules. On the other hand, the science of *Recht* must address the science of extralegal ends; law depends, therefore, on the study of human ends undertaken by philosophers, sociologists, anthropologists, economists, psychologists, and other social scientists. Lawyers must be aware of these ends if law is to serve them well. The two sciences of *Recht* relate in that the technical science of *Recht* serves the normative science of ends. What the science of *Recht* (as opposed to the science of ends) requires is, above all, a technical legal system that makes *Recht* serviceable to the social, political, and economic ends of society.

The division of legal science into a system of laws that presuppose and are controlled by a separate system of social, normative, economic ends is not simply the fantasy of a nineteenth-century German scholar.[15] On the contrary, Jhering's thesis that law is a manmade product for the achievement of social and economic ends is the fundamental idea underlying the creation and writing of the German BGB. The BGB, therefore, needs to be understood as both a continuation of the scientific approach to law initiated by Leibniz and rejuvenated by Savigny and as the first scientific code that abandons the effort to revive the connection between law and a transcendent ethics through science. With the BGB, *Recht* emerges in a new form as a pure technical object that is, in its nature, nothing but a means to an end.

That the BGB incorporates Jhering's understanding of a technical legal science in the service of nonlegal ends is clearly attested to by Gottlieb Planck. Planck, the head of the commission responsible for writing the BGB and one of the most influential of the code's founding fathers, expressly imagined the BGB as a tool in the hands of lawyers and judges for the pursuit of social ends. In his published commentary to the code, designed to help Germany's jurists in their attempts to use the new system, he writes that everything depends on a clear understanding of the "leading ideas" that animate the code. "For the correct understanding of a *Gesetz*," Planck argues, "two moments are of decisive importance.

Positive Legal Science and the End of Justice   141

On the one hand is the economic and social end that the *Gesetz* pursues, and on the other, the technical-juridical means that are appropriate to reaching the end."[16] Like Jhering, Planck fully endorses the basic idea that the code must bring a technical jurisprudence into the service of social and economic ends.

This chapter argues that the BGB, the last and most scientifically rigorous of the German legal codes, actualizes modern *Recht* as a product of science. The BGB must be seen within the tradition of legal science that this book has traced from Leibniz through the ALR to Savigny and Jhering. Severed from its pre-scientific ground in an insightful and ethical activity, law must justify itself. The need *Recht* has of justification has brought about the subordination of *Recht* to its reasons and grounds.

For Leibniz, as for Savigny and even Svarez, the reasons for law were at least purportedly transcendent—they sought to connect the laws of this world with a higher justice. This is no longer the case within the BGB. While the BGB remains a scientific codification, the nature of its science undergoes a radical and fateful change. Divorced from any and all connection to an ethical reason or a deeper ground, law emerges in its modern form as positive law: namely, as a pure technical means for the pursuit of social, economic, and ultimately political ends.

The BGB and the Science of Abstraction

In 1874, the new German parliament appointed a committee of eleven jurists to the so-called first commission responsible for writing a German civil code. The members of the first commission were professors, judges, and legal officials who had been weaned on the writings of Savigny's legal historical school. While this new generation of jurists rejected Savigny's faith that science could reveal the historical unity of the German *Volk*, they fully internalized his basic methodological innovation: namely, that the ground and reason for law *(Recht)* comes to be given by legal scientists themselves. Savigny's scientific jurisprudence served as the intellectual background of the German BGB of 1900.

Written over nearly one-quarter of a century, the BGB adopts Savigny's faith in the productive and creative power of legal science. As the culmination of nearly a century of scientific analysis of law, the German BGB is rightly considered the most technically advanced legal code ever written. It has been termed a "masterwork" of judicial science,[17] and the English legal historian Frederic William Maitland jealously referred to it as "the best code that the world has yet seen."[18] If law, as this book argues, has come to be a product of science, the BGB stands as the most lucid expression of the scientific essence of law.

The scientific character of the BGB is most clearly visible in the code's overwhelming tendency toward abstraction. The BGB is composed of highly abstract rules that bear little connection to any vital legal relations. They do not arise from out of the emotional furnace of actual social and legal disputes, and there is little of the colorful detail that marks the specific origins of many of the rules from the Roman law and the ALR. Rather, the language of the code has the arid crispness of "dispassionate objectivity and strict moral self-discipline" that aims for "clarity and concision through its rigorous conceptualism and almost total rejection of detailed casuistry."[19]

An example of the BGB's austere abstraction can be found in the seemingly simple case of a purchase of goods. Whereas the ALR lays out the rules governing a sales contract in 362 paragraphs providing examples, solutions, and justifications for all kinds of situations, the BGB covers the sales contract in 82 terse paragraphs that offer neither examples nor justifications. The sales contract is directly regulated by BGB paragraph 433, which requires certain actions on the part of both buyer and seller.[20]

> §433. By the contract of sale the seller of a thing is bound to deliver the thing to the purchaser and to transfer ownership of the thing. The seller of a right is bound to transfer the right to the purchaser, and if the right entitles one to the possession of a thing, to deliver the thing. The purchaser is bound to pay to the seller the purchase price agreed upon and to take delivery of the thing purchased.[21]

While paragraph 433 seems plain enough, it is unlikely to decide any case that actually would come before a court. Most contract disputes involve questions about whether one party was indeed the seller or whether a sales contract was ever concluded. On these and other questions, the sections of the BGB dealing with a purchase contract are silent. As one commentator has quipped, "We see that anyone who thinks he has found the answer to his sales question within the eighty paragraphs of the law of sale is one hundred per cent mistaken."[22]

Positive Legal Science and the End of Justice 143

Instead, a full legal evaluation of the validity and meaning of any particular sales contract requires an understanding of the various concepts that comprise the legal contract for buying and selling goods. The abstract method of the BGB works through intersecting levels of rules.[23] Faced with a case involving a contractual sale of goods, a judge under the BGB first turns to the rules governing sales contracts themselves. These specific rules cover circumstances unique to sales contracts—for example, implicit warranties and the specific moment at which a sale is concluded. But the law governing sales contracts is also found within the sections of the BGB that deal with two-party contracts. As a result, a judge must turn to a second level of rules that includes the BGB's discussion of mutual contracts (BGB, §320ff). Further, if the question arises whether a contract exists at all, a judge will need to consult a third level of the code, namely, the section on the "Contractual Relations Based on Contracts"; here the judge will find definitions and rules regulating the existence of contracts in general (BGB, §305ff).

In addition, a fourth level of laws lies outside the realm of contracts altogether. Since a contract is simply one kind of legal obligation, the resolution of contractual disputes also is governed by rules regulating obligations, contractual or otherwise. These rules are dealt with in the "General Part" of Book II of the BGB, which addresses the "Law of Obligation." Rules from this fourth level of abstraction require, for example, that contracts be carried out with regard to commercial customs (BGB, §242) and state that contracts are void upon the emergence of an intervening circumstance that makes the fulfillment of the contract impossible (BGB, §275).

A fifth level of abstraction moves beyond the realms of obligation and contract and into the legal concepts contained in the "General Part" or *Allgemeiner Teil* of the BGB. The 240 paragraphs that comprise the "General Part" contain those overarching principles that apply to all the areas of civil law, including the simple contract of sale. Accordingly, the sales contract must be executed by valid legal subjects and must involve private declarations of will that carry legal consequences (BGB, §116–144). Finally, there is the section of the "General Part" addressing the general rules governing contracts (BGB, §145–157). It is here that one learns that all contracts are to be interpreted in accordance with *"Treu und Glauben* [i.e., *bona fides* or good faith] and with respect to commercial customs" (BGB, §157).

The abstract presentation of the *Gesetz* in which basic legal activities such as sales contracts are "dissected into their parts" is at once the BGB's great advance and its great danger. It is dangerous because the rules are so distant from actual situations in which everyday legal relations arise that the application of the rules to particular cases is subject to abuse or error by either unscrupulous or incompetent judges. One potentially chaos-inducing consequence of the BGB's abstract technique is that it requires judges not to simply apply the laws *(Gesetz)* to cases in a mechanical way, but to explicate and interpret the rules in every case. Further, it seems undeniable that "a consequence of this system (beginning with the most general rules, and always placing the more general rules before the more special) [is] that it complicates the treatment of even so simple a case as the sale of a chattel, in that it may necessitate recourse to various provisions in the various books of the codification."[24] From the point of view of a common citizen looking to buy a car, the BGB must seem impenetrable. For all its vaunted coherence and logic, the BGB is striking in its inaccessibility.

At the same time, however, trained jurists find in the BGB's technique a unique advantage, since they can quickly abstract any case that arises into its basic legal concepts and then resolve the case with certitude by recombining the concepts in accordance with the rules set out in the code. The legal concepts in the BGB approximate an "alphabet of *Recht*" *(Rechtsalphabet)* that comprises the "simple elements of *Recht*."[25] Just as Leibniz had hoped to break *Recht* into foundational elements and then reconstruct it in order to decide particular cases, the great value of the BGB's technical abstraction is not that it allows only for a shorter and more economical code, but more importantly, that it "essentially facilitates the understanding, intellectual mastery and thus the usefulness *(Handhabung)* of valid *Recht*."[26] *Recht*, more than 200 years after Leibniz laid out the groundwork of a technical legal science, was finally to be comprehended in an abstract system of elemental concepts through which its entirety could be known and determined with certainty.

And yet, just as Leibniz eventually rejected the ideal of geometrical construction, the BGB abandons the dream of mechanical codification. The youthful Leibniz boasted that a six-year-old child could accurately apply the laws in his legal code. The ALR expressly required that all cases not clearly subsumed by the code be referred to a legislative legal commission rather than allow judges discretion in applying the *Gesetz*. In contrast, the BGB, against nearly all prior codifications, denies the possibility of a systematic presentation of the laws that would be so precise as to obviate the need for judicial interpretation. Rather, the BGB seeks to address the admitted insufficiency of its legal rules through a science of legal interpretation.

The BGB's embrace of judicial interpretation to address its unavoidable lacunae does not mean that the German code dispenses with the systematic certainty that is the goal of legal science. Even as the BGB abandons the codifier's faith in a complete rendering of laws, it does not give judges carte blanche to interpret the code according to their own economic or political views. Instead, the BGB incorporates interpretation into its inner structure. Legal interpretation is not an exercise in arbitrary reasoning, but follows definite rules of interpretation that are presupposed by the codifiers. Within the BGB, legal interpretation forms a necessary part of any certain and scientific approach to law.[27]

The Scientific Handling of *Recht*: Interpretation and the *Rechtsordnung*

As a product of the scientific jurisprudence of the nineteenth century, the BGB presupposes a particular approach that governs its interpretation and application. The first paragraph of the first draft of the BGB lays out the code's scientific ground: "For relations in which the law *(Gesetz)* contains no rule, the rules given for legally similar relations find application. In the absence of such rules the principles given in themselves from out of the spirit of the legal order [*Rechtsordnung*] are controlling."[28]

The idea that the positive laws in the code are to be interpreted according to principles "given" from out of the "spirit of the *legal order*" mirrors the conclusions reached by Bernard Windscheid in his *Textbook on Roman Law*.[29] Windscheid, arguably the most influential member of the first commission and the author of the best-regarded and most influential course book on nineteenth-century German law, holds that the application of a legal code depends on a second and higher source of law found in a scientifically constructed legal order *(Rechtsordnung)*. Just as Leibniz set positive laws within a legal order founded in the science of justice, Windscheid and the authors of the BGB subordinate the particular laws of the code to a science of justice as it exists in the legal order.

Since interpretation of the BGB requires looking through *Gesetz* to the kernel of the legal order, any attempt to comprehend the BGB depends on a prior understanding of the legal order. While paragraph 1 of the BGB's draft was left out of the final version, it was excised only because its subordination of *Gesetz* to the legal order *(Rechtsordnung)* was considered obvious and thus unnecessary.[30] This is made clear by the five-volume *Motive* in which the BGB's authors offer their commentary on the scientific underpinnings of the code. According to the *Motive*, no *Gesetz* can ever hope to be complete and sufficient on its own: "The attempt to achieve a completeness of this kind would be a non-starter."[31] As Andreas von Tuhr, one of the leading commentators on the BGB, writes, interpretation of *Gesetze* in the code is not based on the words themselves, but "rather in the significance that accrues to them in their totality with the entirety of *Gesetz* and the other parts of the legal order."[32] It is the legal order, as the second source of *Recht*, that unifies the codified laws and gives them their meaning and application. The scientific interpretation of *Recht* requires one to know what the *Motive* calls "the true system of *Recht*—the inner togetherness of its legal rules;"[33] interpretation of *Gesetz*, therefore, depends on a prior knowledge of *Recht* as it exists in the legal order, that is, the *Rechtsordnung*.[34]

At times, the legal order appears as a natural order prior to the positing of *Gesetz*. For example, the *Motive* claims that the legal order has a basis in natural reason: "The legal order," states the *Motive*, "fulfills a command of reason and ethics, insofar as it recognizes the legal capacity *(Rechtsfähigkeit)* of man without regard to his individuality and without regard to his will."[35] In declaring slavery foreign to the German legal world and by granting every man (women are a noted exception)[36] equal legal capacity, the BGB claims to be merely "fulfilling" a natural and rational moral principle, "the principle of legal equality and the commonality of *Recht*."[37] This suggests that the positive grant of legal capacity and subjective *Recht* is, at least according to the *Motive*, a manifestation of a natural ethical order of *Recht*.

The presumed naturalness of the legal order, however, cannot be sustained. Even as the *Motive* supports the equal capacity of men as legal actors upon a rational legal order, it importantly distinguishes between the legal order and the ethical order of society itself. Insofar as the legal order fulfills the command of reason, it plays an intermediate role between reason and the posited legal order. As one of the leading contemporary commentators on the BGB writes, "Beyond the legal order standing equal to it yet flowing from other sources and protected by other means, stands the ethical order."[38] Indeed, the intermediate role of the legal order is confirmed in the *Motive*'s later discussion of legal transactions *(Rechtsgeschäfte)*. A legal act exists insofar as "a *will* directed to the production of a legal effect activates itself, and the *word (Spruch) of the legal order (Rechtsordnung)* actualizes the legally willed form by recognizing this will in the legal world."[39] The capacity to act legally *(Rechtsfähigkeit)* is not a natural possession of every man but rather a power granted by the "word of the legal order," a saying that grants and posits the legal world. The legal order *(Rechtsordnung)* awards *Recht* with its word; thus, the legal order stands as a constructed order between an unknowable ideal of justice and the posited system of laws.

The BGB's science of *Recht* demands that *Recht* conform to the posited will of the legal order, just as 100 years earlier the ALR required that *Recht* conform to the posited will of the king. What has changed is that the good posited in the legal order is no longer seen to be knowable according to a principle of sovereign and thus transcendent justice. Leibniz imagined that the legal order extended to the realm of divine justice that governs the interpretation of law by expressing the ethical imperative to act charitably, and Savigny found a non-positivist legal order in the institutional embodiment of a Christian ethical world. Even Svarez, who saw the will of the king as the ultimate *ratio* for law, believed that the king's will was governed by a rational idea of the common good. For Leibniz, Savigny, and Svarez, the legal order of society was seen as a transcendent and rational, albeit willful, second source of law. The BGB, however, rejects all transcendent grounds for law even as it furthers the fundamental scientific drive to justify law through science.

What distinguishes the BGB from preceding scientific codes is its characteristic construction of the legal order as the embodiment of justice. For Windscheid, Jhering, and the BGB's codifiers, the continued embrace of a second source of *Recht* is divorced from its ethical grounding in reason. Not only are the positive laws *(Gesetze)* of the code willed by the legal order *(Rechtsordnung)* as technical means to legal ends, but also, and more radically, the legal order itself is willed and constructed. The problem for the legal scientists behind the BGB was which worldly, material, and ultimately contingent scientific principles of justice could succeed in justifying *Recht* as it is expressed in the legal order.

The Legal Order and the Balancing of Social and Economic Interests

The first principle of law within the BGB's legal order is the protection of a subjective realm of personal freedom. As was shown in Chapter 6, the protection of subjective freedom is, for Savigny, a necessary consequence of the Christian imperative to pursue the good to the best of one's ability. Savigny's double source thesis holds that positive law has its scientific ground in an ethical world. Following Savigny, the jurists behind the BGB also imagined that the positive laws in the code are guaranteed by a higher second source of law located in the legal order. However, the possibility of a rational scientific ground of law is precisely what the BGB's jurists deny. In the BGB, the legal principle guaranteeing every subject a realm of free will is not a legal principle at all. Instead, the first principles of law are sought in the social and economic interests of the legal order. As Planck writes in a revealing passage cited above, the guiding ends of *Gesetz* are found not in logic and reason but in the social and economic interests that inform the legal order.

The BGB takes as the foundation of *Recht* the legal order's grant of legal capacity and legal subjectivity, which begins at the completion of birth (BGB, §1). Only legal subjects are awarded the power to enter into legal relations and to prevent others from interfering with their actions in their sphere of freedom. As Windscheid writes, "Law *(Recht)* is a power of will or a realm of the will granted by the legal order *(Rechtsordnung).*"[40] The *Motive* notes that the *legal order's* grant of legal capacity *(Rechtsfähigkeit)* must be without consideration of racial, sexual, or other characteristics.[41] Yet, the power of the legal order to grant free will to legal subjects is so complete that the will of the legal subject belongs fully to the legal order: "the will that commands in subjective *Recht* is only the will of the legal order, not the will of the rights bearing subject."[42]

Since only the *will* of the legal order grants legal capacity to citizens and gives them their sphere of freedom, the realm of subjective freedom is seen as posited and contingent; it is also, therefore, changeable and even revocable. This can be seen clearly in the BGB's consideration of mistaken contracts. We saw in the previous chapter that Savigny grounds legal capacity in an ethically existing fact of freedom that requires the recognition of all freely made agreements. As a result, Savigny argues that freely made contracts are enforceable even when they are made in error and lead to potentially unfair outcomes.

The BGB, on the contrary, makes the legal order's grant of legal capacity contingent on extralegal social and economic interests. The interest in avoiding unfairness to potentially weaker or disadvantaged persons who enter into contracts without full knowledge of the circumstances, for example, leads the BGB to empower judges to void contracts that are agreed to in error. Thus, a person who contracts to buy a Jaguar mistakenly believing himself to be buying a British roadster rather than a wild cat can rescind his willful declaration, according to the BGB, "if it may be assumed that he would not have made his declaration with knowledge of the facts and with reasonable appreciation of the situation" (BGB, §119). A judge must look beyond the strict requirements of the law and decide each case according to the social and economic interests embodied in the legal order.

The BGB's willingness to turn to the spirit of the legal order as a way of avoiding unfairness is manifest in its regulation of property law. Section 903 of the BGB grants to every legal subject who is the owner of a thing the right "to deal with [his] things as he pleases and to exclude others from any interference" with his use and enjoyment of his property. The owner's seemingly absolute property right, however, is limited by social and economic interests. As a result, one can only exercise his property right over a thing "to the extent that it is not contrary to the law or rights of third parties." When someone seeking to avoid a grave danger, for example, takes refuge on my land or takes possession of my car, I, as the owner, am not entitled to prohibit the other's use of my property if that use "is necessary for the avoidance of a present danger and the damage threatened is disproportionally great compared to the damage caused" me as owner (§904, §228). There are, in other words, social interests of the legal order—here the desirability of allowing people to take reasonable measures to avoid great harm to themselves—that trump the grant of private property rights.

The BGB also recognizes that economic interests can override its grant of subjective rights to private property. For example, a landowner who generally has the right to exclude others from his property is not entitled to prohibit the "intrusion of gases, vapors, smells, smoke, soot, heat, noises, shocks, and similar interferences coming from another piece of land," at least to the extent that the unwelcome emissions "only immaterially prejudice" his use of his land. Even if the emission causes "substantial prejudice," a proprietor cannot exclude them as long as the quantity of emissions conforms to local custom (§906). The *Motive* explains that the practical result of the rule is that only "excessive emissions" are limited and suggests that the "determination of excessive emissions" must take into consideration social and economic interests. In balancing those interests, a judge must ask about the reasonable level of emissions that are customary in different regions.[43] Further, even if the emissions exceed the customarily permitted level, the emissions may be allowed in order to accommodate economic growth. In interpreting the code, therefore, a judge is to prohibit economically valuable emissions only when they have an "extremely harmful" effect on the use of another's land.[44]

While judges are not empowered to supplement the *Gesetze* with their own subjective ethical and political intuitions,[45] the inclusion of open-ended standards as "general clauses"[46] means that judges are free to temper the strict application of the laws in accordance with the social and economic interests of the legal order. In family law, for example, the BGB originally held that a husband, as head of a family, had the right to decide all important decisions regarding family life, including where the family will live. At the same time, however, the code holds that a wife is not obligated to follow her husband's decision when it is a misuse of his rights *(Misbrauch seines Rechts)* (BGB, §1354). In such cases, a judge is required to balance the strictly enforceable rights of one party (husbands) against the economic and social interests of others in society (wives). In the interest of fairness, Planck writes in the *Deutsche Juristen-Zeitung* in 1899, the BGB seeks to "weaken" the strict application of legal rules by requiring judges to take "equitable consideration of the interests of others."[47]

The systematic recourse to concepts like "fairness" *(Billigkeit)*,[48] "commercial customs" *(Verkehrssitte)*,[49] "important grounds" *(wichtige Gründe)*,[50] "good morals" *(guten Sitten)*,[51] and *bona fides (Treu und Glabue)*,[52] reflects

Positive Legal Science and the End of Justice 151

a recognition on the part of the codifiers that abstract legal rules cannot justly be applied to concrete cases without allowing for considerations of equity.[53] Whoever willfully causes damage to another in a manner that is contrary to good values *(gegen die guten Sitten)* is obligated to compensate for the injury. Even someone *not* responsible for damage caused by him shall—where compensation cannot be obtained by a third party—compensate for the damage as fairness demands under the circumstances *(Billigkeit nach den Umständen)* (§829). By including these general clauses in the "General Part" of the BGB and in the general parts of two specific divisions of the code, the codifiers sought to replace the ideal of judges as automatons with that of judges who are under an obligation of "thoughtful obedience" to the laws.[54] Like Roman praetors who could instruct a judge *(judex)* to render decisions by *bona fides* or good faith, the codifiers freed judges to weaken and correct the strict legal propositions by balancing them against social and economic interests. By interpreting *Gesetze* in accord with the interests embodied in the legal order, judges could bring equitable considerations of fairness (what in German is called *Billigkeit*) to bear on legal decisions.

The BGB's Principle of Justice: Fairness and Equality

The recourse to fairness *(Billigkeit)* as the second and higher source of *Recht* in the BGB means that a judge can and should balance legal rules against social and economic interests in the pursuit of fairness. The content of fairness as a principle of justice, however, is highly ambivalent. On the one hand, the BGB's usage of *Billigkeit* has an ancient and important lineage. While the German *billig* has its roots in the stem *Bild* (in English, "image") and originally was an adjective meaning wondrous and powerful, by the seventeenth and eighteenth centuries (around the time the ALR was conceived and written) it had come to be used in the expression *recht und billig,* in which *recht* signifies what is required by *Gesetz* and *billig* names what is required by natural law.[55] Only in a world in which *Recht*—as this book has argued—loses its meaning as natural law, does the need arise for legal science to appeal to fairness *(Billigkeit)* as a new word to say what *Recht* once said. In its association with justice beyond the letter of the positive laws, the German *billig* is associated with the English "equity," which opposes the strict application of law.

Equity is derived from the Latin *aequitas* that translates the Greek *epieikeia* (literally, according to what is proper or most one's own). Aristotle distinguished *epieikeia* from both distributive and corrective justice, which repay what is due according to determinative measures. In contrast to such inflexible measures of justice as legal rules, *epieikeia* is flexible, like the leaden rule used by Lesbian builders; just as that rule is not rigid and can be bent to the shape of the stone, so too is *epieikeia* made to fit the circumstances of a case.[56] Because of its flexibility, *epieikeia* looks beyond the rule and appears as a correction of strict legal justice.[57] And since it is concerned with what is most proper, *epieikeia* bids a judge to judge freely and justly. It asks us to look "at the whole story; to consider not what sort of a person an actor is now, but what sort of person he has been or is usually."[58] Understood as equity, the BGB's appeal to the legal order's spirit of fairness as a second source of law demands that judges correct the code's general provisions in the interest of a higher and absolute insight into the ethical activity of justice.

On the other hand, the BGB's requirement of equitable judgment makes it clear that fairness, at least as it appears in the BGB, is more concerned with equality than with equity. A judge seeking to apply the principle of fairness was neither to impose his subjective evaluation of fairness nor to rely on an ideal measure of ethical behavior. Rather than act from an insightful vision of justice, the judge "must content himself with an average measure."[59] The demand for fairness is designed to ensure the preservation of societal standards by correcting legal rules when they contradict established norms that are equally applicable to everyone. This is especially true in the economic sphere. Planck, for example, accepts that formal legal equality leads often to material inequality. As a result, he argues that fairness requires the code to "work actively against the social ills" of inequality.[60] Within the BGB's legal system, therefore, the interest of fairness rejects equitable justice in favor of equality.

The equation of fairness with equality was widespread in nineteenth-century German legal scholarship. As Windscheid remarks in the middle of the century, "the opposition between *Recht* and fairness is in everyone's mouth," although, he cautions, few understand it. Even the best legal philosophers "see the essence of fairness in the production of equality . . . That is a mistake."[61] And yet, Windscheid sees it as an understandable and even acceptable mistake. Since the actual meaning of

Positive Legal Science and the End of Justice 153

fairness *(Billigkeit)*—the full actualization of the true and natural law given through a necessarily unique and insightful vision—is an impossible ideal, he argues that *"Recht*, to be applicable, must appear as a rule."[62] The rule for deciding individual cases cannot be attuned to each individual case; instead, decisions must follow the legal rules. Equitable decisions are, by definition, ruleless, unjustifiable, and, at least in appearance, unjust. Only when decisions conform to rules do they actualize the spirit of justice manifest in the legal order: namely, the spirit of equal treatment.[63]

Even more than Windscheid, it is Jhering who articulates the emerging connection between justice, fairness, and equality that infuses the spirit of the legal order actualized by the BGB. After having "consciously avoided" speaking about justice *(Gerechtigkeit)* for the first 365 pages of *Der Zweck im Recht*, Jhering asserts that "the practical aim of justice is the production of equality."[64] Equality, in other words, must be seen as the first and highest end of *Recht*.[65]

Jhering's construction of the relation between justice and equality works on two levels. First, equality contributes to material justice insofar as it establishes an equilibrium between a violation of the law and its penalty: punishment should be proportional to the crime. Second, it leads to formal justice when it ensures the uniformity of treatment of all legal subjects under the laws. While a judge's main responsibility is the administration of formal justice in the application of rules to individual cases, he can be empowered—as judges are by the BGB—to apply the formally equal laws according to the standard of material justice. In either case, what makes a judge's decision just as opposed to arbitrary is that it "corresponds to *Gesetz*"; it is *"gesetzmässig."* To the extent a decision departs from formal *Gesetzmässigkeit*—in accordance with fairness and the balancing of social and economic interests—it does so in the name of material equality.[66] In either case, the essence of legal justice is equality understood in opposition to arbitrariness, which Jhering understands to be the epitome of injustice.[67]

That law, insofar as it is governed by ends, must seek equality as the essence of justice begs the question, "What is it then that is so great about equality that we use it to measure the highest concept of *Recht*—which is what justice is."[68] Why, Jhering asks, must law seek equality when all of nature glories in difference and distinction? Indeed, equality appears to be an "ugly trait," rooted in the feelings of jealousy and resentment.[69] The will to equality is the will that "no one should have it better than me." If I am miserable, "so must everyone else be miserable."[70] Equality, it seems, is an unlikely choice as the final end of law.

In spite of the disadvantages attached to equality, Jhering insists that equality is the necessary and highest striving of fairness and justice. He argues that we strive for equality not because we value equality in itself, but "because it is the condition of the *welfare* of society."[71] The value of equality is that it hides or denies the differences that exist by nature and which threaten to "become a highly dangerous menace."[72] The benefit of equality—the pursuit of both material and formal equilibrium—is that it helps to preserve the social order.

Jhering helpfully contrasts his definition of justice as equality in the service of order with what he takes to be Leibniz's identification of justice with fitness. For Leibniz, justice pursues a kind of equality that is grounded in the principle of the "fitness of thing," which "demands a certain satisfaction for the expiation of an evil action."[73] Modeled on divine vengeance, "fitting" punishment is exercised in accord with the principle of reason rather than passion. It has its source in wisdom tempered by charity, and its actualization produces an aesthetic feeling of pleasure in the existence of something good in itself. Understood as fitness, justice must be done even if it has no practical effect.[74] For Jhering, however, there is no legal value in the aesthetic pleasure of the punishment fitting the crime. The demand for equalization inherent in law can be justified only by proving that equality effectively serves a practical purpose: namely, "the equal distribution of burdens and the resulting fixity of social order."[75] As Jhering writes:

> The practical interest in the constancy and growth of society is, therefore, what dictates to it the principle of equality in this sense [of equilibrium between law and social interests], and not in the sense of an a priori categorical imperative of equality to be actualized in all human relations; if experience were to prove that the practical interests of society were better preserved through inequality, then inequality would deserve priority.[76]

The utility of equality as the first principle of law is its legitimating power. When certain members of society are treated unequally and

Positive Legal Science and the End of Justice 155

given less in the distribution of social goods, their interest in the common ends of the society are weakened. A society must secure the devotion of its members, and equality is the best means to that end. Lacking any value in itself, equality is valuable because it is effective in securing Jhering's highest end—the preservation of the societal order.

The emergence of fairness, equality, and legitimacy as the highest values of *Recht* is itself a fitting development of the rise of science as a way of knowing the law. Indeed, it is the logical and necessary culmination of the compulsion to know law as a product of science that this book has named the gift of science.

And yet, the BGB recognizes that the scientific effort to know law with certainty must fail. The "old dream" of the scientific approach to *Recht* is that there is a single, fast, unchangeable *Recht* of reason; in the science that underlies the BGB, this dream is now recognized as an error.[77] Confronted with the failure of science to fully justify *Recht* now understood as *Gesetz*, nineteenth-century jurists saw no alternative but to bracket out the question of justice.

In the place of justice, the jurists behind the BGB set the legitimating capacity of *Billigkeit*, the "norm of comportment that rationally balances the reign of rules," with what Max Weber calls *sachlicher* (in English, "more material") ends.[78] The so-called rational and scientific *Recht* of the BGB is grounded in the principle of the equality of social and economic interests. Instead of rules or transcendent ideals of justice, the codifiers behind the BGB recognize only "what the community thinks is *Recht*."[79] Only that is *Recht* when and "because [the state] has recognized it, has spoken it out as *Recht*."[80] *Recht*, in other words, must first be spoken out *(gesetzt)* by society, and then reconfigured in the scientific creation of the legal order.

The Reign of Legality and Legitimacy of Norms

Having rejected Leibniz's conviction in the scientific knowability of divine reason and Savigny's science of the historically existing *Volksgeist*, the codifiers behind the BGB were thrust back on the assertion—first actualized in the ALR—that law is whatever the legislator says it is. For Svarez, however, the subordination of *Recht* to *Gesetz* was not a rejection of the reign of a scientific worldview, but was itself the result of a scientific approach to natural law that discovers *Recht* to be posited in the rational will of the king. Since the BGB rejects every science of law that relies on a transcendent theory of justice, it seems to be caught between its rejection of all scientific determinations of justice and the imperative to scientifically justify law in order to preserve its authority.

The claim that the BGB, as positive code, has its origin in a scientific metaphysics, has been thought to be a contradiction. Horst Jakobs, for example, argues that the BGB suffers from a divide between its scientific and codificatory impulses.[81] On the one hand, Jakobs names the BGB "the codification of positivism."[82] The BGB, he argues, is a code of "created *Gesetz* whose rules" are not in need of external or extralegal legitimation.[83] On the other hand, however, Jakobs rightly sees that the BGB's scientific foundation compels it to justify its *Gesetze* by looking past the posited laws themselves.

What Jakobs's charge—that the BGB's embrace of science as a second source of law contradicts its legal positivism—misses is the very nature of legal positivism itself. Like many contemporary legal theorists, Jakobs sees the essence of positive law to lie merely in its being posited by a sovereign power. This common understanding of positive law, however, misses the mark.

As this book has sought to show, the essence of positive law is its need for scientific justification. Positive law needs reasons to justify its authority, and it seeks its grounds in science. The common idea that positive law retains its obligatory force simply by virtue of being posited by a sovereign is an absurdity; as H. L. A. Hart has shown, commands and coercive threats may give rise to obedience but not to obligation.[84] Instead, positive law must seek to justify its authority, a task complicated by the loss of law's traditional foundations in natural law, religion, and custom. And yet, denied its natural authority, positive law cannot eschew justification; on the contrary, it is law whose need for justification is palpable.[85] Science, as the modern approach to giving reasons and justifications, comes to be both a symptom of positive law and, more importantly, an essential component of law itself. Law, as positive law, *is* a product of science.

Against all previous scientific codes that sought to actualize an ideal of reasoned justice, the BGB offers a wholly technical *Recht* in the service of equally allotted social and economic values. The will at the ground of the BGB is not the will of a Christian God; nor is it the rational will of a sovereign; nor is it the living Christian will of a *Volkswille*. Instead, it is the general, vague, and ultimately contested idea of fairness: the legitimate balancing of social and economic interests. *Recht* is not, as it was for Leibniz and Savigny, a product of a necessary scientific knowing of the ethical world. And yet *Recht* continues to be known as a product of science. What is changed is that *Recht* itself comes to be a servant *(Magd)* of the juristically determined legal social and economic ends.[86] *Recht*, in other words, is the means for the achievement of the ends adopted by the jurists who form and administer the scientifically constructed legal order.

The reign of legality in the BGB, therefore, differs from that of the ALR. The BGB's insistence on legality *(Gesetzmäßigkeit)* includes but is not limited to the conformity of positive *Recht* to the "calculable rules" of legislative will, as in the ALR;[87] in addition, positive *Recht* must conform to increasingly calculable social and economic needs of the state. *Recht*, in other words, is to be measured by the will both of the legislator posited in *Gesetz* and of the popular will manifest in the social and economic needs of society. *Recht* is again dependent on its legality, but that legality is now understood as the conformity both to *Gesetz (Gesetzmäßigkeit)* and to the material interests of others *(Billigkeit)*.[88]

Once the technique of *Recht* makes *Recht* subservient to both social and economic interests, *Recht* itself threatens to fade away behind the presence and power of the jurisprudentially posited legal order. *Recht*, and with it man as well, becomes a mere means to the will of the legal order, whether that will is justified according to the common happiness, general ethical maxims, or the demands of economic efficiency. In any case, *Recht* retreats behind the pursuit of interests and assumes its new status as a handmaid of power, nothing other than the legitimate use of violence in the name of the legal state.

That the agents of power are no longer Gods, kings, nations, or legislators, but are instead the nameless jurists and bureaucrats who draft and apply the new legal codes in conformity with social and economic ends, is little consolation. On the contrary, the impersonal rule of technical legality and bureaucratic capitalism means that there is no actual master to whom one can protest on ethical grounds.[89] What Weber powerfully names the "masterless slavery" or *Herrenlose Sklaverei*[90] does not simply shield those who hold power from the slings and arrows of the powerless. The powerful even as much as the powerless are incapable of resisting the progressive march of ever-increasing economic and social rationalization in the name of efficiency and social justice. What is required once *Recht* itself comes under the dominion of technique is that man as well as *Recht* becomes merely a means, a cog in the machine of social and economic progress.

As Weber so clearly sees, the impersonal rationality of bureaucratic legal science presents the greatest threat imaginable to individualism and the possibility of individual human freedom. What needs to be seen as well is that legal freedom is not only endangered from without by the sociological rise of bureaucratic institutions, but, more importantly, threatened from within by the necessary demands of legal science itself. The technical compulsion to submit *Recht*—and with it justice—to reasons and grounds makes *Recht* a means in the battle of interests that paves the way for a universal servility in which individual freedom is sacrificed to the "benevolent feudalism" of the welfare state.[91] With the transformation of *Recht* into *Gesetz*, the "cage of the new bondage, *das Gehäuse für die neue Hörigkeit*" is set in place;[92] all that remains is for the masses of men to be made *gefügig*—man, in other words, must be made to fit in the cage of the *"gesetzmäßige" Wirkung materieller Interessen*—the " 'legal' effects of material interests."[93]

For all of its technical mastery, therefore, the BGB is a monument to the failure of the scientific effort to save *Recht* from its descent into *Gesetz*. The dream of legal science—to set law upon a man-made foundation that would replace the lost insightful ground of law—has failed. Moreover, it was an impossible dream. The insightful unity of *Recht* is simply no longer to be discovered, nor is it to be created.[94] The great ambition of legal science—to rejuvenate the entirety of legal and ethical relations through a scientific code—collided with an even greater force: "*Das Ganze lebt überhaupt nicht mehr,* the whole simply lives no more."[95] Once science, in relentless pursuit of truth, clears away all attempts to elevate the reasons for law beyond the needs and interests of man, the legal scientist is left with the conclusion that law, as positive law, is subordinate to human will. Law, in other words, comes to be indistinguishable from *Gesetz*.

Conclusion

> The holiest and most powerful that the world has hitherto possessed has bled to death under our knives.
>
> —Friedrich Nietzsche, *The Gay Science*

That law has fallen to earth from heaven is not reversible. It is what Nietzsche calls the death of God. Once the natural connection with the divine is severed, all efforts to support the enchantment of the world with science are destined to fail. This book has told a history of that failure.

The failure of science to bring about a rebirth of law, however, is neither the end of history nor the end of law. As long as the legal ideal of justice is still heard, albeit faintly, in its connection with transcendence—as long as we can still make sense of the idea of justice that connects us with our friends and fellow citizens without the need for law and contracts—there is the possibility that acts of justice will inspire, ennoble, and enable some to heed the call. The call and those who can hear it are rare, and yet it persists: when a pharmaceutical company foregoes legal rights and agrees to treat its neighbors with the dignity due persons; when a doctor spends hours operating to save a young child without thinking whether she is insured; when a teacher sits in his office for hours upon hours, week after week, guiding his student along the painful, even excruciating, ascent from the cave into the light; when a friend speaks honestly and plainly, lovingly showing you your error—in all these instances both grand and delicate, we are witness to the actuality of the thoughtful and ethical activity of justice.

All the more terrible, depressing, and humiliating must the everyday subjection of law to a product of science strike those who have glimpsed the beauty of law's active presence in themselves and others. From Leibniz to Savigny, the scientific effort to rejuvenate law strove to hold fast law's connection to justice. Even as law was subordinated to the rationality of science, the science of justice set out to actualize the universal dignity of man. The search for certainty and rules was still guided by the beautiful dream of transcendence. Finally, the BGB brought the historical development of the scientific approach to law to its unavoidable conclusion. Abandoning the scientific effort to replace the lost world of natural law with a scientifically grounded ethics, the authors of the BGB emptied law of all content and constructed a purely formal and technical legal apparatus that is distinguished by its serviceability to any and all ends.

For those of us living through the divorce of law from justice, the rules of law appear naked, stripped bare of any claim to a higher good. We may praise law for its legitimacy, its fairness, or its efficiency, but we do not love it for its justice. The sequestering of justice in the world beyond leaves this world prisoner to the whim of calculating bureaucrats, legislators, and judges. With the reduction of law to policy, the weighing of interests, and the overwhelming demand that law achieve political and social ends, the ethical ideal of law as justice has fled the earth. Law, the last bastion of the ethical world's resistance to the rule of scientists and experts, has succumbed to the lure of social engineering.[1] Just as man has become a human resource in the service of whatever social or commercial end, so too is law nothing in itself.

Might it be, however, that consciousness of the death of God—what Heidegger renames the sway of *Technik*—can open a path to redemption? "The nearer we bring ourselves to the peril," Heidegger writes, "the more brightly do the ways into what saves begin to lighten up, the more questioning we become. For asking is the fitness of thinking."[2] To bring the transformation of law into a product of science into question is the highest ambition of *The Gift of Science*. Like every meaningful question, it seeks to open a path to thinking. Whether the science of law can give way to an art of legislation that would summon the just, the true, and the beautiful—what Plato in the *Phaedrus* names *to ekfanestaton*,[3] the most purely shining-forth—is the question of our age.

NOTE ON SOURCES

NOTES

INDEX

Note on Sources

In lieu of a bibliography listing the hundreds of books and articles cited in or consulted for *The Gift of Science*, I provide here a guide to the most essential and influential texts and authors that inform this work. Please note that all translations of the epigraphs, with the exception of the quotation from Pierre Claustres, are mine. All translations in the text are my own unless otherwise noted. The original quotations of the epigraphs, given only in translation in the book, can be found on the Web at *www.vernunft.org*. Those interested can also find there a complete bibliography.

Part I

Leibniz published few books. Most of the primary sources are essays and letters published in scattered collections available in English, Latin, German, and French. The most essential text for general work on Leibniz's philosophy is C. I. Gerhardt's collection, *Die Philosophische Schriften* (New York: Georg Olms Verlag, 1996). This is the standard six-volume collection of Leibniz's writings, primarily in Latin and French. The best English-language version of Leibniz's work is *Philosophical Papers and Letters*, edited by Leroy Loemker (Boston: Kluwer Academic Publishers, 1989). In addition to reliable translations, Loemker also provides a helpful correspondence to the Gerhardt edition. For Leibniz's specifically legal texts, the most invaluable collection is volume 2 of *Textes Inédits*, edited by Gaston Grua (Paris: Presses Universitaires de France, 1948); Grua includes many of the most important drafts and outlines of Leibniz's previously unpublished legal writings. Also helpful is Patrick Riley's collection in English of *Leibniz' Political Writings* (Cambridge: Cambridge University Press, 1996).

Note on Sources

There are only a few secondary sources that specifically address Leibniz's legal thought. The only English text is Patrick Riley's *Leibniz' Universal Jurisprudence* (Cambridge, MA: Harvard University Press, 1996), which offers an important account of the connection between Leibniz's thinking about justice and his broader philosophical project. In German, Hans-Peter Schneider's *Justitia Universalis* (Frankfurt am Main: Vittorio Klostermann, 1967) is a rich and detailed source regarding Leibniz's legal thinking. Also, Hartmut Schiedermair's book, *Das Phänomen der Macht und die Idee des Rechts bei Gottfried Wilhelm Leibniz* (Wiesbaden: Franz Steiner Verlag, 1970), while less comprehensive, is insightful and well worth reading. Peter König's article "Das System des Rechts und die Lehre von dem Fiktionen bei Leibniz" (published in *Entwicklung der Methodenlehre in Rechtswissenschaft und Philosophie Vom 16. Bis Zum 18. Jahrhundert*, edited by Jan Schröder [Wiesbaden: Franz Steiner Verlag, 1998]) is the single best analysis of Leibniz's systematic legal thinking I have found. Klaus Luig's article, "Die Privatrechtsordnung im Rechtssystem von Leibniz" (pubished in *Grund- und Freiheitsrechte von der Ständischen zur Spätbürgerlichen Gesellschaft*, edited by Günther Birtsch [Göttingen; Vandenhoeck & Ruprecht, 1987]) is a helpful guide through the technical aspects of Leibniz's legal system.

In exploring Leibniz's relation to the scientific revolution and the scientific metaphysics that emerges from it, I relied most heavily on Martin Heidegger's lecture courses, *Metaphysische Anfangsgründe der Logik im Ausgang von Leibniz* (Frankfurt am Main: Vittorio Klostermann, 1990) and *Der Satz vom Grund* (Pfullingen: Verlag Günther Neske, 1965). Finally, Konrad Moll's brilliant three-volume study, *Der Junge Leibniz. Eine Wissenschaft für ein Aufgeklärtes Europa: Der Weltmechanismus Dynamischer Monadenpunkte als Gegenentwurf zu den Lehren von Descartes und Hobbes* (Stuttgart: Friedrich Frommann Verlag, 1996) sets all of Leibniz's early work, his jurisprudence included, in the context of his scientific metaphysics.

Part II

There is virtually nothing written in English about the Prussian *Allgemeines Landrecht*. In referring to the text of the code, I relied on Hans Hattenhauer's edited version (Berlin: Luchterhand Verlag, 1996) that, in addition to a short introduction, contains a timeline and, given the ALR's girth, a helpful index. Hermann Conrad and Gerd Kleinheyer have given political theorists and legal scholars a great gift by collecting all of Svarez's virtually unknown and certainly underappreciated speeches and essays in a single volume: *Vorträge über Recht und Staat von Carl Gottlieb Svarez (1746–1798)* (Cologne: Westdeutscher Verlag, 1960). These comprise the essential primary sources on the ALR.

I was surprised and thrilled to discover that Wilhelm Dilthey, one of Germany's great thinkers of the late nineteenth century, turned his ever-insightful glance on the ALR. His short book, "Das Allgemeine Landrecht" remains far and away the best inquiry into the underlying spirit of the ALR (volume 12 of Dilthey's complete works, published as *Zur Preussischen Geschichte*, ed. Erich Weniger [Stuttgart: B. G. Teubner Verlagsgesellschaft m.b.H., 1985]). It is also a brilliant work of cultural history. Andreas Schwennicke's *Die Entstehung der Einleitung des Preußischen Allgemeinen Landrechts von 1794* (Frankfurt am Main: Vittorio Klostermann, 1993) is a provocative and thoughtful inquiry into the ALR's relation to constitutionalism. Finally, two leading German legal historians, Franz Wieacker and Hans Thieme, provide excellent jumping-off points for research into the ALR and codification more generally. Wieacker's *Privatrechtsgeschichte der Neuzeit: Unter Besonderer Berücksichtigung der Deutschen Entwicklung* (Göttingen: Vandenhoeck & Ruprecht, 1996) well deserves its status as a classic. It is available in a somewhat unreliable and abridged English translation (*A History of Private Law*, trans. Tony Weir [Oxford: Oxford University Press, 1995]). Thieme's essays on the ALR and many other topics in legal history are collected in *Ideengeschichte Und Rechtsgeschichte. Gesammelte Schriften*, ed. Hans Thieme (Cologne: Böhlau Verlag GmbH & Cie, 1986).

Part III

Savigny's writings are widely available in German in multiple editions. Many are out of print. Whenever possible, I cite to recent reprints that are generally available. The key texts that I used include the following: "Vom Beruf Unsrer Zeit Für Gesetzgebung Und Rechtswissenschaft," reprinted in *Politik Und Neuere Legislation*, ed. Hidetake Akamatsu and Joachim Rückert (Frankfurt am Main: Vittorio Klostermann, 2000); *System Des Heutigen Römischen Rechts* (Aalen: Scientia Verlag, 1981); and *Vermischte Schriften* (Aalen: Scientia Verlag, 1981). A few English translations of Savigny exist, including *Of the Vocation of Our Age for Legislation and Jurisprudence*, trans. Abraham Hayward (London: Littlewood, 1831).

The secondary source literature on Savigny in Germany is vast and inversely proportional to the near total absence of English commentary. By far the most comprehensive and also the best book on Savigny is Joachim Rückert's *Idealismus, Jurisprudenz Und Politik Bei Friedrich Carl von Savigny* (Ebelsbach: Verlag Rolf Gremer, 1984). In addition, Dieter Nörr's *Savignys Philosophische Lehrjahre* (Frankfurt am Main: Vittorio Klostermann, 1994) sets Savigny's work in the context of his early interest in German romantic philosophy. Hans Kiefner's essays on Savigny are particularly enlightening, especially his exploration of Savigny's relation to Friedrich Hölderlin in "Ideal Wird, Was Natur War" (*Quad Fiorentini* 9 [1980]: 515–522). The English reader can find a short but helpful account of Savigny's role in German jurisprudence in James Q. Whitman's *The Legacy of Roman Law in the German Romantic Era: Historical Vision and Legal Change* (Princeton, NJ: Princeton University Press, 1990).

While there are countless editions of the BGB—including those now on the Web—the text of the code has undergone many changes, deletions, and additions. I used a reprint of the original text published by C. H. Beck'sche Verlagsbuchhandlung (1996). I also made frequent use of the English translation of the BGB, *The German Civil Code*, by Simon L. Goren (Littleton, CO: Fred B. Rothman & Co., 1994). I was lucky to find a used copy of the *Motive zu dem Entwurfe eines Bürgerlichen Gesetzbuches für das Deutsche Reich*. The explanations of the code in the *Motive* are fascinating and worthwhile for anyone interested in law as well as those studying legal history. I cite to the official edition published by Verlag von J. Guttentag (1888). Finally, Bernard Windscheid's *Lehrbuch des Pandektenrechts*, 9th ed. Aalen: Scientia Verlag, 1963)—while technically a secondary source—is so essential to any understanding of the BGB that I list it here.

The best secondary sources on the BGB are the commentaries published around the time it came into effect. Gottlieb Planck, one of the main authors of the code, published an especially useful analysis in the introduction to his *Bürgerliches Gesetzbuch Nebst Einführungsgesetz* (Berlin: J. Guttentag, Verlagsbuchhandlung, 1897). Andreas von Tuhr's three-volume commentary, *Der Allgemeine Teil des Deutschen Bürgerlichen Rechts*, is also insightful (Berlin: Verlag von Duncker & Humblot, 1957). I rely heavily on both of them in the text. In English, Basil Markensinis's "The Legacy of History on German Contact Law" (in *Foreign Law and Comparative Methodology* [Oxford: Hart Publishing, 1997]) is a good introduction to the intricate system in the BGB.

Any effort to understand late nineteenth-century German legal thought must go through the work of Rudolf von Jhering. Jhering's two great works are *Geist des Römischen Rechts auf den Verschiedenen Stufen seiner Entwicklung* (Aalen: Scientia Verlag, 1993) and *Der Zweck im Recht* (Liepzig: Breitkopf and Härtel, 1893). These works are the direct fundament of nearly all twentieth-century American jurisprudence. The latter has been partially translated as *Law as a Means to an End*, trans. Isaac Husik (Union, NJ: The Lawbook Exchange, 1999).

Philosophical and Theoretical Background

The Gift of Science is a work of political theory and philosophy as much as it is a work of legal history. While writing this book, I was reading, teaching, and writing about the major thinkers of the Western tradition, from Plato and Aristotle to Nietzsche, Weber, and Heidegger. Many of these works find resonance in *The Gift of Science:* most especially, Martin Heidegger's "Die Frage nach der Technik" (in *Die Technik und die Kehre* [Pfullingenen: Verlag Günther Neske, 1991]) and Heidegger's lecture course on Kant, "Die Frage nach dem Ding" (Tübingen: Max Niemeyer Verlag, 1975). A full appreciation of my statement, "Once law seeks to reassert its rightful authority through scientific guarantees of its certainty, the technique of law comes to overwhelm its morality" (pp. 6–7), is not possible without a prolonged meditation on Heidegger's texts from which it flows.

Notes

Preface

1. "The one thing of value in the world is the active soul. This every man is entitled to; this every man contains within him, although, in almost all men, obstructed, and as yet unborn. The soul active sees absolute truth and utters truth and creates." Ralph Waldo Emerson, *The Essential Writings of Ralph Waldo Emerson*, ed. Brooks Atkinson (New York: The Modern Library, 2000), 47.
2. *Ereignis* is a word too rich to translate or to develop fully in its many senses here. For the relation between *Ereignis*, transcendence, and law, see Heidegger's statement: "Das Ereignis ist das Gesetz, insofern es die Sterblichen zu ihrem Wesen versammelt und darin halt." Martin Heidegger, *Unterwegs zur Sprache* (Pfullingen: Verlag Günther Neske, 1960), 259.
3. I first encountered this analogy in a conversation with Philippe Nonet.
4. See, e.g., *Whalen v. Union Bag & Paper*, 101 N.E. 805 (1913).
5. See, e.g., *Boomer v. Atlantic Cement*, 357 N.E.2nd 870 (1970).
6. John Rawls, *A Theory of Justice* (Cambridge, MA: Harvard University Press, 1971), 11.
7. G. W. F. Hegel, *Grundlinien der Philosophie des Rechts*, ed. Johannes Hoffmeister (Hamburg: Felix Meiner Verlag, 1955), §93 (addendum); Marianne Constable, *The Law of the Other: The Mixed Jury and Changing Conceptions of Citizenship, Law, and Knowledge* (Chicago: University of Chicago Press, 1994), 74.
8. Aristotle, *The Nicomachean Ethics*, ed. G. P. Goold, trans. H. Rackham (Cambridge, MA: Harvard University Press, 1990), 1133a7. See also the insightful discussion in Jill Frank, *A Democracy of Distinction: Aristotle and the Work of Politics* (Chicago: University of Chicago Press, 2004), 138ff.
9. Jacques Derrida, "The Force of Law: The Mystical Foundation of Authority," *Cardozo Law Review* 11 (1990): 945; Drucilla Cornell, *The Philosophy of the Limit* (New York: Routledge, 1992), 134.

10. Friedrich Carl von Savigny, "Vom Beruf unsrer Zeit für Gesetzgebung und Rechtswissenschaft," in *Politik und Neuere Legislation*, ed. Hidetake Akamatsu and Joachim Rückert (Frankfurt am Main: Vittorio Klostermann, 2000), 237.
11. Martin Heidegger, *Vorträge und Aufsätze* (Stuttgart: Günther Neske, 1954), 178.

Introduction

1. Christina Börner, *Kodifikation des Common Law* (Zurich: Schulthess Juristische Medien AG, 2001).
2. Pio Caroni, "Kodifikation und Dekodifikation des Privatrechts in der Heutigen Rechtsentwicklung," in *Kodifikace a Dekodifikace Soukromého Práva V Dnesním Právním Vyvoji*, ed. Karel V. Maly and Pio Caroni (Prague: Karolinum nakladatelství Univerzity Karlovy, 1998), 41ff. See Manlio Bellomo, *The Common Legal Past of Europe 1000–1800*, trans. Lydia G. Cochrane (Washington, DC: Catholic University of America Press, 1995), 27. See also Maria Luisa Murillo, "The Evolution of Codification in the Civil Law Legal Systems: Towards Decodification and Recodification," *Journal of Transnational Law & Policy* 11 (2001): 172–173.
3. There is, however, a sporadic movement for recodification, although the meaning of codification has largely changed. Murillo, "The Evolution of Codification in the Civil Law Legal Systems," 176–177. See also Reinhard Zimmermann, "Codification: History and Present Significance of an Idea— Apropos of the Recodification of Private Law in the Czech Republic," *European Review of Private Law* 3 (1995).
4. The English-language legal world has virtually ceased to think and write seriously about codification outside a purely historical context. For a historical account of the codification movement in the United States, see Börner, *Kodifikation des Common Law*; and Charles M. Cook, *The American Codification Movement*, ed. Paul L. Murphy (Westport, CT: Greenwood Press, 1981). Two political histories of German codification in the nineteenth century are Michael John, *Politics and the Law in Late Nineteenth-Century Germany* (Oxford: Clarendon Press, 1989); and Margaret Barber Crosby, "The Civil Code and the Transformation of German Society" (doctoral thesis, Brown University, 2001). See also Lindsay Farmer, "Reconstructing the English Codification Debate: The Criminal Law Commissioners, 1833–1845," *Law and History Review* 18, no. 2 (2004).
5. See Anthony Sebok, *Legal Positivism in American Jurisprudence* (New York: Cambridge University Press, 1998), 7ff.
6. Joseph Raz, *The Authority of Law: Essays on Law and Morality* (New York: Oxford University Press, 1983), 47.
7. Sebok, *Legal Positivism in American Jurisprudence*, xii.

8. Pierre Clastres, *Archaeology of Violence*, trans. Jeanine Herman (New York: Semiotext(e), 1994), 58.
9. See, e.g., H. L. A. Hart, *The Concept of Law* (Oxford: Oxford University Press, 1961). See also Jules Coleman, "Incorporationism, Conventionality, and the Practical Difference Thesis," in *Hart's Postscript*, ed. Jules Coleman (New York: Oxford University Press, 2001), 115–116.
10. Richard A. Posner, "The Law and Economics Movement," in *The Economic Structure of the Law: The Collected Economic Essays of Richard A. Posner*, ed. Francesco Parisi (Northampton, MA: Edward Elgar Publishing, 2000), 7, 5.
11. While most normative theorists offer themselves as critics of positive law, they share the need to justify law with science, which I argue is the essential mark of the positivist approach to law. See generally, Ronald Dworkin, *Law's Empire* (Cambridge, MA: Harvard University Press, 1986); John Rawls, *A Theory of Justice* (Cambridge, MA: Harvard University Press, 1971); Jürgen Habermas, *Between Facts and Norms*, trans. William Rehg (Cambridge, MA: MIT Press, 1998).
12. Oliver Wendell Holmes Jr., letter to Sir Frederick Pollock, Feb. 1, 1920 (cited approvingly in Richard A. Posner, *The Problems of Jurisprudence* [Cambridge, MA: Harvard University Press, 1990], 83). See also, agreeing, Stanley Fish, "Almost Pragmatism: Richard Posner's Jurisprudence," *University of Chicago Law Review* 57 (1990): 1459.
13. John Austin, *The Province of Jurisprudence Determined*, ed. Wilfred E. Rumble (Cambridge: Cambridge University Press, 1995), 21ff.
14. "Wir können diesen Begriff der Positivität demnach auf die Formel bringen, daß das Recht nicht nur durch Entscheidung *gesetzt* (das heißt ausgewählt) wird, sondern auch kraft Entscheidung (also kontingent und änderbar) *gilt.*" Niklas Luhmann, *Rechtssoziologie*, 3rd ed. (Opladen: Westdeutscher Verlag GmbH, 1987), 210 (emphasis in original). See also Niklas Luhmann, *Legitimation Durch Verfahren* (Frankfurt am Main: Suhrkamp, 1997), 21; and Rainer Maria Kiesow, *Das Alphabet des Rechts* (Frankfurt am Main: Fischer Taschenbuch Verlag, 2004), 144ff.
15. Oliver Wendell Holmes Jr., "The Path of Law," in *The Collected Works of Justice Holmes*, ed. Sheldon M. Novick (Chicago: University of Chicago Press, 1995).
16. To understand the claim made in this paragraph, it would be helpful to read and meditate on Martin Heidegger's essay, "Die Frage Nach der Technik," in *Die Technik und die Kehre* (Pfullingen: Verlag Günther Neske, 1991).
17. Max Weber, *Wirtschaft und Gesellschaft* (Tübingen: J. C. B. Mohr, 1980), 124–125.
18. See, e.g., John, *Politics and the Law in Late Nineteenth-Century Germany.*
19. Sten Gagnér, *Studien zur Ideengeschichte der Gesetzgebung* (Uppsala: Almquist & Wiksells Boktryckeri Aktiebolag, 1960). See especially 53–55, 70–74, 347ff.

20. Friedrich Nietzsche, "Götzen-Dämmerung," in Friedrich Nietzsche, *Kritische Studienausgabe*, vol. 6, ed. Giorgio Colli and Mazzino Montinari (Munich: Deutscher Taschenbuch Verlag, 1988), 72–73.

Part I Introduction

1. Leibniz, letter to Kaiser Leopold, August 1671, in Gottfried Wilhelm Leibniz, "Allgemeiner Politischer und Historischer Briefwechsel," vol. 1, in *Sämtliche Schriften und Briefe*, ed. Leibniz-Archiv Hannover (Darmstadt: Otto Reichl Verlag, 1923), 57.
2. Ibid., 61.
3. See Kurt Dickerhof, "Leibniz' Bedeutung für die Gesetzgebung Seiner Zeit" (inaugural dissertation, Albert-Ludwig-Universität, 1941), 6.
4. Huntington Cairns, *Legal Philosophy from Plato to Hegel* (London: Oxford University Press, 1949), 297.
5. Hans-Peter Schneider concludes that "Man wird deshalb nicht fehlgehen zu vermuten, daß Leibniz . . . die *Reconcinnation* des römischen Rechts und die Emendation der Jurisprudenz als seine eigentliche Lebensaufgabe betrachtet hat." Hans-Peter Schneider, *Justitia Universalis* (Frankfurt am Main: Vittorio Klostermann, 1967), 52 (emphasis in original).
6. In Lucy Prenant, *Oeuvres choisies de Leibniz*, at p. 33, cited in ibid. Leibniz came from a long tradition of lawyers. For further accounts of the centrality of Leibniz's codification efforts to his personal and philosophical thinking, see Gustav Hartmann, "Leibniz Als Jurist und Rechtsphilosoph," in *Festgabe Herrn Dr. Rudolph von Jhering zum Doktorjubiläum am 6. August 1892* (Aalen: Scientia Verlag, 1979), 31ff. See also Adolf Trendelenburg, "Leibnizens Anregung zu einer Justizreform," in *Kleine Schriften*, ed. Adolf Trendelenburg (Leipzig: Verlag von S. Hirzel, 1871).
7. See generally, Paul Hazard, *The European Mind: The Critical Years (1680–1715)*, trans. J. Lewis May (New Haven, CT: Yale University Press, 1953); H. R. Trevor-Roper, *The Crisis of the Seventeenth Century* (New York: Harper & Row, 1968). And see Rudolf W. Meyer, *Leibniz und die Europäische Ordnungskrise* (Hamburg: Hannischer Gildenverlag, 1948).
8. Jacob Burckhardt, *The Civilization of the Renaissance in Italy*, trans. S. G. C. Middlemore (New York: Penguin Books USA, 1990), 98.
9. Konrad Moll, *Der Junge Leibniz. Eine Wissenschaft für ein Aufgeklärtes Europa: Der Weltmechanismus Dynamischer Monadenpunkte als Gegenentwurf zu den Lehren von Descartes und Hobbes*, vol. 3 (Stuttgart-Bad Cannstatt: Friedrich Frommann Verlag, 1996), 32–33.
10. Riley dedicates only one three-page section of his book to "Leibniz' Codification of *Caritas Sapientis* in His Late Writings"; even here, attention is focused less on *ius* than on justice. See Patrick Riley, *Leibniz' Universal Jurisprudence* (Cambridge, MA: Harvard University Press, 1996), 182–185.

11. See, most perceptively, Peter König, "Das System des Rechts und die Lehre von dem Fiktionen bei Leibniz," in *Entwicklung der Methodenlehre in Rechtswissenschaft und Philosophie vom 16. bis zum 18. Jahrhundert,* ed. Jan Schröder (Stuttgart: Franz Steiner Verlag, 1998). See also Klaus Luig, "Leibniz und die Prinzipien des Vertragrechts," in *Gesellschaftliche Freiheit und Vertragliche Bindung in Rechtsgeschichte und Philosophie,* ed. Jean-François Kervégan and Heinz Mohnhaupt (Frankfurt am Main: Vittorio Klostermann, 1999); Schneider, *Justitia Universalis;* Klaus Luig, "Die Privatrechtsordnung im Rechtssystem von Leibniz," in *Grund- und Freiheitsrechte von der Ständischen zur Spätbürgerlichen Gesellschaft,* ed. Günther Birtsch (Göttingen: Vandenhoeck & Ruprecht, 1987); Klaus Luig, "Die Rolle des Deutschen Rechts in Leibniz' Kodifikationsplänen," *Ius Commune* 5 (1975); Klaus Luig, "Leibniz als Dogmatiker des Privatrechts," in *Römisches Recht in der Europäischen Tradition,* ed. Okko Behrends, Malte Diesselhorst, and Wulf Eckart Voss (Ebelsbach: Verlag Rolf Gremer, 1985); Klaus Luig, "Die Wurzeln des Aufgeklärten Naturrechts bei Leibniz," in *Naturrecht–Spätaufklärung–Revolution,* ed. Otto Dann and Diethelm Klippel (Hamburg: Felix Meiner Verlag, 1995).
12. Riley, *Leibniz' Universal Jurisprudence,* 5.
13. Schneider, *Justitia Universalis.*
14. Leroy E. Loemker, "Introduction," in Gottfried Wilhelm Leibniz, *Philosophical Papers and Letters,* ed. Leroy E. Loemker (Boston: Kluwer Academic Publishers, 1989), 1.
15. Kuno Fischer, *Geschichte der Neueren Philosophie,* vol. 2 (Heidelberg: Verlagsbuchhandlung von Friedrich Bassermann, 1867), 16.
16. Riley, *Leibniz' Universal Jurisprudence,* 274.
17. Ibid.

1. Beyond Geometry

1. M. H. Hoeflich, "Law and Geometry: Legal Science from Leibniz to Langdell," *The American Journal of Legal History* 30 (1986): 99.
2. Aristotle, *Metaphysics,* trans. G. Cyril Armstrong (Cambridge, MA: Harvard University Press, 1990), 1077b12ff.
3. Aristotle, *The Physics,* ed. G. P. Goold, trans. Philip H. Wicksteed and Francis M. Cornford (Cambridge, MA: Harvard University Press, 1996), 193b34ff.
4. Aristotle, *Metaphysics,* 1092a17.
5. See generally, Martin Heidegger, *Platon: Sophistes* (Frankfurt am Main: Vittorio Klostermann, 1992), 100.
6. Maximillian Herberger, *Dogmatik zur Geschichte von Begriff und Methode in Medizin und Jurisprudenz* (Frankfurt am Main: Vittorio Klostermann, 1981). See esp. ch. 6.
7. Nicholas Rescher, "Leibniz and the Concept of a System," *Studia Leibnitiana* 13 (1981): 122.

8. Patrick Riley, *Leibniz' Universal Jurisprudence* (Cambridge, MA: Harvard University Press, 1996), 14.
9. Gottfried Wilhelm Leibniz, "Nova Methodus Discendae Docendaeque Jurisprudentiae," in *Philosophische Schriften*, ed. Leibniz-Forschungsstelle der Universität Münster, vol. 2 (Berlin: Akademie-Verlag, 1971), §5. See also Riley, *Leibniz' Universal Jurisprudence*, 12.
10. "Tota fere Theologia magnam partem ex Jurisprudentia pendet." Leibniz, "Nova Methodus," §5. Elsewhere he writes: "Theologia est divina quaedam jurisprudentia, nostrae cum Deo societatis jura explicans. Ergo universalis jurisprudentia etiam ipsi fundamenta substernit." G. W. Leibniz, *Textes Inédits*, vol. 1, ed. Gaston Grua (Paris: Presses Universitaires de France, 1948). Cited in Hans-Peter Schneider, *Justitia Universalis* (Frankfurt am Main: Vittorio Klostermann, 1967), 421.
11. "Juris prudentia est scientia justi seu scientia libertatis et officiorum seu scientia juris proposito aliquo casu seu facto." Leibniz, "Initium Institutionum Iuris Perpetui," in *Mittheilungen aus Leibnizens Ungedruckten Schriften*, ed. Georg Mollat (Leipzig: Verlag von H. Haessel, 1893), 1.
12. Aristotle, *The Nicomachean Ethics*, ed. G. P. Goold, trans. H. Rackham (Cambridge, MA: Harvard University Press, 1990), Bk. VI.
13. "Systema est veritatum inter se et cum principiis suis connexarum congeries." Christian Wolff, *Logic*, §889, cited in Rescher, "Leibniz and the Concept of a System," 116.
14. See, e.g., Schneider, *Justitia Universalis*, 338ff.
15. A. P. d'Entrèves, *Natural Law. An Introduction to Legal Philosophy*, 7th ed. (London: Hutchinson & Co., 1963), 7. See also John Hostler, *Leibniz' Moral Philosophy* (London: Duckworth, 1975), 56.
16. D'Entrèves also attributes the ambiguity in natural law thinking to the failure to distinguish clearly between meanings of "nature." His distinction between the historical and philosophical approaches to natural law is helpful, but only as far as it goes. See d'Entrèves, *Natural Law. An Introduction to Legal Philosophy*, 7ff.
17. The relation between *physis* and law is less than clear to modern sensibilities. For a fascinating discussion of the law of *physis*, I recommend Philippe Nonet, "Antigone's Law," *Law, Culture and the Humanites* (forthcoming).
18. Gottfried Wilhelm Leibniz, "Discourse on Metaphysics," in *Philosophical Papers and Letters*, ed. Leroy E. Loemker (Boston: Kluwer Academic Publishers, 1989), 310. Translation emended.
19. Ibid., 311.
20. Riley, *Leibniz' Universal Jurisprudence*, 57.
21. Leibniz, "Discourse on Metaphysics," 311.
22. Ibid.
23. Gottfried Wilhelm Leibniz, *New Essays on Human Understanding*, ed. Karl

Ameriks and Desmond M. Clarke, trans. Peter Remnant and Jonathan Bennett (Cambridge: Cambridge University Press, 1996), 427.
24. Riley, *Leibniz' Universal Jurisprudence*, 267.
25. Gottfried Wilhelm Leibniz, "Critical Thoughts on the General Part of the Principles of Descartes," in *Philosophical Papers and Letters*, ed. Leroy E. Loemker (Boston: Kluwer Academic Publishers, 1989), 387.
26. See, e.g., Schneider, *Justitia Universalis*; Huntington Cairns, *Legal Philosophy from Plato to Hegel* (London: Oxford University Press, 1949).
27. Samuel von Pufendorf, *De Officio Hominis et Civis Juxta Legem Naturalem Libri Duo*, ed. James Brown Scott, trans. Frank Gardner Moore, The Photographic Reproduction of the Edition of 1682 (Buffalo: William S. Hein & Co., 1995).
28. Thomas Hobbes, *De Corpore Politico* (Bristol England: Thoemmes Press, 1994), 123.
29. Thomas Hobbes, *Leviathan*, ed. Richard Tuck (Cambridge: Cambridge University Press, 1994), §15, 216. See Samantha Frost, "Faking It: Hobbes's Thinking-Bodies and the Ethics of Dissimulation," *Political Theory* 29, no. 1 (2001): 36–42.
30. Riley, *Leibniz' Universal Jurisprudence*, 207.
31. Gottfried Wilhelm Leibniz, "Meditation on the Common Concept of Justice," in *Political Writings*, ed. Patrick Riley (Cambridge: Cambridge University Press, 1996), 50.
32. Ibid.
33. Hartmut Schiedermair, *Das Phänomen der Macht und die Idee des Rechts bei Gottfried Wilhelm Leibniz*, ed. Kurt Müller and William Totok (Wiesbaden: Franz Steiner Verlag, 1970), 156.
34. Ibid., 336.
35. Leibniz, *New Essays on Human Understanding*, 371.
36. Ibid., 425.
37. Leibniz, letter to Johannes Georg Graevius, June 7, 1671, in Gottfried Wilhelm Leibniz, "Philosophischer Briefwechsel," vol. 1, in *Sämtliche Schriften und Briefe*, ed. Leibniz-Forschungsstelle der Universität Münster (Darmstadt: Otto Reichl Verlag, 1926).
38. René Descartes, *Meditationes de Prima Philosophia*, trans. George Heffernan (Notre Dame, IN: University of Notre Dame Press, 1990).
39. Gottfried Wilhelm Leibniz, "Meditations on Knowledge, Truth, and Ideas," in *Philosophical Papers and Letters*, ed. Leroy E. Loemker (Boston: Kluwer Academic Publishers, 1989), 293–294 (emphasis added).
40. See Gottfried Wilhelm Leibniz, letter to Antoine Arnauld, March 23, 1690, in *Philosophical Papers and Letters*, ed. Leroy E. Loemker (Boston: Kluwer Academic Publishers, 1989), 360.
41. Ibid.

2. The Force of Law

1. "In Philosophia Morali und Iurisprudentia habe ich vor estlich *Elementa Iuris Naturalis*, so ein kleines Werck seyn, aber viel in sich begreifen wird, mit solcher clarheit und kürze, daß auch die wichtigsten Fragen Iuris Gentium und publici von jeden vernünftigen Menschen, wenn er nur dem darinn vorgeschriebenen Methodo folgen will, erörtet werden können." Leibniz, letter to Herzog Johann Friedrich, Oct. 1671, in Gottfried Wilhelm Leibniz, "Philosophischer Briefwechsel," vol. 1, in *Sämtliche Schriften und Briefe*, ed. Leibniz-Forschungsstelle Münster (Darmstadt: Otto Reichl Verlag, 1926), 162.
2. "*Elementa Iuris Naturalis* ut mole exigua, ita pondere magna erunt, continebunt enim ex solis justi definitionibus deductas demonstrationes." Leibniz, letter to Louis Ferrand, Jan. 31, 1672, in Gottfried Wilhelm Leibniz, "Allgemeiner Politischer und Historischer Briefwechsel," vol. 1, in *Sämtliche Schriften und Briefe*, ed. Leibniz-Archiv Hannover (Darmstadt: Otto Reichl Verlag, 1923), 180.
3. "Ex his definitionibus omnia duco. . . ." Ibid., 181.
4. Ibid.
5. "Der ausbund Römischer Rechte, oder Elementa Iuris Romani hodieque attendendi, brevis et certi können bestehen in einer einigen Tafel, etwa in größe einer großen Holändischen Land-charte, darinnen alle Haupt-Regeln also begriffen, daß aus deren combination alle vorfallende fragen entschieden, und aller actionen, exceptionen und replicarum etc . . . mit fingern gezeigt werden können, dergleichen noch nie vorgenommen, viel weniger gesehen worden." Leibniz, letter to Emperor Leopold, Aug. 1671, in ibid., 60.
6. Leibniz, letter to Louis Ferrand, Jan. 31, 1672, in ibid., 181.
7. Leibniz, letter to Herzog Johann Friedrich, Oct. 1671, in Leibniz, "Philosophischer Briefwechsel," vol. 1, 162. Leibniz, letter to Emperor Leopold, Aug. 1671, in Leibniz, "Allgemeiner Politischer und Historischer Briefwechsel," vol. 1, 60.
8. Leibniz, letter to Emperor Leopold, Aug. 1671, in Leibniz, "Allgemeiner Politischer und Historischer Briefwechsel," vol. 1, 60.
9. Leibniz, letter to Louis Ferrand, Jan. 31, 1672, in ibid., 181. See also G. W. Leibniz, *Textes Inédits*, ed. Gaston Grua, vol. 2 (Paris: Presses Universitaires de France, 1948), 603.
10. Leibniz, letter to Emperor Leopold, Aug. 1671, in Leibniz, "Allgemeiner Politischer und Historischer Briefwechsel," 60–61.
11. Ibid., 61.
12. Ibid.
13. Gothofredi Guillelmi Leibniz, "Ratio Corporis Juris Reconcinnandi," in *Opera Omnia*, ed. Ludovici Dutens (Geneva: Fratres de Tournes, 1768), §39.

14. "Ex his Elementa Iuris Naturalis Tabulasque Elementorum Iuris Communis mihi vindico. . . ." Leibniz, letter to Louis Ferrand, Jan. 31, 1672, in Leibniz, "Allgemeiner Politischer und Historischer Briefwechsel," vol. 1. Leibniz was at the time assistant to the court assessor, Hermann Andreas Lasser.
15. G. W. Leibniz, "Dissertatio De Arte Combinatoria," in *Die Philosophische Schriften*, ed. C. I. Gerhardt, vol. 4 (New York: Georg Olms Verlag, 1996), 35ff. For the partial English translation, see Gottfried Wilhelm Leibniz, *Philosophical Papers and Letters*, ed. Leroy E. Loemker (Boston: Kluwer Academic Publishers, 1989), 73ff.
16. Leibniz, "Dissertatio De Arte Combinatoria," 32–33.
17. Gottfried Wilhelm Leibniz, "Elements of Natural Law," in *Philosophical Papers and Letters*, 131.
18. G. W. Leibniz, "Preface to the General Science," in *Leibniz Selections*, ed. Philip P. Wiener (New York: Charles Scribner's Sons, 1951), 12.
19. Leibniz, "Elements of Natural Law," 131.
20. Ibid., 132–133.
21. Gottfried Wilhelm Leibniz, letter to the *Kurfürst* von Mainz, Mar. 27, 1669, in Leibniz, "Allgemeiner Politischer und Historischer Briefwechsel," vol. 1, 21.
22. "Sed exigua haec sunt et arctis limitibus comprehensa; itaque obstruendus est fons mali superiore manu, quod melius fieri non posse quam Codice novo condito jam dudum prudentibus visum est." Leibniz, "Praefatio Novi Codicis," in *Textes Inédits*, vol. 2, 626.
23. "Wir haben soviel methodos, und ist doch keiner der zu wege bringe daß eine jede lex, proposition, decision, oder consequenz unter ihren Grund und ration, daraus sie fließet, gebracht werde, da doch solches der einige weg die gleichsam luxurirende Strahlen wie durch ein fern-glas abzuschneiden, und den Kern rein zu bekommen." Leibniz, letter to Emperor Leopold, Aug. 1671, in Leibniz, "Allgemeiner Politischer und Historischer Briefwechsel," vol. 1, 60.
24. Wilhelm Gottfried Leibniz, "Bedenkenswerte Bemerkungen über die Jurisprudenz," in *Politische Schriften*, ed. Hans Heinz Holz (Frankfurt am Main: Europäische Verlagsanstalt, 1967). See also Kurt Dickerhof, "Leibniz' Bedeutung für die Gesetzgebung Seiner Zeit" (inaugural dissertation, Albert-Ludwig-Universität, 1941), 29.
25. Leibniz, letter to Kaiser Leopold, Aug. 1671, in Leibniz, "Allgemeiner Politischer und Historischer Briefwechsel," vol. 1, 60.
26. Leibniz, "Dissertatio de Arte Combinatoria."
27. Ibid., 58. For English, see Leibniz, *Philosophical Papers and Letters*, 82.
28. Leibniz, "Dissertatio de Arte Combinatoria," 58.
29. Ibid., 39ff.
30. Ibid., 44ff. For English, see Leibniz, *Philosophical Papers and Letters*, 80ff.

31. *The Digest of Justinian*, Latin text ed. Theodor Mommsen and Paul Krueger, English translation ed. Alan Watson, vol. 2 (Philadelphia: University of Pennsylvania Press, 1985), 479, D.17.1.2. (Gaius).
32. Gerhard Otte, "Leibniz und die Juristische Method," *Zeitschrift für Neuere Rechtsgeschichte* 5 (1983): 5.
33. "Jurisprudentia enim cum in aliis geometriae similis est, tum in hoc quod utraque habet elementa, utraque casus. Elementa sunt simplicia, in geometria figurae triangulus, circulus, etc. in Jurisprudentia actus, promissum, alienatio, etc. Casus: complexiones horum, qui utrobique variabiles sunt infinites." Gottfried Wilhelm Leibniz, "Nova Methodus Discendae Docendaeque Jurisprudentiae," in *Philosophische Schriften*, ed. Leibniz-Forschungsstelle der Universität Münster, vol. 1, reprint of 1930 ed. (Berlin: Akademie-Verlag, 1971), 82.
34. Leibniz, "Dissertatio de Arte Combinatoria," 58.
35. "Alle vorgegebene Fragen nach den Gemeinen Römischen Rechten auflösen könne." Letter to Herzog Johann Friedrich, Oct. 1671, in Leibniz, "Philosophischer Briefwechsel," vol. 1. See, however, Gerhard Otte, who argues that Leibniz never intended his *ars combinatoria* to be a method for the solution of cases: Otte, "Leibniz und die Juristische Method," 9.
36. "Haec juris naturalis elementa, sic enim nominabuntur, animam Jurisprudentiae continent." Letter to Johanne Albrecht Portner, August 6, 1671, in Leibniz, "Allgemeiner Politischer und Historischer Briefwechsel," vol. 1.
37. Leibniz, letter to Emperor Leopold, Aug. 1671, in ibid., 60.
38. Otte, "Leibniz und die Juristische Method," 8–9.
39. Leibniz, "Dissertatio de Arte Combinatoria," 58–59.
40. Ibid., 59–60.
41. "Si nihil per se concipitur, nihil omnino concipitur." Cited in Heinrich Schepers, "Leibniz' Arbeiten zu Einer Reform der Kategorien," *Zeitschrift für Philosophische Forschung* 20 (1966): 583. One potential answer to the riddle of humanly knowable concepts depends on Leibniz's differentiated understanding of the clarity of our knowledge of a complex concept. As Dennis Plaisted argues, Leibniz admits that artists can recognize an artwork as beautiful even if they cannot analyze their conclusion down to its primitive conceptions. It is possible, therefore, to have a clear conception of something without being able to analyze it into its component parts. Leibniz, therefore, can differentiate clear and distinct concepts in which, for example, an assayer can distinguish gold not merely by its appearance but also by describing its properties, from clear yet indistinct concepts. What this means, as Plaisted rightly sees, is that Leibniz adopts a graded "scale of conception." There is, in other words, the possibility of arriving at complex conceptions "in direct proportion to the degree to which we conceive of its component concepts." See Dennis Plaisted, "Leibniz's Argument for Primitive Concepts," *Journal of the History of Philosophy* 41, no. 3 (2003): 336–340.

42. Peter König, "Das System des Rechts und die Lehre von dem Fiktionen bei Leibniz," in *Entwicklung der Methodenlehre in Rechtswissenschaft und Philosophie vom 16. bis zum 18. Jahrhundert*, ed. Jan Schröder (Stuttgart: Franz Steiner Verlag, 1998), 139n9; Schepers, "Leibniz' Arbeiten zu einer Reform der Kategorien," 547. See also Otte, "Leibniz und die Juristische Method," 8.
43. Schepers, "Leibniz' Arbeiten zu einer Reform der Kategorien," 545. See G. W. Leibniz, "Modalia Iuris," in *Textes Inédits*, vol. 2, 605.
44. Schepers, "Leibniz' Arbeiten zu einer Reform der Kategorien," 545.
45. "Caeterum ut Capita utilia vel inutilia reperiantur, adhibenda disciplina est, ad quam res variandae, aut totum ex iis compositum pertinet." Leibniz, "Dissertatio de Arte Combinatoria," 96.
46. The passage from the Digest (D.1.1.10 [Ulpian]) reads: "Practical Wisdom in *ius* [*Iuris prudentia*] is a taking note of divine and human things, moreover the science of justice and injustice." *The Digest of Justinian*, vol. 1, 2.
47. "Specimen Quaestionum Philosophicarum ex Jure Collectarum," in *Philosophische Schriften*, vol. 1, 73. See Kuno Fischer, *Geschichte der Neueren Philosophie*, vol. 2 (Heidelberg: Verlagsbuchhandlung von Friedrich Bassermann, 1867), 77.
48. Gottfried Wilhelm Leibniz, *New Essays on Human Understanding*, ed. Karl Ameriks and Desmond M. Clarke, trans. Peter Remnant and Jonathan Bennett (Cambridge: Cambridge University Press, 1996), 371.
49. "Ita est ergo: omnes certatim in jus naturae tradendum nunc incumbunt: et veterum gliscit paulatim neglectus, et quisquis tamen eos intelligit, fatebitur mecum opinor, demonstrationibus tamen certis hactenus caremus, praeter pauca Aristotelis et Hobbii. Jctorum Romanorum non extare nunc librum in quo plura de jure naturali, maioreque elegantia et claritate (iis qui dictionis eruditae et rerum veterum sunt intelligentes) sint demonstrata quam Corpus Juris; ut credam nec Euclidem nec Cartesium, si se huic doctrinae applicuissent, potuisse scribere rotundius profundiusque, quam Ulpianum et Papinianum: ut quivis his non lectis intellectisque magnum se juris naturae et gentium consultum fore sperat, procul a janua sit aberratus." Letter to Graevius, June 7, 1671, in Leibniz, "Philosophischer Briefwechsel," vol. 1. See also the letter to Lambert Van Velthuysen, April 6 or 16, 1670, in Leibniz, "Philosophischer Briefwechsel," vol. 1, 39–40.
50. "Specimen Quaestionum Philosophicarum ex Jure Collectarum," in Leibniz, *Philosophische Schriften*, vol. 1. See also Fischer, *Geschichte der Neueren Philosophie*, 77.
51. Leibniz, *New Essays on Human Understanding*, 371.
52. Gottfried Wilhelm Leibniz, "Monodologie," in *Die Philosophische Schriften*, vol. 6, 607, §3. For English, see Leibniz, *Philosophical Papers and Letters*, 643.
53. Gottfried Wilhelm Leibniz, "On the Radical Origination of Things," in *Philosophical Papers and Letters*, 488.

54. Ibid., 489.
55. Gottfried Wilhelm Leibniz, "A New System of the Nature and the Communication of Substances, as Well as the Union between the Soul and the Body," in *Philosophical Papers and Letters*, 457.
56. Gottfried Wilhelm Leibniz, "Studies in Physics and the Nature of Body," in *Philosophical Papers and Letters*, 139–140. "*Dantur indivisiblia seu inextensa*, alioquin nec initium nec finis motus coporisive intelligi potest. Demonstratio haec est: datur initium finisque spatii, corporis, motus, temporis alicujus: esto illud, cujus initium quaeritur, expositum linea *ab*, cujus punctum medium *c*, et medium inter *a* et *c* sit *d*, et inter *a* et *d* sit *e*, et ita porro: quaeratur initium sinistrorsum, in latere *a*. Ajo *ac* non esse initium, quia ei adimi potest *dc* salvo initio; nec *ad*, quia *ed* adimi potest, et ita porro; nihil ergo initum est, cui aliquid dextrorsum adimi potest. Cui nihil extensionis adimi potest, inextensum est; initium ergo corporis, spatii, motus, temporis (punctum nimirum, conatus, instans) aut nullum, quod absurdum, aut inextensum est, quot erat demonstrandum." Leibniz, *Die Philosophische Schriften*, vol. 4, 228–229.
57. Leibniz, "On the Radical Origination of Things," 486.
58. Ibid.
59. Leibniz, "A New System," 309.
60. Kuno Fischer, *Gottfried Wilhelm Leibniz. Leben, Werke und Lehre*, 5th ed. (Heidelberg: Carl Winters Universitätsbuchhandlung, 1920), 326.
61. "De Ipsa Natura sive de Vi Insita Actionibusque Creaturarum, Pro Dynamicis suis Confirmandis Illustrandisque," in Leibniz, *Die Philosophische Schriften*, vol. 4, 509.
62. Gottfried Wilhelm Leibniz, "On the Correction of Metaphysics and the Concept of Substance," in *Philosophical Papers and Letters*, 433.
63. Leibniz, letter to Herzog Johann Friedrich, Oct. 1671, in Leibniz, "Philosophischer Briefwechsel," vol. 1, 108–109.
64. G. W. Leibniz, "De Jure et Iustita," in *Textes Inédits*, vol. 2, 618.
65. Ibid.
66. "Jus est potentia moralis." *Definitionum Iuris Specimen*, cited in Leibniz, *Textes Inédits*, vol. 2, 721.
67. Gottfried Wilhelm Leibniz, "Codex Iuris Gentium (Praefatio)," in *Political Writings*. See also Leibniz, "Elements of Natural Law," 137.
68. Leibniz, "On the Correction of Metaphysics and the Concept of Substance," 433; Leibniz, *Die Philosophische Schriften*, vol. 4, 468.
69. Gottfried Wilhelm Leibniz, "Specimen Dynamicum," in *Philosophical Papers and Letters*, 435.
70. Martin Heidegger, *Metaphysische Anfangsgründe der Logik im Ausgang von Leibniz*, 2nd ed. (Frankfurt am Main: Vittorio Klostermann, 1990), 99–101.
71. Aristotle, *Metaphysics*, trans. G. Cyril Armstrong (Cambridge, MA: Harvard

University Press, 1990), Bk.9.III.1046b30. See also Martin Heidegger, *Aristotle's Metaphysics Θ 1–3*, trans. Walter Brogan and Peter Warnek (Bloomington: Indiana University Press, 1995), 137ff.
72. Aristotle, *Metaphysics*, Bk.9.III.1046b36–1047a8.
73. Ibid., 1047a.
74. Heidegger, *Aristotle's Metaphysics Θ 1–3*, 151.
75. Leibniz, "On the Correction of Metaphysics and the Concept of Substance," 433. See Martin Heidegger, *Metaphysische Anfangsgrunde der Logik im Ausgang von Leibniz*, 101.
76. Ibid. See also Leibniz, *Die Philosophische Schriften*, vol. 4, 470.
77. Leibniz, *New Essays on Human Understanding*, 169.
78. "Praeexistentis jam nisus sui, sive virtutis agendi." Leibniz, "On the Correction of Metaphysics and the Concept of Substance," 433. See also Leibniz, *Die Philosophische Schriften*, vol. 4, 470.
79. Gottfried Wilhelm Leibniz, "The Monadology," in *Philosophical Papers and Letters*, §18, 644; §7, 643.
80. Gottfried Wilhelm Leibniz, "Ad Elementa Iuris Civilis," in *Textes Inédits*, vol. 2, 706.
81. "Porro ipsa prudentia dicastica duas rursum partes habet, scientiam et peritiam, scientiam *juris naturalis*, peritiam *juris positivi*." Leibniz, letter to Conring, January 13/23, 1670, in Leibniz, "Philosophischer Briefwechsel," vol. 1, 29.
82. Leibniz, letter to Conring, January 13/23, 1670, in ibid.
83. "Scientiam juris arbitrarii docere, est leges receptas cum legibus optimae Respublicae conferre." Leibniz, *Textes Inédits*, vol. 2, 614.
84. Gottfried Wilhelm Leibniz, "The Principles of Nature and of Grace Based on Reason," in *Philosophical Papers and Letters*, 639.
85. Leibniz, *Die Philosophische Schriften*, 232; for English, Leibniz, *Philosophical Papers and Letters*, 142.
86. Leibniz, "The Principles of Nature and of Grace," 639; Leibniz, *Die Philosophische Schriften*, vol. 6, 603.
87. Leibniz, "On the Radical Origination of Things," 489. See also Nicholas Rescher, "Leibniz and the Concept of a System," *Studia Leibnitiana* 13 (1981): 119.
88. Leibniz, "Studies in Physics and the Nature of Body," 142. "*Nihil est sine ratione*, cujus consectaria sunt, quam minimum mutandum, inter contraria medium eligendum, *quidvis* uni addendum, ne quid alterutri adimatur, multaque alia, quae in *scientia* quoque *civili* dominantur." Leibniz, *Die Philosophische Schriften*, vol. 4, 232 (emphasis in original).
89. Leibniz, *Die Philosophische Schriften*, 309. See Martin Heidegger, *Der Satz vom Grund* (Pfullingen: Günther Neske, 1957), 44. The following relies heavily on Heidegger's discussion of Leibniz in the third hour of his lecture course, *Der Satz vom Grund*.

90. Luc Ferry, *Homo Aestheticus: The Invention of Taste in the Democratic Age*, trans. Robert de Loaiza (Chicago: University of Chicago Press, 1993), 156–157.
91. Patrick Riley, *Leibniz' Universal Jurisprudence* (Cambridge, MA: Harvard University Press, 1996), 7.
92. Friedrich Wilhelm Joseph Schelling, *Über das Wesen der Menschlichen Freiheit* (Stuttgart: Philipp Reclam jun. GmbH, 1995).
93. Riley, *Leibniz' Universal Jurisprudence*, 7.

3. Leibniz's *Systema Iuris*

1. Hans-Peter Schneider, *Justitia Universalis* (Frankfurt am Main: Vittorio Klostermann, 1967), 86–92.
2. Gottfried Wilhelm Leibniz, letter to Johann Lincker, April 1678, in Leibniz, "Allgemeiner Politischer und Historischer Briefwechsel," vol. 2, in *Sämtliche Schriften und Briefe*, ed. Leibniz-Archiv Hannover (Darmstadt: Otto Reichl Verlag, 1927), 333. See also the letter to Johann Paul Hocher, July 7, 1678, in Leibniz, "Allgemeiner Politischer und Historischer Briefwechsel," vol. 2, in *Sämtliche Schriften und Briefe*, 346–352. See Schneider, *Justitia Universalis*, 91.
3. MATERIAM Systematis faciunt Leges ipsae; in quibus illud observandum est, quod in lapidibus ex quibus molimur aedificium, debent enim ita esse secti ut inter se commode firmiterque conjungi possint, deinde, ut nullus sit locus vacuus, ita in legibus coordinandis requiritur, tum ut ne pugnent inter se, tum ut nullum negotium dubium relinquant. Tale System Legum hactenus quidem non extat, quin tamen confici possit, ego dubitare non possum. Sed vulgus in contrarium abit, credunt enim infinita esse negotia, quae complecti omnia sit supara humanas vires: quod ita esset fateor, si propositum nobis esset enumerare omnes casus; sed qui universalia novit, is facile innumerabilem rerum copiam in classes dividere potest, ita ut nihil eum effugere possit (emphasis in original). Gottfried Wilhelm Leibniz, "De Legum Interpretatione, Rationibus, Applicatione, Systemate," in *Philosophische Schriften*, ed. Leibniz-Forschungsstelle der Universität Münster, vol. 6 (Berlin: Akademie-Verlag, 1999), 2791.
4. "Bildung von Kategorien, von Klassen untereinander in prädikamentaler Abhängigkeit stehender Begriffe." Heinrich Schepers, "Leibniz' Arbeiten zu Einer Reform der Kategorien," *Zeitschrift für Philosophische Forschung* 20 (1966): 561.
5. See Schneider, *Justitia Universalis*, 88–89. See also Peter König, "Das System des Rechts und die Lehre von dem Fiktionen bei Leibniz," in *Entwicklung der Methodenlehre in Rechtswissenschaft und Philosophie vom 16. bis Zum 18. Jahrhundert*, ed. Jan Schröder (Stuttgart: Franz Steiner Verlag, 1998), 144.
6. The following presentation of the structure of the *Systema Iuris* and the *Tabula Iuris* draws upon the insightful account in König, "Das System des Rechts und die Lehre von dem Fiktionen bei Leibniz," 144–145.

7. G. W. Leibniz, "Tractatio," in *Textes Inédits*, ed. Gaston Grua, vol. 2 (Paris: Presses Universitaires de France, 1948), 797.
8. The underlining can be seen in Leibniz's manuscript, available on microfilm housed at the Berlin Academy of Science.
9. G. W. Leibniz, "Systema Iuris," in *Textes Inédits*, vol. 2, 820.
10. Ibid. (Citing D.50.17.9 (Ulpian): "Semper in obscuris quod minimum est sequimur.") *The Digest of Justinian*, Latin text ed. Theodor Mommsen and Paul Krueger, English translation ed. Alan Watson, vol. 4 (Philadelphia: University of Pennsylvania Press, 1985), 957.
11. G. W. Leibniz, "Tabula Iuris," in *Textes Inédits*, vol. 2, 791–792.
12. Leibniz, "Systema Iuris," §8, 12, 16. See König, "Das System des Rechts und die Lehre von dem Fiktionen bei Leibniz," 148n38.
13. Leibniz, "Systema Iuris," §22.
14. Klaus Luig, "Die Privatrechtsordnung im Rechtssystem von Leibniz," in *Grund- und Freiheitsrechte von der Ständischen zur Spätbürgerlichen Gesellschaft*, ed. Günther Birtsch (Göttingen: Vandenhoeck & Ruprecht, 1987), 357.
15. "De essentia juris realis est ut alii excludantur, quasi moralis saepes rem circumderit." G. W. Leibniz, "Notae in Tabulam Jurisprudentiae," in *Textes Inédits*, vol. 2, 804.
16. "Persona hoc jure affecta quasi res consideratur." Leibniz, "Systema Iuris," §34. See also G. W. Leibniz, "Praefatio Tabulae Juris," in *Textes Inédits*, vol. 2, 786.
17. Luig, "Die Privatrechtsordnung im Rechtssystem von Leibniz," 358.
18. Leibniz, "Tabula Iuris," 793. See also König, "Das System des Rechts und die Lehre von dem Fiktionen bei Leibniz," 153.
19. G. W. Leibniz, "De Postulationibus," in *Textes Inédits*, vol. 2, 750. Klaus Luig, "Leibniz und die Prinzipien des Vertragrechts," in *Gesellschaftliche Freiheit und Vertragliche Bindung in Rechtsgeschichte und Philosophie*, ed. Jean-François Kervégan and Heinz Mohnhaupt (Frankfurt am Main: Vittorio Klostermann, 1999).
20. "Sunt enim communia omnium jurium, sunt communia omnium realium, sunt alia communia aliorum, sunt propriae unicuique juri causae, quae omnia non nisi factorum ordine disponi possunt." Leibniz, "Praefatio Tabulae Juris," 784.
21. "Synopsis singularum juris materiarum, novo systemati accomodata." Eduard Bodemann, *Die Leibniz-Handschriften der Königlich-Öffentlichen Bibiliothek zu Hannover* (Hannover, 1895), 33–34. See Schneider, *Justitia Universalis*, 89n297.
22. Schneider, *Justitia Universalis*, 89.
23. Ibid., 89n297.
24. See König, "Das System des Rechts und die Lehre von dem Fiktionen bei Leibniz," 144–145.
25. Gottfried Wilhelm Leibniz, "De Legum Interpretatione, Rationibus, Applica-

tione, Systemate," in *Philosophische Schriften*, vol. 4 (Berlin: Akademie-Verlag, 1999), 2781.
26. Gustav Hartmann, "Leibniz als Jurist und Rechtsphilosoph," in *Festgabe Herrn Dr. Rudolph von Jhering zum Doktorjubiläum am 6. August 1892* (Aalen: Scientia Verlag, 1979), 94 (citing "de methodo legum seu de systemate ex pluribus legibus concinnando").
27. "Et si semel methodum facti eligere voluit, cur non continuavit, cur non subdivisit personas & res ex physicis & ethicis, v.g. Personas in surdos, mutos, coecus; hermaphroditos, perfectos; viros, foeminas, impuberes, minores, adultos. . . . Cur, inquam, non ita titulos juris distribuit, & in singulis quid juris esset, explicuit?" Leibniz, *Nova Methodus*, cited in König, "Das System des Rechts und die Lehre von dem Fiktionen bei Leibniz," 146n28.
28. "Duplex enim methodus est, ut jura ipsa ordine percensentes, atque unicuique immorantes explicemus, ex quibus causis nasci, intendi, infringi, tollique possit. Ita enim quod facti est, juri subjicimus, quemadmodum supra subjeceramus jura facto." Leibniz, "De Legum Interpretatione, Rationibus, Applicatione, Systemate," 92, cited in Hartmann, "Leibniz als Jurist und Rechtsphilosoph," 94. See also Leibniz, "De Postulationibus," 750.
29. Leibniz, "De Postulationibus," 750.
30. "Sed ne inutiles hoc loco divisiones persequamur, considerandum est quod diximus omne quod hic petitur esse Actum, cumque actus a nobis definitus sit voluntatis effectus, actus autem illi tantum desiderentur in judicio qui sunt in potestate, sequitur, habita effectus qui in volentis potestate est sponte sequatur. Sufficit ergo in definitione Actus persequi notionem voluntatis omissa notione effectus." Ibid., 751.
31. Jus Civile est Systema Legum Civitatis.
    Civitatis est societas inita felicitatis causa.
    Lex est enuntiatio circa agenda aut omittenda vim cogendi habens.
    Systema est collectio enuntiationum apta ad docendum.
    Leibniz, "De Legum Interpretatione, Rationibus, Applicatione, Systemate," 2781 (emphasis in original).
32. Leibniz, "Systema Iuris," 819.
33. "GENERALIA id est jus in genere significans jurisprudentiam, non, ut infra id quod producit actionem vel exceptionem." Ibid.
34. "Jus in genere a causa, modificatione et dissolutione abstrahens." Ibid., 823.
35. "Huc concursus et cumulatio actionum." Ibid.
36. "Habe das arcanum motus gefunden . . . Demonstrationes de jurisprudentia naturali ex hoc solo principio: quod justitia sit caritas sapientis." Leibniz, letter to Herzog Johann Friedrich, in Leibniz, "Allgemeiner Politischer und Historischer Briefwechsel," vol. 1, 23.
37. Gottfried Wilhelm Leibniz, "Codex Iuris Gentium (Praefatio)," in *Political Writings*, ed. Patrick Riley (Cambridge: Cambridge University Press, 1996),

170ff; G. W. Leibniz, *Die Philosophische Schriften*, ed. C. I. Gerhardt, vol. 3 (New York: Georg Olms Verlag, 1996), 386ff.
38. Leibniz, "Codex Iuris Gentium (Praefatio)," 170.
39. Ibid., 175.
40. Ibid., 171. Leibniz, *Die Philosophische Schriften*, vol. 3, 386 (emphasis in the Latin original).
41. Cf. Werner Schneiders, "Naturrecht und Gerechtigkeit bei Leibniz," *Zeitschrift für Philosophische Forschung* 20 (1966): 631. "[Leibniz'] Ausgangspunkt ist im allgemeinen die Tugend der Gerechtigkeit, nicht die Norm der Gerechtigkeit."
42. Leibniz, *Die Philosophische Schriften*, vol. 3, 387.
43. "Wirklichen Inhalt enthält Leibniz' Bestimmung der Gerechtigkeit zunächst nur dadurch, daß die rightige Liebe sich vor allem als Gottesliebe erweist." in Schneiders, "Naturrecht und Gerechtigkeit bei Leibniz," 641.
44. "Quia autem sapientia caritatem dirigere debet, hujus quoque definitione opus erit. Arbitror autem notioni hominum optime satisfieri, si *sapientiam* nihil aliud esse dicamus quam ipsam scientiam felicitatis." Leibniz, *Die Philosophische Schriften*, vol. 3, 387.
45. Ibid., 387–389.
46. See Schneiders, "Naturrecht und Gerechtigkeit bei Leibniz," 610–611.
47. Leibniz, "Codex Iuris Gentium (Praefatio)," 173.
48. Ibid.
49. Ibid.
50. Gottfried Wilhelm Leibniz, "Elementa Juris Civilis," in *Philosophische Schriften*, ed. Leibniz-Forschungsstelle der Universität Münster, vol. 2 (Berlin: Akademie-Verlag, 1966), 465. See also Schneiders, "Naturrecht und Gerechtigkeit bei Leibniz," 619.

Part II Introduction

1. "Es ist ein alter Wunsch, der, wer weiß wie spät, vielleicht einmal in Erfüllung gehen wird: daß man doch einmal, statt der endlosen Mannigfaltigkeit bürgerlicher Gesetze, ihre Prinzipien aufsuchen möge; denn darin kann allein das Geheimnis bestehen, die Gesetzgebung, wie man sagt, zu simplifizieren. Aber die Gesetze sind hier auch nur Einschrankungen unserer Freiheit auf Bedingungen, unter denen sie durchgängig mit sich selbst zusammenstimmt; mithin gehen sie auf etwas, was gänzlich unser eigen Werk ist, und wovon wir durch jene Begriffe selbst die Ursache sein können." See Immanuel Kant, *Kritik der Reinen Vernunft* (Hamburg: Felix Meiner Verlag GmbH, 1990), B358. See also G. W. F. Hegel, *Grundlinien der Phiosophie des Rechts*, ed. Johannes Hoffmeister (Hamburg: Felix Meiner Verlag, 1955), §212.
2. Franz Wieacker, *Privatrechtsgeschichte der Neuzeit: Unter Besonderer Berück-*

sichtigung der Deutschen Entwicklung, Reprint of 2nd revised ed. of 1967 ed. (Göttingen: Vandenhoeck & Ruprecht, 1996), 323. See also Walter Demel and Werner Schubert, *Der Entwurf eines Bürgerlichen Gesetzbuchs für das Königreich Bayern von 1811* (Ebelsbach: Verlag Rolf Gremer, 1986), LXIV; Franz Löher, *Das System des Preußischen Landrechts in Deutschrechtlicher und Philosophischer Begründung* (Paderborn: Junfermann, 1852).

3. Wieacker, *Privatrechtsgeschichte der Neuzeit: Unter Besonderer Berücksichtigung der Deutschen Entwicklung*, §19, 323.
4. Franz Wieacker, "Aufstieg, Blüte und Krisis der Kodifikationsidee," in *Festschrift für Gustav Boehmer* (Bonn: Ludwig Röhrscheid Verlag, 1954), 35.
5. Wieacker, *Privatrechtsgeschichte der Neuzeit: Unter Besonderer Berücksichtigung der Deutschen Entwicklung*, 323.
6. Ibid. See also Paul Koschaker, *Europa und das Römische Recht*, 4th unedited ed. (Munich: C. H. Beck'sche Verlagsbuchhandlung, 1966).
7. The few apparent exceptions are largely interested in Leibniz as a theorist of justice rather than as a forerunner of modern legal codes; see Huntington Cairns, *Legal Philosophy from Plato to Hegel* (London: Oxford University Press, 1949), 295–335. For a more recent account, see Patrick Riley, *Leibniz' Universal Jurisprudence* (Cambridge, MA: Harvard University Press, 1996).
8. For an account of the breadth of the nineteenth-century adoption of legal codes, see Csaba Varga, *Codification as a Socio-Historical Phenomenon*, trans. Sándor and Judit Petrányi and Csaba Varga Sezenyi (Budapest: Akademiai Kiado, 1991).
9. Adolf Trendelenburg, "Leibnizens Anregung zu einer Justizreform," in *Kleine Schriften*, ed. Adolf Trendelenburg (Leipzig: Verlag von S. Hirzel, 1871), 245. A reprint of the report can be found in Trendlenburg's essay, and also in Johann Wilhelm Bernhard von Hymmen, ed., *Beyträge zu der Juristischen Litteratur in dem Preußischen Staaten Zweite Sammlung*, vol. 2 (Berlin: Voss, 1778), 263ff.
10. Fuchs's assignment to the juridical faculty in Frankfurt will reappear, nine years later, in the documents preparing Friedrich I's order from March 1709, which set in motion the process of judicial reform that would later become the Prussian ALR.
11. Thilo Ramm, "Die Friderizianische Gesamtkodifikation und der Historische Rechtsvergleich," in *Das Preußische Allgemeine Landrecht. Politische, Rechtliche und Soziale Wechsel—und Fortwirkungen*, ed. Jörg Wolff (Heidelberg: C. F. Müller Verlag, Hüthig GmbH, 1995), 3.
12. See Svarez's statement of the need for the universal grounding principles of *Recht* in the body of the ALR in Andreas Schwennicke, *Die Entstehung der Einleitung des Preußischen Allgemeinen Landrechts von 1794* (Frankfurt am Main: Vittorio Klostermann, 1993), 315n87.
13. Carl Gottlieb von Svarez, *Vorträge über Recht und Staat*, ed. Hermann Conrad and Gerd Kleinheyer (Cologne: Westdeutscher Verlag, 1960), 464.

14. "Die Franzosen ließen sich durch Wissenschaftlichkeitsfragen ohnehin nicht irritieren. . . . Die Anlehnung an Natur(Wissenschaft) und Geist(eswissenschaft) erschien ihnen als Juristen fremd." Rainer Maria Kiesow, *Das Alphabet des Rechts* (Frankfurt am Main: Fischer, 2004), 52.

4. From the *Gesetzbuch* to the *Landrecht*

1. "Eben so wenig kann ich solche Sätze, die dahin abzielen, die Unterthanen des Staats über den wahren Zweck des Staats zu belehren; ihn mit den wohlthätigen Regeln und Maximen nach welchen er beherrscht wird, bekannt zu machen; ihm den vernunftmäßigen Grund seiner Verpflichtung zum Gehorsam gegen die Gesetze und seinen Landesherrn zu zeigen, und das enge Band dieser Verpflichtung mit der Conservation der öffentlichen und PrivatGlückseligkeit sichtbar zu machen, für unnutz und überflüßig ansehen." *GstA Merseburg*, Report 84, Division XVI Nr. 7, vol. 88, fol. 71v, cited in Andreas Schwennicke, *Die Entstehung Der Einleitung Des Preußischen Allgemeinen Landrechts Von 1794*, vol. 61 (Frankfurt am Main: Vittorio Klostermann, 1993), 60n250.
2. "Vielmehr befürchte ich im Gegentheile gewiß nicht ohne Grund, daß es das Vertrauen der Unterthanen, sowie ihre Zufriedenheit mit der Regierung, unter welcher sie leben, gar sehr schwächen dürfte, wenn man gegenwärtig durch Übergehung und Weglaßung dieser Sätze eine Mißbilligung derselben zu erkennen geben, und den Verkündigungen dererjenigen, welche den Preußischen Staat der Despotie beschuldigen, einen so scheinbaren Vorwand liefern wollte." Ibid., 60.
3. See *Allgemeines Landrecht für die Preussischen Staaten von 1794*, ed. Hans Hattenhauer, 3rd expanded ed. (Berlin: Luchterhand Verlag, 1996), 16.
4. Friedrich Nietzsche, "Der Antichrist," in *Kritische Studienausgabe*, ed. Giorgio Colli and Mazzino Montinari, vol. 6 (Munich: Deutscher Taschenbuch Verlag GmbH & Co. KG, 1988), 239–242. For a more detailed account of Nietzsche's thinking about positive law, see Philippe Nonet, "What Is Positive Law?" *The Yale Law Journal* 100 (1990): 667–699. See also Roger Berkowitz, "Friedrich Nietzsche, the Code of Manu, and the Art of Legislation," *Cardozo Law Review* 24 (2003): 1131–1149.
5. Gerhard Buchda, "Die Spruchtätigkeit der hallischen Juristenfakultät in ihrem äußeren Verlauf," 266 (cited in Peter Krause, "Einführung," in *Entwurf eines Allgemeinen Gesetzbuches für die Preußischen Staaten*, ed. Peter Krause, in *Carl Gottlieb Svarez Gesammelte Schriften*, ed. Peter Krause, vol. 1 [Stuttgart: Friedrich Fromann Verlag, 1996], xxi–xxii).
6. Krause, "Einführung," xxii–xxviii.
7. "Welches sich bloß auf die Vernunft und Landesverfassungen gründet." Hattenhauer, "Einführung," 1.
8. The title of Cocceji's code, medieval in its style and length, reflects the

scholastic nature of his work: "Projekt des Corporis Juris Fridericiani das ist Seiner Königlichen Majestät in Preusen in der Vernunft und Landesverfassungen gegründete Landsrecht, worinnen das Römische Recht in eine natürliche Ordnung und richtiges Systema, nach denen dreyen Objectis juris gebracht: Die General-Principia, welche in der Vernunft gegrundet sind, bey einem jeden Objecto Festgesetzt und die nötigen Conclusiones, als so viel Gesetze, daraus deducirt: Alle Subtilitäten und Fictiones, nicht weniger was auf den Teutschen Statum nicht applicable ist, ausgelassen: Alle zweifelhafte Jura, welche in denen Römischen Gesetzen vorkommen, oder von denen Doctoribus gemacht worden, decidirt und solchergestalt ein Ius certum und universale in allen Dero Provinzen statuirt wird." Cited in ibid., 2.
9. Krause, "Einführung," xxxvi.
10. See, most vociferously, ibid., xxixff.
11. Marginal remark by Friedrich to the proposed code by Cocceji, cited in Hattenhauer, "Einführung," 2.
12. "Dissertation sur les raisons d'établir ou d'abroger les lois," cited from the German translation, in Friedrich the Great, "Über die Gründe, Gesetze Einzuführen oder Abzuschaffen," in *Die Werke Friedrichs des Großen*, ed. Gustav Berthold Volz (Berlin: Verlag von Reimar Hobbing, 1913), 32.
13. Ibid., 38.
14. "Allerhöchste Königliche Cabinetts-Ordre die Verbesserung des Justiz-Wesens betreffend vom 14. April 1780." Reprinted in Hattenhauer, *Allgemeines Landrecht für die Preußischen Staaten von 1794*, 37ff.
15. Krause, "Einführung," xxxix–xl.
16. Hattenhauer, "Einführung," 3.
17. See, e.g., Adolf Stölzel, *Carl Gottlieb Suarez* (Berlin: Verlag von Franz Dahlen, 1885), 274–275.
18. Hattenhauer, "Einführung," 5.
19. For Svarez, see Stölzel, *Carl Gottlieb Svarez*. For Ernst Ferdinand Klein, see Michael Kleensang, *Konzept der Bürgerlichen Gesellschaft bei Ernst Ferdinand Klein* (Frankfurt am Main: Vittorio Klostermann, 1998).
20. Hattenhauer, "Einführung," 6.
21. Ibid.
22. Schwennicke, *Die Entstehung der Einleitung des Preußischen Allgemeinen Landrechts von 1794*, 378ff.
23. But see Schwennicke, amending the received wisdom. Ibid.
24. Hattenhauer, "Einführung," 5.
25. Christoph Goßler, cited in ibid., 6.
26. Erik Wolf, "Carl Gottlieb Svarez," in *Grosse Rechtsdenker der Deutschen Geistesgeschichte* (Tübingen: J. C. B. Mohr, 1963), 462.
27. Hattenhauer, "Einführung," 12.
28. Schwennicke, *Die Entstehung der Einleitung des Preußischen Allgemeinen Landrechts von 1794*, 49ff.

29. Ibid., 52.
30. Hattenhauer, "Einführung," 14; Schwennicke, *Die Entstehung der Einleitung des Preußischen Allgemeinen Landrechts von 1794*, 55.
31. See more generally, Hans Hattenhauer, "Das ALR im Widerstreit der Politik," in *Kodifikation Gestern und Heute. Zum 200. Geburtstag des Allgemenen Landrechts für die Preußischen Staaten*, ed. Detlef Merten and Waldemar Schreckenberger (Berlin: Duncker & Humblot, 1995), 45ff.
32. Ernst Ferdinand Klein, *System des Preußischen Civilrechts* (Halle: Verlag der Buchhandlung des Waisenhauses, 1835), 23.
33. Stölzel, *Carl Gottlieb Suarez*, 274–275. See also Hans Thieme, "Zum 175. Geburtstag des Allgemeinen Landrechts," in *Die Zeit des Späten Naturrechts*, ed. Hans Thieme (Cologne: Böhlau Verlag, 1986), 771.
34. See, e.g., Hattenhauer, "Das ALR im Widerstreit der Politik," 45.
35. "*Das allgemeine Gesetzbuch enthält die Vorschriften, nach welchen die Rechte und Verbindlichkeiten der Einwohner des Staats, . . . zu beurtheilen sind*" (emphasis added). Paragraph 1 of the ALR, printed in *Allgemeines Landrecht für die Preussichen Staaten von 1794*, ed. Hans Hattenhauer, 3rd expanded ed. (Berlin: Luchterhand Verlag, 1966), 57.
36. Letter from von Danckelmann to von Carmer, Oct. 28, 1793, reprinted in Hans Thieme, "Die Preußische Kodifikation," in *Ideengeschichte und Rechtsgeschichte. Gesammelte Schriften*, ed. Hans Thieme (Cologne: Böhlau Verlag GmbH & Cie, 1986), 758–759).
37. "Für den Einwohner des Staats, ist es, im allgemeinen, genug, daß er wiße, daß z.B. auf Begehung dieser oder jener That, die Todes-Strafe gesetzt sey. Er wird dadurch die Gefahr, in die er sich, durch deren Begehung, setzt, [erkennen], und es würde gewiß überflüßig seyn, ihn mit der Lehre von er Imputation und allen mitigantibus et aggravantibus bekannt zu machen." Letter from von Danckelmann to von Carmer, Oct. 28, 1793, reprinted in ibid.
38. See Nietzsche's account of such an aristocratic positivism in his discussion of the Code of Manu. Nietzsche, "Der Antichrist," 239–247. See Berkowitz, "Friedrich Nietzsche, the Code of Manu, and the Art of Legislation."
39. Letter from von Danckelmann to von Carmer, Oct. 28, 1793, reprinted in Thieme, "Die Preußische Kodifikation," 759.
40. Ibid., 758.
41. Ibid.
42. "Die Legislation ist in meinen Augen so wenig ein Stück der Jurisprudenz als ein attribut des Justiz Departementes, sondern ein Werck der Politik, das die Concurrenz aller Departements erfordert, wenn die Gesetze Zutrauen und willige Folge Leistung finden sollen." Ibid., 759 (citing the quotation as comments found in Stölzel, *Carl Gottlieb Svarez*, 379).
43. "Auch bin ich von dem großen Werthe eines wahren philosophischen Natur Rechts sowohl für den Gesetzgeber als für den Richter vollkommen

überzeugt." Letter from von Carmer to von Danckelmann, Nov. 8, 1793, reprinted in Thieme, "Die Preußische Kodifikation," 759–764.
44. "Da es nun, wie Ewr. Wohlgeb. Selbst bemerken, noch keinen allgemein anerkannten Codex des Natur Rechts giebt, auf den der Gesetzgeber verweisen könnte, so muß er sich schon die Mühe nehmen, auch solchen Sätzen, welche bereits im Natur Recht enthalten zu seyn scheinen, die positive Sanction beyzulegen, um allen Zweifeln: was iuris naturalis sey od. Nicht, zuvor zu kommen." Letter from Svarez to Friedrich Philipp Karl Böll, April 10, 1785, reprinted in Schwennicke, *Die Entstehung der Einleitung des Preußischen Allgemeinen Landrechts von 1794*, 129–130.
45. "Zufördest setzt das Natur Recht ... allemal etwas Gegebenes, etwas Positives voraus." Letter from von Carmer to von Danckelmann, Nov. 8, 1793, reprinted in Thieme, "Die Preußische Kodifikation," 760.
46. "Die Begriffe selbst [müssen] erst festgesetzt seyn." Cited in ibid.
47. "Denn wenn aus Begriffen richtige Folgerungen hergeleitet werden sollen, so müssen die Begriffe selbst erst festgesetzt seyn; und dieß kann, bey Rechts-Materien in der bürgerlichen Gesellschaft, nicht füglich anders, als durch den erklärten Willen des Gesetzgebers geschehen." Ibid.
48. Ibid.
49. See Martin Heidegger, *Der Ursprung des Kunstwerkes* (Stuttgart: Philipp Reclam jun., 1992), 7–8.
50. See Philippe Nonet, "Technique and Law," in *Legality and Community*, ed. Robert A. Kagan, Martin Krygier, and Kenneth Winston (New York: Rowman & Littlefield, 2002), 53.
51. "Nul ne peut être puni qu'en vertu d'une loi établie et promulguée antérieurement au délit et légalement appliquée." Ibid., 54–55.
52. "Man nennt die bloße Übereinstimmung oder Nichtübereinstimmung einer Handlung mit dem Gesetze ohne Rücksicht auf die Triebfeder derselben die Legalität (Gesetzmäßigkeit), diejenige aber, in welcher die Idee der Pflicht aus dem Gesetze zugleich die Triebfeder der Handlung ist, die Moralität (Sittlichkeit) derselben." Immanuel Kant, *Die Metaphysik der Sitten* (Cologne: Könemann Verlagsgesellschaft, 1995), 219.
53. Wolfgang Kersting, *Wohlgeordnete Freiheit* (Frankfurt am Main: Suhrkamp Taschenbuch Verlag, 1993), 178.
54. Kant, *Die Metaphysik der Sitten*, 218–219.
55. Cf. Nonet, "Technique and Law," 55.
56. Max Weber, *Wirtschaft und Gesellschaft* (Tübingen: J. C. B. Mohr, 1980), 124–125.
57. Ibid., 125.
58. Ibid., 494.
59. Ibid.
60. Ibid., 565.
61. Ibid., 562.

62. Ibid., 565.
63. Ibid., 563.

5. The Rule of Law

1. Erik Wolf, "Carl Gottlieb Svarez," in *Grosse Rechtsdenker der Deutschen Geistesgeschichte* (Tübingen: J. C. B. Mohr, 1963), 450; Hans Thieme, "Die Preußische Kodifikation," in *Ideengeschichte und Rechtsgeschichte*, ed. Hans Thieme (Cologne: Böhlau Verlag, 1986), 717. Adolf Stölzel, *Carl Gottlieb Svarez* (Berlin: Verlag von Franz Dahlen, 1885), 281; Carl Gottlieb Svarez, *Vorträge über Recht und Staat*, ed. Hermann Conrad and Gerd Kleinheyer (Cologne: Westdeutscher Verlag, 1960), xiv.
2. Carl Gottlieb Svarez, "Kronprinzenvorträge," in Svarez, *Vorträge über Recht und Staat*, 453.
3. Ibid., 454.
4. Ibid., 454–455.
5. "[D]aß wir von Natur berechtigt sind, alles das zu tun, was zu unserer Glückseligkeit dient." Ibid., 3.
6. "Hier fängt also das Gebiet der Moral an. Ihr kommt es zu, den Menschen zu belehren, in welcher natürlichen und untrennbaren Verbindung die Wohlfahrt eines jeden einzelnen Menschen mit dem Wohl und der Glückseligkeit seiner Nebenmenschen stehe, daß nur edle, großmütige und wohlwollende Gesinnungen der Natur und Würde unsers unsterblichen Geistes gemäß sind." Ibid., 457.
7. Aristotle, *The Nicomachean Ethics*, ed. G. P. Goold, trans. H. Rackham, vol. Aristotle: 19 (Cambridge, MA: Harvard University Press, 1990), Bk. V; Immanuel Kant, *Die Metaphysik der Sitten* (Cologne: Könemann Verlagsgesellschaft, 1995), 230ff.
8. Aristotle, *The Nicomachean Ethics*, Bk. V, ch. 6, 1134a. See also "Epi koinonon biou pros to einai autoarkeian, eleutheron kai ison." Ibid.
9. Aristotle further divides political justice into distributive justice and corrective justice, the two standards by which political and legal affairs in a *polis* are to be governed.
10. "Der Begriff des Rechts, sofern er sich auf eine ihm correspondirende Verbindlichkeit bezieht, (d.i. der moralische Begriff desselben) betrifft erstlich nur das äußere und zwar praktische Verhältniß einer Person gegen eine andere, sofern ihre Handlungen als Facta aufeinander (unmittelbar oder mittelbar) Einfluß haben können." Kant, *Die Metaphysik der Sitten*, 230.
11. "Ein *strictes* (enges) Recht kann man also nur das völlig äußere nennen. Dieses gründet sich nun zwar auf dem Bewußtsein der Verbindlichkeit eines jeden nach dem Gesetze." Ibid., 232. See also Wolfgang Kersting, *Wohlgeordnete Freiheit* (Frankfurt am Main: Suhrkamp Taschenbuch Verlag, 1993), 112–116. What exactly Kant means by a consciousness of one's ob-

ligation to obey *Gesetz* remains unclear; his attempt to ground obligation outside of free will does contradict the essence of his critical philosophy.
12. Aristotle, *The Nicomachean Ethics*, 1129b12–30.
13. Ibid., 1129b26–27.
14. Kant, *Die Metaphysik der Sitten*, 231.
15. "Der Gegenstand dieser Wissenschaft sind [sic] bloß die natürlichen Rechte des Menschen gegen andre außer ihm und unter diesen nur solche, die er nötigenfalls mit Gewalt und Zwang auszuüben befugt ist." Svarez, "Kronprinzenvorträge," 456.
16. Jan Schröder, "Gottfried Achenwall, Johann Stephan Pütter und die Elementa Iuris Naturae," in *Anfangsgründe des Naturrechts*, ed. Jan Schröder (Frankfurt am Main: Insel Verlag, 1995), 336ff.
17. "Daher kann unter Menschen, die in einer bürgerlichen Gesellschaft und unter Gesetzen leben, nicht mehr davon die Frage sein, was für Befugnisse und Obliegenheiten unter ihnen nach dem Naturrechte stattfinden, sondern es kommt alles darauf an, was die Gesetze des Staats über ihre Rechte und Pflichten bestimmen." Svarez, *Vorträge über Recht und Staat*, 582.
18. "Daß jedes Mitglied derselben für seine Person und sein Vermögen der möglichsten Sicherheit gegen alle gewaltsamen Angriffe und Störungen andrer genießen solle." Svarez, "Kronprinzenvorträge," 464.
19. Ibid., 460–461.
20. Ibid., 463.
21. Ibid., 464.
22. Ibid.
23. Ibid., 581.
24. Ibid., 464–465.
25. Ibid., 581.
26. Ibid.
27. Ibid.
28. Ibid., 582.
29. Ibid., 464.
30. John Locke, *Two Treatises of Government*, ed. Peter Laslett (New York: Cambridge University Press, 1988). See Bk. II, ch. 9, 131.
31. "Er hat die vollkommenste Freiheit, die Kräfte seines Körpers, die Fähigkeiten seines Geistes zu bilden." Svarez, "Kronprinzenvorträge," 458.
32. Wilhelm Dilthey, "Das Allgemeine Landrecht," in *Zur Preussischen Geschichte*, ed. Erich Weniger (Stuttgart: B. G. Teubner Verlagsgesellschaft, 1985), 199.
33. Lon Fuller, *The Morality of Law* (New Haven, CT: Yale University Press, 1969), 98.
34. The eight virtues of legality are developed by Lon Fuller, in *The Morality of Law*.
35. Joseph Raz, *The Authority of Law: Essays on Law and Morality* (New York: Oxford University Press, 1983), 213.

36. "Hier hat die gesetzgebende Macht keine andre Regel, die sie bindet, als den Zweck des Staats, d.h. die Erhaltung und Befestigung der gemeinen Ruhe und Sicherheit, die Erleichterung und Begünstigung der Mittel, wodurch einem jeden einzelnen die Gelegenheit verschafft werden kann, seine Privatglückseligkeit ohne Beeinträchtigung und Beleidigung anderer zu befördern, und die Aufrechterhaltung der Staatsverbindung selbst als der notwendigen Bedingung, unter welcher nur jene Zwecke erreicht werden können." Svarez, "Kronprinzenvorträge," 586.
37. Carl Gottlieb Svarez, "Über den Zweck des Staats," in *Vorträge über Recht und Staat*, 640.
38. "Wir finden nämlich in einem jeden wohleingerichteten Staate eine Menge von Anordnungen und Ausübungen der Obergewalt, denen wir uns alle ohne Murren sogar mit Freuden unterwerfen, ohnerachtet sie bloß dahin abzielen, zum Besten nicht des Ganzen, sondern gewisser einzelnen Mitglieder des Staats unvolkommene Pflichten in volkommene, bloße moralische Befugnisse in Zwangsrechte zu verwandeln." Ibid., 641.
39. See, e.g., Angela Taeger, " 'Im Familienglück Lebt die Vaterlandsliebe'—Dynamik und Rechtliche Ramhung der Ehe im Preußen des 19. Jahrhunderts," in *Das Preußische Allgemeine Landrecht*, ed. Jörg Wolff (Heidelberg: C. F. Müller Verlag, 1995), 201.
40. "Allgemeines Landrecht für die Preussischen Staaten von 1794," in *Allgemeines Landrecht für die Preussischen Staaten, von 1794* ed. Hans Hattenhauer, 3rd expanded ed. (Berlin: Luchterhand Verlag, 1996), Pt. I, Title 8, §83, 106.
41. Ibid., Pt. II, Title 7, §37, 440.
42. Svarez, "Über den Zweck des Staats," 642.
43. Ibid., 643.
44. "§. 73. Ein jedes Mitglied des Staats ist, das Wohl und die Sicherheit des gemeinen Wesens, nach dem Verhältnis seines Standes und Vermögens, zu unterstützen verpflichtet."
45. See Andreas Schwennicke, *Die Entstehung der Einleitung des Preußischen Allgemeinen Landrechts von 1794*, vol. 61 (Frankfurt am Main: Vittorio Klostermann, 1993), 311.
46. "§.50. Das allgemeine Wohl ist der Grund der Gesetze.

    §.51. Der Staat ist verpflichtet, für die innere und äußere Ruhe und Sicherheit seiner Mitglieder zu sorgen.

    §.52. Er ist berechtigt, die äußern Handlungen aller, welche seinen Schutz geniessen, diesem Endzweck gemäß anzuordnen.

    §.53. Jeder Bürger des Staats ist schuldig, das Seinige zu Erreichung dieses Endzwecks beyzutragen.

    §.54. Alle einzle Rechte der Bürger des Staats müssen dem Endzweck der allgemeinen Ruhe und Sicherheit untergeordnet werden."

    These paragraphs remained as part of the Prussian code, albeit in a slightly

altered form, up until the last published draft, but were excised from the final version of the ALR that came into power in 1794. Cited in Schwennicke, *Die Entstehung der Einleitung des Preußischen Allgemeinen Landrechts von 1794*, 299.
47. Ibid.
48. Section 77 of Klein's draft of the introduction to the code reads, "Das Wohl des Staats und seiner Einwohner ist der Zweck der bürgerlichen Vereinigung, und das allgemeine Ziel der Gesetze." See Ibid., 310.
49. As expressed by Friedrich II in his secret testament from 1768 (cited in ibid., 306).
50. See especially Svarez, "Über den Zweck des Staats," 641ff.
51. Locke, *Two Treatises of Government*, Bk. II, ch. 11, 355.

Part III Introduction

1. Hans Hattenhauer, "Einführung," in *Allgemeines Landrecht für die Preussischen Staaten von 1794*, ed. Hans Hattenhauer, 3rd expanded ed. (Berlin: Luchterhand Verlag, 1996), 23.
2. Cited in James Sheehan, "The German States and the European Revolution," in *Revolution and the Meaning of Freedom in the Nineteenth Century*, ed. Isser Woloch (Stanford, CA: Stanford University Press, 1996), 251.
3. A sampling of the output includes: J. N. Borst, *Einige Grundlinien für eine Vernünftige Gesetzgebung des Civilprocesses mit Vergleichenden Bemerkungen über den Gemeinen Teutschen, Baierischen, Preußischen und Französischen Proceß* (Nuremberg: Friedrich Campe, 1810); Alexander Müller, *Die Fortbildung der Gesetzgebung im Geiste der Zeit, und über die Hindernisse Derselben Besonders in Deutschland, Mit Hinblick auf den Deutschen Gesetz- und Rechts-Zustand, und die Legislatorischen Vorarbeiten; Sodann über die Zweckmäßigsten Mittel zu einer Guten Gresetzgebung Überhaupt zu Gelangen, Mittelst Angabe der Vornehmsten Hieher Gehörenden Literatur-Quellen für Fremde und Einheimische Bürgerliche Gesetzgebung* (Cologne: Büschler, 1836); J. F. L. Duncker, *Das Recht, aus dem Gesetz des Lebens als Leitfaden eines Gesetzbuchs Entwickelt* (Berlin: Duncker & Humblot, 1831); H.[einrich] Zoepfl, "Ueber das Verhältniß des Rationalen und Nationalen Rechtes, Mit Rücksicht auf die Neuen Gesetzbücher," *Zeitschrift für deutsches Recht und deutsche Rechtswissenschaft* 3 (1840); C. A. F. Graun, *Versuch über die Principien der Bürgerlichen Gesetzgebung; in Besonderer Beziehung auf das Bürgerliche Recht des Preuszischen Staates* (Berlin: Verlag von G. Crantz, 1841); A. L. Reyscher, *Ueber die Bedürfnisse Unserer Zeit in der Gesetzgebung Mit Besonderer Rücksicht auf den Zustand der Leztern in Württemberg* (Stuttgart and Tübingen: Verlag der J. G. Cotta'schen Buchhandlung, 1828).
4. F. Vierhaus, *Die Entstehungsgeschichte des Entwurfes eines Bürgerlichen Gesetzbuches für das Deutsche Reich* (Berlin: Verlag von J. Guttentag, 1888), 19.

5. Michael John, *Politics and the Law in Late Nineteenth-Century Germany* (Oxford: Clarendon Press, 1989), 15.
6. James Q. Whitman, *The Legacy of Roman Law in the German Romantic Era: Historical Vision and Legal Change* (Princeton, NJ: Princeton University Press, 1990), 101.
7. Ibid., 233. See also pp. 116–117.
8. Ibid., 150.
9. Ibid., 232–234.
10. Friedrich Carl von Savigny, "Vom Beruf Unsrer Zeit für Gesetzgebung und Rechtswissenschaft," in *Politik und Neuere Legislation*, ed. Hidetake Akamatsu and Joachim Rückert (Frankfurt am Main: Vittorio Klostermann, 2000). A. F. J. Thibaut, "Ueber die Nothwendigkeit eines Allgemeinen Bürgerlichen Rechts für Deutschland," in *Thibaut und Savigny. Zum 100 Jährigen Gedächtnis des Kampfes um ein Einheitliches Bürgerliches Recht für Deutschland*, ed. Jacques Stern (Berlin: Verlag Franz Vahlen, 1914), 37.
11. "Bannstrahl gegen die Kodifikation," in Hattenhauer, "Einführung," 24.
12. Stefan Riesenfeld, "The Influence of German Legal Theory on American Law: The Heritage of Savigny and His Disciples," *American Journal of Comparative Law* 37 (1989): 1–2.
13. Joachim Rückert, *Idealismus, Jurisprudenz und Politik bei Friedrich Carl von Savigny* (Ebelsbach: Verlag Rolf Gremer, 1984), 57–58.

6. From Reason to History

1. "Man stelle sich die Wohllust vor, mit welcher ich nun manche meiner Sätze oder Beweiße bey ihm fand!" A reprint of Hugo's *Civilistische Magazin* from 1790 was published in 1810 as Gustav Hugo, *Civilistisches Magazin*, 3rd shortened ed. (Berlin: August Mylius, 1810), 10–18. The citation is at p. 11. See also R. Stintzing and Ernst Landsberg, *Geschichte der Deutschen Rechtswissenschaft* (Munich and Berlin: R. Oldenbourg, 1910), 11.
2. Hugo, *Civilistisches Magazin*, 15 (citing Leibniz).
3. Rudolf von Jhering, "Friedrich Karl von Savigny," *Jherings Jahrbücher für Dogmatik* 5 (1861): 354.
4. See, e.g., Erik Wolf, *Grosse Rechtsdenker der Deutschen Geistesgeschichte*, 4th revised and expanded ed. (Tübingen: J. C. B. Mohr [Paul Siebeck], 1963), 527ff.
5. Friedrich Karl von Savigny, "Ueber den Zweck der Zeitschrift für Geschichtliche Rechtswissenschaft," in *Vermischte Schriften*, ed. Friedrich Karl von Savigny (Aalen: Scientia Verlag, 1981), 105.
6. Savigny, letter to Zimmer, in 1814, cited in Pio Caroni, "Savigny und die Kodifikation," *Zeitschrift für Rechtsgeschichte* (German division) 86 (1969):

129. The letter can be found in *Zeitschrift für Rechtsgeschichte* (German division) 56 (1936): 394, 395.
7. See Friedrich Karl von Savigny, *Juristische Methodenlehre Nach Der Ausarbeitung Des Jakob Grimm*, ed. Gerhard Wesenberg (Stuttgart: K. F. Koehler Verlag, 1951); Friedrich Carl von Savigny, *Vorlesungen über Juristische Methodologie 1802–1842*, ed. Aldo Mazzacane (Frankfurt am Main: Vittorio Klostermann, 1993); Friedrich Carl von Savigny, "Institutionen, Winter 1808," in *Idealismus, Jurisprudenz und Politik bei Friedrich Carl von Savigny*, ed. Joachim Rückert (Ebelsbach: Verlag Rolf Gremer, 1984).
8. Pierre Clastres, *Archaeology of Violence*, trans. Jeanine Herman (New York: Semiotext(e), 1994), 58.
9. Savigny, *Juristische Methodenlehre nach der Ausarbeitung des Jakob Grimm*, 76.
10. Friedrich Carl von Savigny, "Vom Beruf Unsrer Zeit für Gesetzgebung und Rechtswissenschaft," in *Politik und Neuere Legislation*, ed. Hidetake Akamatsu and Joachim Rückert (Frankfurt am Main: Vittorio Klostermann, 2000), 238 [45]. Bracketed page numbers refer to the 1814 edition of Savigny's essay.
11. Ibid., 240 [48]. "Unglücklicherweise nun ist das ganze achtzehnte Jahrhundert in Deutschland sehr arm an großen Juristen gewesen."
12. Ibid., 241 [50].
13. Ibid., 218 [6].
14. See Christoph Mährlein, *Volksgeist und Recht* (Würzburg: Königshausen & Neumann, 2000), 20.
15. Wolf, *Grosse Rechtsdenker der Deutschen Geistesgeschichte*, 493.
16. Friedrich Karl von Savigny, *System des Heutigen Römischen Rechts*, reprint of the Berlin 1840 ed. (Aalen: Scientia Verlag, 1981), vol. 1, 15.
17. Ibid., vol. 1, 14. See Savigny, "Vom Beruf Unsrer Zeit für Gesetzgebung und Rechtswissenschaft," 219 [8].
18. Savigny, "Vom Beruf Unsrer Zeit für Gesetzgebung und Rechtswissenschaft," 219 [8].
19. "Ursprünglich alles positive Recht Volksrecht ist." Savigny, *System des Heutigen Römischen Rechts*, vol. 1, 50.
20. "Mehr als bloße Methodenänderung war ein neues Lebensgefühl, eine veränderte metaphysische Grundhaltung zum Recht das Kennzeichen der 'Historischen Schule.'" See Wolf, *Grosse Rechtsdenker der Deutschen Geistesgeschichte*, 491.
21. "Das Recht hat kein Daseyn für sich, sein Wesen vielmehr ist das Leben der Menschen selbst, von einer besondern Seite angesehen." Savigny, "Vom Beruf Unsrer Zeit für Gesetzgebung und Rechtswissenschaft," 230 [30].
22. "Das Recht hat sein Daseyn in dem gemeinsamen Volksgeist, also in dem Gesammtwillen, der insofern auch der Wille jedes Einzelnen ist." Savigny, *System des Heutigen Römischen Rechts*, vol. 1, 24.

23. Otto Gierke, *Die Historische Rechtsschule und die Germanisten* (Berlin: Gustav Schade, 1903), 7.
24. Savigny, "Vom Beruf Unsrer Zeit für Gesetzgebung und Rechtswissenschaft," 222 [13].
25. Jhering, "Friedrich Karl von Savigny," 364–365.
26. Savigny, "Vom Beruf Unsrer Zeit für Gesetzgebung und Rechtswissenschaft," 230 [30].
27. Joachim Rückert, *Idealismus, Jurisprudenz und Politik bei Friedrich Carl von Savigny* (Ebelsbach: Verlag Rolf Gremer, 1984), 305.
28. "Sein [das Recht] Daseyn aber ist ein selbstständiges." Savigny, *System des Heutigen Römischen Rechts*, vol. 1, 332.
29. "Dadurch entsteht indessen ein Misverhältniß zwischen dem Gesetz und dem Rechtsinstitut, dessen organische Natur in jener abstracten Form unmöglich erschöpft werden kann." Ibid., 44.
30. Ibid., 39.
31. Ibid.
32. "... dieses Unternehmen deshalb fruchtlos bleiben muß, weil es für die Erzeugung der Verschiedenheiten wirklicher Fälle schlechthin keine Gränze giebt." Savigny, "Vom Beruf Unsrer Zeit für Gesetzgebung und Rechtswissenschaft," 226 [22].
33. Ibid., 226 [23].
34. "Auf ähnlicher Weise hat jeder Theil unsres Rechts solche Stücke, wodurch die übrigen gegeben sind: wir können sie die leitenden Grundsätze nennen." Ibid., 226 [22].
35. "Diese heraus zu fühlen, und von ihnen ausgehend den innern Zusammenhang und die Art der Verwandtschaft aller juristischen Begriffe und Sätze zu erkennen, gehört eben zu den schwersten Aufgaben unsrer Wissenschaft, ja es ist eigentlich dasjenige, was unsrer Arbeit den wissenschaftlichen Charakter giebt." Ibid.
36. James Q. Whitman, *The Legacy of Roman Law in the German Romantic Era: Historical Vision and Legal Change* (Princeton, NJ: Princeton University Press, 1990), 150.
37. "Diese Jugendzeit der Völker ist arm an Begriffen, aber sie genießt ein klares Bewußtseyn ihrer Zustände und Verhältnisse." Savigny, "Vom Beruf Unsrer Zeit für Gesetzgebung und Rechtswissenschaft," 219, 20 [9].
38. "Es Erscheint also hierin ein mannichfaltiger Einfluß des Juristenstandes auf das positive Recht.... Wer das Recht zu seinem Lebensberuf macht, durch seine größere Sachkenntniß mehr als Andere auf das Recht Einfluß haben wird." Savigny, *System des Heutigen Römischen Rechts*, vol. 1, 48–49.
39. "Das Recht ist im besondern Bewußtseyn dieses Standes nur eine Fortsetzung und eigenthümliche Entwicklung des Volksrechts." Ibid., 45.
40. Ibid.
41. Ibid., 45–49.

42. "Indessen entsteht durch die dem Stoff gegeben wissenschaftliche Form, welche seine inwohnende Einheit zu enthüllen und zu vollenden strebt, ein neues organisches Leben, welches bildend auf den Stoff zurück wirkt, so daß auch aus der Wissenschaft als solcher eine neue Art der Rechtserzeugung unaufhaltsam hervorgeht." Ibid., 46–47.
43. Ibid., 49 (emphasis in original).
44. Savigny, "Vom Beruf Unsrer Zeit für Gesetzgebung und Rechtswissenschaft," 221 [12]. The classical ideal of politics animated Gustav Hugo's *Naturrecht*, which Savigny knew well. See Gustav Hugo, *Naturrecht* (1809), §5 (cited in Rückert, *Idealismus, Jurisprudenz und Politik bei Friedrich Carl von Savigny*, 266–267).
45. "Ohnehin liegt in der einseitigen Beschäftigung mit einem gegebenen positiven Rechte die Gefahr, von dem bloßen Buchstaben überwältigt zu werden." Savigny, "Vom Beruf Unsrer Zeit für Gesetzgebung und Rechtswissenschaft," 227 [24].
46. "In jedem Grundsatz sehen sie zugleich einen Fall der Anwendung, in der Leichtigkeit, womit sie so vom allgemeinen zum besondern und vom besondern zum allgemeinen übergehen, ist ihre Meisterschaft unverkennbar." Ibid., 231 [30–31].
47. ". . . ohne die Anschaulichkeit und Lebendigkeit einzubüßen." Ibid., 231 [31].
48. Volume one of *Die Zeitschrift für Geschichtliche Rechtswissenschaft* appeared in 1815, edited by Savigny, Karl Friedrich Eichhorn, and Johann Friedrich Ludwig Göschen.
49. Savigny, "Ueber den Zweck der Zeitschrift für Geschichtliche Rechtswissenschaft," vol. 1, 105.
50. Ibid., 107.
51. Ibid., 109.
52. "Dieses also ist die allgemeine Frage: In welchem Verhältniß steht die Vergangenheit zur Gegenwart, oder das Werden zum Seyn?" Ibid., 109.
53. Ibid.
54. Ibid., 110.
55. Wolf, *Grosse Rechtsdenker der Deutschen Geistesgeschichte*, 479.
56. Savigny, *System des Heutigen Römischen Rechts*, vol. 1, 15.
57. Savigny, "Ueber den Zweck der Zeitschrift für Geschichtliche Rechtswissenschaft," vol. 1, 111.
58. Clastres, *Archaeology of Violence*, 58.
59. Savigny, *System des Heutigen Römischen Rechts*, vol. 1, 15.
60. "Die geschichtliche Schule nimmt an, der Stoff des Rechts sei durch die gesammte Vergangenheit der Nation gegeben, doch nicht durch Willkür, so daß er zufällig dieser oder ein anderer sein könnte, sondern aus dem innersten Wesen der Nation selbst und ihrer Geschichte hervorgegangen." Savigny, "Ueber den Zweck der Zeitschrift für Geschichtliche Rechtswissenschaft," vol. 1, 113.

61. "Die Gestalt aber, in welcher das Recht in dem gemeinsamen Bewußtseyn des *Volks* lebt, ist nicht die der abstracten Regel, sondern *die lebendige Anschauung* der Rechtsinstitute in ihrem organischen Zusammenhang, so daß, wo das Bedürfniß entsteht, sich der Regel in ihrer logischen Form bewußt zu werden, diese erst durch einen künstlichen Prozeß aus jener *Totalanschauung* gebildet werden muß." Savigny, *System des Heutigen Römischen Rechts*, vol. 1, 16 (emphasis added).
62. "Die besonnene Thätigkeit jedes Zeitalters aber müsse darauf gerichtet werden, diesen mit innerer Nothwendigkeit gegebenen Stoff zu durchschauen, zu verjüngen und frisch zu erhalten." Savigny, "Ueber den Zweck der Zeitschrift für Geschichtliche Rechtswissenschaft," vol. 1, 113.
63. John E. Toews, "The Immanent Genesis and Transcendent Goal of Law: Savigny, Stahl, and the Ideology of the Christian German State," *American Journal of Comparative Law* 37 (1989): 139. See also Franz Wieacker, "Friedrich Karl von Savigny," *Zeitschrift der Savigny Stiftung* (Roman division) 72 (1955): 21–22.
64. "Der Charakter derselben [die Strenge historische Methode der Rechtswissenschaft] besteht nicht, wie einige neuere Gegner unbegreiflicherweise gesagt haben, in ausschließender Anpreisung der Römischen Rechts: auch nicht darin, daß sie die unbedingte Beybehaltung irgend eines gegebenen Stoffs verlangte, was sie vielmehr gerade verhüten will, wie sich dieses oben bey der Beurtheilung des Oesterreichischen Gesetzbuch gezeigt hat. Ihr Bestreben geht vielmehr dahin, jeden gegebenen Stoff bis zu seiner Wurzel zu verfolgen, und so sein organisches Prinzip zu entdecken, wodurch sich von selbst das, was noch Leben hat, von demjenigen absondern muß, was schon abgestorben ist, und nur noch der Geschichte angehört." Savigny, "Vom Beruf Unsrer Zeit für Gesetzgebung und Rechtswissenschaft," 276 [117–18].
65. Richard A. Posner, "Past-Dependency, Pragmatism, and Critique of History in Adjudication and Legal Scholarship," *University of Chicago Law Review* 67 (2000): 573, 586; see also Richard A. Posner, "Savigny, Holmes, and the Law and Economics of Possession," *Virginia Law Review* 86 (2000): 541.
66. Savigny, *System des Heutigen Römischen Rechts*, vol. 1, xv.
67. Savigny, "Vom Beruf Unsrer Zeit für Gesetzgebung und Rechtswissenschaft," 230–231 [29–31].
68. "Vielmehr besteht das Wesen derselben [Die geschichtliche Ansicht der Rechtswissenschaft] in der gleichmäßigen Anerkennung des Werthes und der Selbständigkeit jedes Zeitalters, und sie legt nur darauf das höchste Gewicht, daß der lebendige Zusammenhang erkannt werde, welcher die Gegenwart an die Vergangenheit knüpft, und ohne dessen Kenntniß wir von dem Rechtszustand der Gegenwart nur die äußere Erscheinung wahrnehmen, nicht das innere Wesen begreifen." Savigny, *System des Heutigen Römischen Rechts*, vol. 1, xv.

69. Savigny, "Vom Beruf Unsrer Zeit für Gesetzgebung und Rechtswissenschaft," 231 [31–32].
70. Ibid., 231 [30].
71. "Nach der Methode, die ich für die rechte halte, wird in dem Mannichfaltigen, welches die Geschichte darbietet, die höhere Einheit aufgesucht, das Lebensprinzip, woraus diese einzelnen Erscheinungen zu erklären sind, und so das materiell Gegebene immer mehr vergeistigt." Friedrich Karl von Savigny, "Recension. N. Th. V. Gönner, Über Gesetzgebung und Rechtswissenschaft in Unserer Zeit," in *Vermischte Schriften*, ed. Friedrich Karl von Savigny (Aalen: Scientia Verlag, 1981), vol. 15, 140–141.
72. "Dadurch wird also gerade umgekehrt das ursprünglich Gegebene verwandelt und vergeistigt, indem Dasjenige, was zuerst als todter, materieller Stoff erschien, nunmehr als lebendige Kraft und Thätigkeit des Volkes angeschaut wird." Ibid., 141–142.
73. Rückert, *Idealismus, Jurisprudenz und Politik bei Friedrich Carl von Savigny*, 235 ff.
74. Dieter Nörr, *Savignys Philosophische Lehrjahre* (Frankfurt am Main: Vittorio Klostermann, 1994), 61ff.
75. Hans Kiefner, "Lex Frater a Fratre. Institution und Rechtsinstitut bei Savigny," *Rechtstheorie* 9, no. 2 (1979). See also Hans Kiefner, "*Der Junge Savigny* (Marburg 1795–1808)," in *Akademische Feier aus Anlaß der 200 Wiederkehr des Geburtstags von Friedrich Carl von Savigny*, ed. H. G. Leser (Marburg: Fachberaich Rechtswissenschaft der Philipps-Universität Marburg an der Lahn, 1979); Hans Kiefner, "Der Einfluß Kants auf Theorie und Praxis des Zivilrechts im 19. Jahrhundert," in *Philosophie und Rechtswissenschaft*, ed. J. Blühdorn and J. Ritter (Frankfurt am Main: Vittorio Klostermann, 1969), 3–25.
76. Hans Kiefner, "Ideal Wird, Was Natur War," *Quad Fiorentini* 9 (1980): 515–522; Rückert, *Idealismus, Jurisprudenz und Politik bei Friedrich Carl von Savigny*, 141; Nörr, *Savignys Philosophische Lehrjahre*, 39.
77. Nörr, *Savignys Philosophische Lehrjahre*.
78. The quotation, along with an explanation of its provenance, is included in the published collection of Savigny's material on codification. See Friedrich Carl von Savigny, *Politik und Neuere Legislationen. Materialien zum "Geist der Gesetzgebung,"* ed. Hidetake Akamatsu and Joachim Rückert (Frankfurt am Main: Vittorio Klostermann, 2000), 158. See also the helpful discussions in Kiefner, "Ideal Wird, Was Natur War," and in Rückert, *Idealismus, Jurisprudenz und Politik bei Friedrich Carl von Savigny*.
79. Friedrich Hölderlin, "Hyperion, or the Hermit in Greece," in *Hyperion and Selected Poems*, ed. Eric L. Santner, trans. Willard R. Trask (New York: Continuum, 1990), 51 (translation emended).
80. "Ein ursprüngliches Recht kann bestehen ohne Rechtswissenschaft, aber in einem gebildeten Zustand muß Rechtswissenschaft hinzutreten, oder

das Recht selbst wird untergehen in flacher, charakterloser Unbedeutenheit [!]." Friedrich Carl von Savigny, "Institutionen, Winter 1808," ed. Rückert and printed in Rückert, *Idealismus, Jurisprudenz und Politik bei Friedrich Carl von Savigny*, 428.
81. Kiefner, "Ideal Wird, Was Natur War," 520.
82. Savigny, "Vom Beruf Unsrer Zeit für Gesetzgebung und Rechtswissenschaft," 280–281 [125].
83. "[N]ur ist eine nothwendige Bedingung nicht mit in Rechnung gebracht, die Fähigkeit nämlich wahre Erfahrungen zu *machen*." Ibid., 281–282 [127] (emphasis added).
84. Ibid., 282 [127].
85. "Glauben Sie mir, wer auch nur in anderen Dingen, in Poesie, Geschichte, Wissenschaft aller Art der Wahrheit mit treuem liebevollem auge nachgeforscht hat, sich selbst und eitlen Schein vergessend, dem kommt diese Übung des inneren Sinnes auch hier im heiligsten zu gute, denn hier und dort ist es doch am Ende der einfältige Kindersinn, dem allein die Wahrheit offenbart wird." Savigny, letter to Jacob Grimm, Dec. 29, 1817, cited in Nörr, *Savignys Philosophische Lehrjahre*, 263.
86. Savigny, *Vorlesungen über Juristische Methodologie 1802–1842*. See also Rückert, *Idealismus, Jurisprudenz und Politik bei Friedrich Carl von Savigny*, 57, 142ff.
87. Savigny, *Vorlesungen über Juristische Methodologie 1802–1842*, 139–140 (emphasis in original).
88. Ibid., 211.
89. "New view for science: *historical* handling in the proper sense, i.e. consideration of legislation as self-advancing in a given time.—. Unity of our science with the history of the state and *Volk*.—. The *system itself* must be thought as advancing . . . In hindsight, this operation [the historical approach to law] presupposes the first two [the philological and the systematic]." Ibid., 88.
90. Ibid., 210.
91. Ibid., 140.
92. ". . . so ist seine wesentliche Leistung doch die Eröffnung einer neuen Sehweise auf das Recht." Nörr, *Savignys Philosophische Lehrjahre*, 294.
93. Letter to the Brothers Grimm from Oct. 27, 1812, cited in Rückert, *Idealismus, Jurisprudenz und Politik bei Friedrich Carl von Savigny*, 333.
94. Nörr, *Savignys Philosophische Lehrjahre*, 263.
95. Friedrich Julius Stahl, *Die Philosophie des Rechts*, Elibron Classics replica ed. of the 1870 ed. by J. C. B. Mohr (Chestnut Hill, MA: Adamant Media Corporation, 2003), 586–587.
96. Ibid., 373.
97. "Jeder hat eine Methode, aber bei wenigen kommt sie zum Bewußtwerden und System. Sie wird aber in ein System dadurch gebracht, daß

wir uns eine Wissenschaft nach den eigenen Gesetzen ihrer Natur vollendet denken, oder ein Ideal von ihr. Seine Anschauung allein führt uns zu einer richtigen Methode." Savigny, *Juristische Methodenlehre Nach der Ausarbeitung des Jakob Grimm,* 11.

98. Horst Hammen, *Die Bedeutung Friedrich Carl v. Savignys für die Allgemeinen Dogmatischen Grundlagen des Deutschen Bürgerlichen Gesetzbuches* (Berlin: Duncker & Humblot, 1983), 24.
99. Savigny, *System des Heutigen Römischen Rechts,* vol. 1, 105.
100. "Jene allgemeine Aufgabe alles Rechts nun läßt sich einfach auf die sittliche Bestimmung der menschlichen Natur zuruck führen." Ibid., 53.
101. See, insightfully, Kiefner, "Lex Frater a Fratre. Institution und Rechtsinstitut bei Savigny," 139.
102. "Jene allgemeine Aufgabe alles Rechts nun läßt sich einfach auf die sittliche Bestimmung der menschlichen Natur zurück führen, so wie sich dieselbe in der christlichen Lebensansicht darstellt." Savigny, *System des Heutigen Römischen Rechts,* vol. 1, 53.
103. "Denn das Christenthum ist nicht nur von uns als Regel des Lebens anzuerkennen, sondern es hat auch in der That die Welt umgewandelt, so daß alle unsre Gedanken, so fremd, ja feindlich sie demselben scheinen mögen, dennoch von ihm beherrscht und durchdrungen sind." Ibid., 53–54.
104. "Die Anerkennung der überall gleichen sittlichen Würde und Freyheit des Menschen." Ibid., 55.
105. "Sollen nun in solcher Berühung freye Wesen neben einander bestehen, sich gegenseitig fördernd, nicht hemmend, in ihrer Entwicklung, so ist dieses nur möglich durch Anerkennung einer unsichtbaren Gränze, innerhalb welcher das Daseyn, und die Wirksamkeit jedes Einzelnen einen sichern, freyen Raum gewinne. Die Regel, wodurch jene Gränze und durch sie dieser freye Raum bestimmt wird, ist das Recht." Ibid., 331–332.
106. "Das Recht dient der Sittlichkeit." Ibid., 332.
107. Ibid., 332, 54.
108. Ibid., 54.
109. Ibid., 344.
110. Ibid., 386.
111. Ibid., 388.
112. Ibid., 390.
113. For what follows, I have relied heavily on Klaus Luig's very helpful treatment of this topic. See Klaus Luig, "Savignys Irrtumslehre," *Ius Commune* 8 (1979): 36–59. See also Hammen, *Die Bedeutung Friedrich Carl v. Savignys für die Allgemeinen Dogmatischen Grundlagen des Deutschen Bürgerlichen Gesetzbuches,* 95ff.
114. Savigny, *System des Heutigen Römischen Rechts,* vol. 3, 3–6.
115. Ibid., 307–309.

116. Ibid., 114. See also p. 341: "Der Irrthum im Allgemeinen wirkt an und für sich gar nicht, schützt also auch nicht gegen den dadurch entstandenen Nachtheil."
117. Ibid., 343.
118. Ibid., 264. See Luig, "Savignys Irrtumslehre," 36.
119. D.50.17.116.2. Savigny cites a number of passages from the *Digests* that oppose his view. See Savigny, *System des Heutigen Römischen Rechts*, vol. 3, 342. See also Luig, "Savignys Irrtumslehre," 37 (citing—to the wrong source—the rule: "cum errantis voluntas nulla sit").
120. See Luig, "Savignys Irrtumslehre," 41.
121. Ibid., 41 (citing Savigny, *System des Heutigen Römischen Rechts*, vol. 3, 355).
122. Savigny, *System des Heutigen Römischen Rechts*, vol. 3, 356.
123. Ibid., 113.
124. Ibid.
125. Luig, "Savignys Irrtumslehre," 43–44.
126. Savigny, *System des Heutigen Römischen Rechts*, vol. 1, 54.

7. The *Bürgerliche Gesetzbuch*

1. Rudolf von Jhering, "Friedrich Karl von Savigny," *Jherings Jahrbücher für Dogmatik* 5 (1861): 355.
2. ". . . daß die Rechte nicht gemacht *wären*, sondern *würden*, daß sie hervorgingen, wie Sprache und Sitte, aus dem Innersten des Volks-lebens und -Denkens, ohne das Medium der Berechnung und des Bewußtseins." Ibid., 364–65 (emphasis in original).
3. ". . . den Werth und die Bedeutung der menschlichen Thatkraft, die Rolle, die der freie Entschluß, die Reflexion und Absicht in der Geschichte spielen, ebenso unterschätzen." Ibid., 369.
4. Ibid.
5. Ibid.
6. Rudolph von Jhering, *Entwicklungsgeschichte des Römischen Rechts* (Leipzig: Breitkopf & Härtel and Duncker & Humblot, 1894), 13.
7. Rudolf von Jhering, "Ist Die Jurisprudenz Eine Wissenschaft?" in *Ist die Jurisprudenz eine Wissenschaft? Jherings Wiener Antrittsvorlesung*, ed. Okko Behrends (Göttingen: Wallstein Verlag, 1998), 67.
8. "Die ganze menschliche Welt mit Einschluß des Rechts und des Sittlichen ist die Schöpfung des Menschen." Jhering, *Entwicklungsgeschichte des Römischen Rechts*, 19.
9. Jhering, "Ist die Jurisprudenz eine Wissenschaft?" 55.
10. See the footnote Jhering adds to his *Geist des Römischen Rechts* in 1883: "uber dem bloß Formalen der juristischen Logik steht als Höheres die substantielle Idee der Gerechtigkeit und Sittlichkeit, und eine Vertiefung in sie, d.h. wie sie in den einzelnen Rechtsinstituten und Rechtssätzen zum Aus-

druck und zur Verwirklichung gelangt, ist nach menem Dafürhalten die schönste und erhabenste Aufgabe, welche die Wissenschaft sich stellen kann. Mein Werk: "Der Zweck im Recht" ist der Lösung dieser Aufgabe gewidmet." Rudolf von Jhering, *Geist des Römischen Rechts auf den Verschiedenen Stufen seiner Entwicklung*, 6th ed., vol. 2 (Aalen: Scientia Verlag, 1993), 361n506a.

11. Jhering, "Ist die Jurisprudenz eine Wissenschaft?" 90–92.
12. "Motto: Der Zweck ist der Schöpfer des ganzen Rechts." Rudolf von Jhering, *Der Zweck im Recht*, 3rd ed., vol. 1 (Leipzig: Breitkopf and Härtel, 1893).
13. Jhering, "Ist die Jurisprudenz eine Wissenschaft?" 68.
14. Clearly, Jhering's scientific overcoming of truth illustrates the *Wille zur Wahrheit* that Nietzsche describes as the self-overcoming of the will to truth, which is the last stage in the unfolding of nihilism. See Friedrich Nietzsche, "Also Sprach Zarathustra," in *Kritische Studienausgabe*, ed. Giorgio Colli and Mazzino Montinari, vol. 4 (Munich: Deutscher Taschenbuch Verlag, 1988), 146ff.
15. The opposition between technical and normative legal theory parallels the distinction between analytic and normative jurisprudence that occupies so much of twentieth- and twenty-first-century Anglo-American jurisprudence. See, e.g., Ronald Dworkin, *Taking Rights Seriously* (Cambridge, MA: Harvard University Press, 1978), 2ff. While not challenging the basic opposition, modern American theorists tend to privilege normative over technical approaches to jurisprudence. See, e.g., Melvin Aron Eisenberg, *The Nature of the Common Law* (Cambridge, MA: Harvard University Press, 1988), 2–3. "All common law cases are decided under a unified methodology, and under this methodology social propositions always figure in determining the rules the courts establish and the way in which those rules are extended, restricted, and applied."
16. "Für das richtige Verständniß eines Gesetzes sind zwei Momente von entscheidener Bedeutung. Es sind dies einerseits der wirthschaftliche und soziale Zweck, den das Gesetz verfolgt, und andererseits die technisch-juristischen Mittel, welche zur Erreichung des Zweckes angewandt werden." G. Planck, *Bürgerliches Gesetzbuch nebst Einführungsgesetz*, vol. 1 (Berlin: J. Guttentag, Verlagsbuchhandlung, 1897), i.
17. Franz Wieacker, *Privatrechtsgeschichte der Neuzeit: Unter Besonderer Berücksichtigung der Deutschen Entwicklung*, Reprint of 2nd revised ed. of 1967 ed. (Göttingen: Vandenhoeck & Ruprecht, 1996), 483.
18. See, e.g., Frederic William Maitland, "The Laws of the Anglo-Saxons," cited in Marcus Dittmann, *Das Bürgerliche Gesetzbuch aus Sicht des Common Law* (Berlin: Duncker & Humblot, 2001), 169.
19. Wieacker, *Privatrechtsgeschichte der Neuzeit: Unter Besonderer Berücksichtigung der Deutschen Entwicklung*, 475.

20. For the following, see ibid. Cf. Bernard Windscheid, *Lehrbuch des Pandektenrechts*, 9th ed., vol. 1 (Aalen: Scientia Verlag, 1963), 111n1.
21. For translations of the BGB, I have consulted *The German Civil Code*, trans. Simon L. Goren (Littleton, CO: Fred B. Rothman & Co., 1994).
22. Konrad Zweigert and Hartmut Dietrich, "System and Language of the German Civil Code 1900," in *Problems of Codification*, ed. S. J. Stoljar (Canberra: Department of Law, Research School of Social Sciences, Australian National University, 1977), 38.
23. Basil Markensinis, "The Legacy of History on German Contact Law," in *Foreign Law and Comparative Methodology* (Oxford: Hart Publishing, 1997), 83.
24. Konrad Zweigert and Hartmut Dietrich, "System and Language of the German Civil Code 1900," 37.
25. Jhering, *Geist des Römischen Rechts auf den Verschiedenen Stufen seiner Entwicklung*, vol. 2, 334ff.
26. Paul Koschaker, *Europa und das Römische Recht*, 4th unedited ed. (Munich: C. H. Beck'sche Verlagsbuchhandlung, 1966), 281. See generally, Andreas von Tuhr, *Der Allgemeine Teil des Deutschen Bürgerlichen Rechts*, vol. 1 (Berlin: Verlag von Duncker & Humblot, 1957), xii–xiii. See also Wieacker, *Privatrechtsgeschichte der Neuzeit: Unter Besonderer Berücksichtigung der Deutschen Entwicklung*, §25, 476ff.
27. "Die Auslegung erfolgt durch den Richter und ihm vorarbeitend durch die Wissenschaft." Tuhr, *Der Allgemeine Teil des Deutschen Bürgerlichen Rechts*, 37. See also Windscheid, *Lehrbuch des Pandektenrechts*, 110.
28. "Auf Verhältnisse, für welche das Gesetz keine Vorschrift enthält, finden die für rechtsähnliche Verhältnisse gegebenen Vorschriften entsprechende Anwendung. In Ermangelung solcher Vorschriften sind die aus dem Geiste der Rechtsordnung sich ergebenden Grundsätze maßgebend." *Entwurf eines Bürgerlichen Gesetzbuches für das Deutsche Reich*, Amtliche ed. (Berlin: Verlag von Guttentag, 1888), 1.
29. Windscheid, *Lehrbuch des Pandektenrechts*, 97ff.
30. Horst Jakobs, *Wissenschaft und Gesetzgebung im Bürgerlichen Recht* (Munich: Ferdinand Schöningh, 1983), 135.
31. "Kein Gesetz kann in dem Sinne vollständig sein, daß es für jedes denkbare, in den Rahmen des von ihm behandelten Rechtsstoffes fallende Verhältniß eine unmittelbare Vorschrift an die Hand gibt. Der Versuch, eine Vollständigkeit dieser Art zu erstreben, wäre verkehrtes Beginnen." *Motive zu dem Entwurfe eines Bürgerlichen Gesetzbuches für das Deutsche Reich*, Amtliche ed., vol. 1 (Berlin: Verlag von J. Guttentag, 1888), 16.
32. "Bei Auslegung wie des Gesetzes so auch der Rechtsgeschäfte (§133) ist nicht der Wortlaut der einzelnen Gesetzesbestimmung maßgebend, sondern die Bedeutung, welche ihr im Zusammenhang mit dem ganzen

Gesetz und den übrigen Teilen der Rechtsordnung zukommt." Tuhr, *Der Allgemeine Teil des Deutschen Bürgerlichen Rechts*, 37.

33. Jakobs, *Wissenschaft und Gesetzgebung im Bürgerlichen Recht*, 134 (quoting, without page citation, the *Motive* to the BGB).
34. Cf. Max Weber, *Wirtschaft und Gesellschaft* (Tübingen: J. C .B Mohr, 1980), 565.
35. "Die Rechtsordnung erfüllt, indem sie die *Rechtsfähigkeit* des Menschen ohne Rücksicht auf seine Individualität und ohne Rücksicht auf seinen Willen anerkennt, ein Gebot der Vernunft und der Ethik." *Motive zu dem Entwurfe eines Bürgerlichen Gesetzbuches für das Deutsche Reich*, vol. 1, 25. See also Windscheid, *Lehrbuch des Pandektenrechts*, 25.
36. *Motive zu dem Entwurfe eines Bürgerlichen Gesetzbuches für das Deutsche Reich*, vol. 1, 26.
37. Ibid., 25.
38. Tuhr, *Der Allgemeine Teil des Deutschen Bürgerlichen Rechts*, 37.
39. "Das Wesen des Rechtsgeschäftes wird darin gefunden, daß ein auf die Hevorbringung rechtlicher Wirkungen gerichteter Wille sich bethätigt, und daß der *Spruch* der Rechtsordnung in Anerkennung dieses Willens die gewollte rechtliche Gestaltung in der Rechtswelt verwirklicht." *Motive zu dem Entwurfe eines Bürgerlichen Gesetzbuches für das Deutsche Reich*, vol. 1, 126 (emphasis added).
40. "Recht ist eine von der Rechtsordnung verliehene Willensmacht oder Willensherrschaft." Windscheid, *Lehrbuch des Pandektenrechts*, §37, 156.
41. *Motive zu dem Entwurfe eines Bürgerlichen Gesetzbuches für das Deutsche Reich*, vol. 1, 25.
42. "Der im subjectiven Recht gebietende Wille (ist) nur der Wille der Rechtsordnung, nicht der Wille des Berechtigen." Windscheid, *Lehrbuch des Pandektenrechts*, §37, 158 n3.
43. *Motive zu dem Entwurfe eines Bürgerlichen Gesetzbuches für das Deutsche Reich*, vol. 3, 267.
44. Ibid., 268.
45. Hans-Peter Haferkamp, "Bemerkungen zur Deutschen Privatrechtswissenschaft Zwischen 1925 und 1935—Dargestellt an der Debatte um die Behandlung der *Exceptio Doli Generalis*," Forum Historiae Juris, http://www.forhistiur.de/index_en.htm (1997): text at n38 (accessed June 2, 2005). Citing Planck: In no way is the judge empowered, "den Vertrag oder das Gesetz durch Aufstellung eiens sozialen Ideals als Richtmaß oder durch Geltendmachung subjektiver sittlicher Anschauungen zu korrigieren."
46. For a discussion of the role of general clauses in the BGB, see Karl Engisch, *Einführung in das Juristische Denken*, 9th ed. (Stuttgart: Verlag W. Kohlhammer, 1997). See also Justus Wilhelm Hedemann, *Die Flucht in der Generalklauseln. Eine Gefahr für Staat und Recht* (Tübingen: Verlag Mohr, 1933).

47. "Das BGB. hat nun das Bestreben, die subjektiven Rechte insoweit abzuschwächen, als die billige Rücksicht auf das Interesse anderer es erfördert." G. Planck, "Die Sociale Tendenz des Bürgerlichen Gesetzbuchs," *Deutsche Juristen-Zeitung* 4, no. 9 (1899): 181.
48. See, e.g., §315, §571, §920, §829, §325, §660, §1361.
49. See, e.g., §151, §157, §242.
50. See, e.g., §626.
51. See, e.g., §138, §817, §819, §826, §1741.
52. See, e.g., §157, §242.
53. Wieacker, *Privatrechtsgeschichte der Neuzeit: Unter Besonderer Berücksichtigung der Deutschen Entwicklung,* §25, 476. See also Rudolf Stammler, *Die Bedeutung des Deutschen Bürgerlichen Gesetzbuches für den Fortschritt der Kultur* (Halle: Max Niemeyer, 1900), 27.
54. Wieacker, *Privatrechtsgeschichte der Neuzeit: Unter Besonderer Berücksichtigung der Deutschen Entwicklung,* §25, 476 (citing Philipp Heck, *Gesetzesauslegung und Interessenjurisprudenz* (Tübingen: Mohr Siebeck Verlag, 1914).
55. Paul Grebe, ed., *Der Große Duden. Etymologie. Herkunftswörterbuch der Deutschen Sprache* (Mannheim: Bibliographisches Institut AG, 1963), 66. By the time of the BGB, however, *billig* had acquired its modern sense of a good value, that which was appropriately priced and even inexpensive or cheap.
56. See Aristotle, *The Nicomachean Ethics,* ed. G. P. Goold, trans. H. Rackham (Cambridge, MA: Harvard University Press, 1990), 1137b30ff. See also Jill Frank, *A Democracy of Distinction: Aristotle and the Work of Politics* (Chicago: University of Chicago Press, 2004), 105.
57. Aristotle, *The Nicomachean Ethics,* 1137b12.
58. Aristotle, *The "Art" of Rhetoric,* ed. John Henry Freese, (Cambridge, MA: Harvard University Press, 1982), 1374b.15ff. See the excellent discussion of Aristotle's use of equity in Frank, *A Democracy of Distinction,* 101ff.
59. Tuhr, *Der Allgemeine Teil des Deutschen Bürgerlichen Rechts,* 34.
60. "Die formale Rechtsgleichheit bei Rechtsverhältnissen . . . führt oft zur materiellen Ungleichheit. Um den sich hieraus ergebenden sozialen Uebelständen thunlichst entgegen zu wirken, stellt das BGB [sic] . . . einige allgemeine Vorschriften auf." Planck, "Die Sociale Tendenz des Bürgerlichen Gesetzbuchs," 182.
61. Bernard Windscheid, "Recht und Rechtswissenschaft," in *Gesammelte Reden und Abhandlungen,* ed. Paul Oertmann (Leipzig: Verlag von Duncker & Humblot, 1904), 10.
62. Ibid., 11.
63. Ibid., 19.
64. "Das praktische Ziel der Gerechtigkeit ist die Herstellung der Gleichheit." Jhering, *Der Zweck im Recht,* vol. 1, 367. For an English translation, see Rudolf von Ihering, *Law as a Means to an End,* trans. Isaac Husik, 4th ed. (Union, NJ: The Lawbook Exchange, 1999), 275ff.

65. Jhering, however, distinguishes the practice of *Recht* from its theoretical connection to *Sittlichkeit* and ethics. See Rudolf von Jhering, *Der Zweck im Recht*, 3rd ed., vol. 2 (Leipzig: Breitkopf and Härtel, 1898).
66. Jhering, *Der Zweck im Recht*, vol. 1, 367–368.
67. Ibid., 364–365.
68. Ibid., 368–369.
69. Ibid., 369.
70. Ibid. For a penetrating look at the relation between equality and resentment, see Friedrich Nietzsche, "Zur Genealogie der Moral," in *Kritische Studienausgabe*, ed. Giorgio Colli and Mazzino Montinari, vol. 5 (Munich: Deutscher Taschenbuch Verlag, 1988). See also Nietzsche, "Also Sprach Zarathustra," 128ff.
71. "Allein nicht darum wollen wir im Recht die Gleichheit, weil sie an sich etwas Erstrebenswertes wäre . . . sondern darum wollen wir sie, weil sie die Bedingung des *Wohles* der Gesellschaft ist." Jhering, *Der Zweck im Recht*, vol. 1, 369.
72. Ibid., 369–370.
73. "Cette justice n'est fondée que dans la convenance, qui demande une certaine satisfaction pur l'expiation d'une mauvaise action." Gottfried Wilhelm Leibniz, "Essais de Theodice," in C. I. Gerhardt, *Die Philosophischen Schriften*, vol. 6 (New York: Georg Olms Verlag, 1996), 141.
74. Ibid.
75. "Aber das Ebenmass das er verlangt scheint weniger den praktischen Zweck der gleichen Vertheilung des Schwergewichts und der dadurch zu erzielenden Festigkeit der socialen Ordnung." Jhering, *Der Zweck im Recht*, vol. 1, 370.
76. "Das praktische Interesse des Bestehens und Gedeihens der Gesellschaft also ist es, welches ihr den Grundsatz der Gleichheit in diesem Sinne dictirt, nicht der aprioristische kategorische Imperative einer in allen menschlichen Verhältnissen zu verwirklichenden Gleichheit: würde die Erfahrung zeigen, dass sie bei der Ungleichheit besser bestehen kann, so würde letztere den Vorzug verdienen." Ibid., 371–372.
77. "Es ist ein alter, nie ausgeträumte Traum der Menschheit, daß es ein einiges, festes, unwandelbares Recht gebe. Dieses Recht sei das Recht der Vernunft. Was der Vernunft entspreche, sei eben deswegen Recht, notwendig, für alle Zeiten, an allen Orten . . . Jetzt ist sie in der Wissenschaft als irrig erkannt." Bernard Windscheid, "Die Aufgaben der Rechtswissenschaft," in *Gesammelte Reden und Abhandlungen*, ed. Paul Oertmann (Leipzig: Verlag von Duncker & Humblot, 1904), 105.
78. "Das Entscheidende bliebe doch: daß diese 'frei' schaffende Verwaltung (und eventuell: Rechtssprechung) nicht, wie wir das bei den vorbürokratischen Formen finden werden, ein Reich der freien Willkür und Gnade,

der persönlich motivierten Gunst und Bewertung bilden würde. *Sondern daß stets als Norm des Verhaltens die Herrschaft und rationale Abwägung, 'sachlicher' Zwecke und die Hingabe an sie besteht.* Auf dem Gebiet der staatlichen Verwaltung speziell gilt gerade der das 'schöpferische' Belieben des Beamten am stärksten verklärenden Ansicht als höchster und letzter Leitstern seiner Gebarung der spezifisch moderne, streng 'sachliche' Gedanke der Staatsraison." Weber, *Wirtschaft und Gesellschaft*, 565 (emphasis added).
79. Windscheid, "Die Aufgaben der Rechtswissenschaft," 105.
80. Ibid.
81. Jakobs, *Wissenschaft und Gesetzgebung im Bürgerlichen Recht*, 135.
82. Ibid., 12.
83. Ibid., 13.
84. H. L. A. Hart, *The Concept of Law* (Oxford: Oxford University Press, 1961), 20.
85. The entirety of modern legal theory can rightly be seen as an anxious attempt to offer law the solace of justification. From Ronald Dworkin and Jürgen Habermas to Richard Posner and Stanley Fish, contemporary legal theorists strive to legitimize positive law through social science. For the surprising convergence between Posner's law and economics and Fish's version of pragmatism, see Stanley Fish, "Almost Pragmatism: Richard Posner's Jurisprudence," *University of Chicago Law Review* 57 (1990): 1459.
86. Windscheid, "Die Aufgaben der Rechtswissenschaft," 102.
87. See Weber, *Wirtschaft und Gesellschaft*, 563.
88. Stammler, *Die Bedeutung des Deutschen Bürgerlichen Gesetzbuches für den Fortschritt der Kultur*, 26–32.
89. Weber, *Wirtschaft und Gesellschaft*, 708.
90. Ibid., 709.
91. Max Weber, "Zur Lage der Bürgerlichen Demokratie in Rußland," in *Gesammelte Politische Schriften*, ed. Johannes Winckelmann (Tübingen: J. C. B. Mohr, 1958), 60.
92. Ibid.
93. Ibid.
94. Friedrich Nietzsche, "Der Fall Wagner," in *Kritische Studienausgabe*, ed. Giorgio Colli and Mazzino Montinari, vol. 6 (Munich: Deutscher Taschenbuch Verlag, 1988), 27.
95. Max Weber, "Zur Lage der Bürgerlichen Demokratie in Rußland," 60.

Conclusion

1. Philippe Nonet, "Green v. Recht," *California Law Review* 75 (1987): 363–364.
2. Martin Heidegger, "Die Frage Nach der Technik," in *Die Technik und die*

Kehre (Pfullingen: Verlag Günther Neske Pfullingen, 1991), 35. The translation is taken from *The Question Concerning Technique*, trans. Roger Berkowitz and Philippe Nonet (unpublished manuscript on file with the author).
3. Plato, "Phaedrus," in *Euthyphro. Apology. Crito. Phaedo. Phaedrus*, ed. G. P. Goold (Cambridge, MA: Harvard University Press, 1995), 250d–250e.

Index

Allgemeiner Teil. See General Part
Allgemeines Gesetzbuch (AGB), 71–73, 78–83, 87, 98–100. See also *Allgemeines Landrecht* (ALR)
Allgemeines Landrecht (ALR), 8–9, 84, 85–86, 87, 94–101, 103, 104, 113, 144, 147, 155, 157, 164; positive law, 8–9, 70, 100–101; natural law codes, 67–70; versus *Allgemeines Gesetzbuch*, 71–73, 79–83, 98–100; history, 73–79
Ananias, ix
Antigone, ix, 4
Aristotle, xii, 20, 46–48, 57, 88, 89–90, 167; geometry, 18. See also *Forum Externum and Internum*
Ars Combinatoria, 25, 35–42
Austin, John, 5

Bacon, Francis, 12, 112
Basketball, x–xii
Bentham, Jeremy, 87
Billigkeit. See Fairness
Boomer v. Atlantic Cement, 169n5
Brothers Grimm, 128
Bürgerliches Gesetzbuch (BGB), 9, 104–106, 107, 108, 140–141, 160; Nazi jurists, 108; science of abstraction, 141–145; alphabet of law, 144; science of interpretation, 145–148; balancing of interests, 148–155

Caesar, Julius, 21–22
Carmer, Johann Heinrich Casimer Graf von, 75–76
Christianity, 130–131, 135, 147
Clastres, Pierre, 1, 4, 6, 7, 122, 163
Cocceji, Samuel von, 74
Code Civil, 67, 68, 103
Codex Leopoldus, 11, 54, 55
Codification, 1–4, 10, 20–21, 60–61, 67–70, 104, 116, 135
Constable, Marianne, 169n7
Cornell, Drucilla, xiv
Crown Prince Lectures, 87–89, 90–97

Danckelmann, Adolf Albrecht Heinrich Leopold von, 80–82
Déclaration des droits de l'homme et du citoyen, 83–84
Derrida, Jacques, xiv
Descartes, René, 17, 26, 32, 40, 41, 43–44, 45, 48
Dilthey, Wilhelm, 67, 94, 165
Double source thesis, 109–111, 138, 148
Dworkin, Ronald, 171n11, 204n15, 209n85

Economics. See Efficiency
Efficiency, x–xii, 10, 134–135, 150, 151–155, 156–157, 160. See also Justice; Law
Elements of law. See Jhering, Rudolf von; Leibniz, Gottfried Wilhelm
Emerson, Ralph Waldo, x
Epieikeia. See Equity
Equality, 130, 151, 152, 153–155
Equity, 152–153, 154–155

211

212   Index

Ethical activity, x, xiii, xiv, 137. *See also* Justice
Euclid, 18, 34, 40, 41, 44

Fairness, x–xii, 150–155, 157, 160. *See also* Justice; Law
Ferrand, Louis, 30, 31
Ferry, Luc, 52
Finnis, John, xiv
Fischer, Kuno, 14
Force of justice, 19, 28–29, 45–53. *See also* Law; Leibniz, Gottfried Wilhelm; Science of law
Force of law. *See* Force of justice
Forum Externum and Internum, 65, 89–91, 100. *See also* Aristotle; Kant, Immanuel
Frank, Jill, 169n8, 207nn56,58
Freedom, 130–132, 148
Free will, 21–23, 134, 148
Friedrich, Johann, 54, 64
Friedrich III, 73
Friedrich the Great, 8, 33, 74–76, 87, 100, 101; Arnold (miller), 75–76, 80
Friedrich Wilhelm II, 77–79, 87
Fuller, Lon, 94–95

Gaddis, William, ix
Gagnér, Sten, 10
Gaius, 37. *See also* Roman law
General Part, 56, 61–63, 132, 133, 143
Geometry. *See* Leibniz, Gottfried Wilhelm
George, Robert, xiv
Gerhardt, C. I., 163
Gesetz. *See* *Ius*; Positive law; *Recht*
Gesetzmäßigkeit. *See* Legality
Graevius, Johann Georg, 26
Gratian, 33. *See also* Roman law
Grisez, Germain, xiv
Grua, Gaston, 55, 60, 163

Habermas, Jürgen, 171n11, 209n85
Hart, H. L. A., 5, 156, 209n84
Hattenhauer, Hans, 74, 103

Hegel, G. W. F., 9, 14, 52, 68, 169n7
Heidegger, Martin, x, xx, 11, 28, 103, 160, 164, 167, 169n2, 170n11, 171n16, 173n5, 181nn71,74,75,89, 190n49
Hobbes, Thomas, 12, 23, 84, 111
Hocher, Johann Paul, 54
Hoeflich, M. H., 17
Hölderlin, Friedrich, 125–126, 166
Holmes, Oliver Wendell, 5
Homer, xii
Hugo, Gustav, 109–110

Ignatius of Loyola, xii
Insight, xii–xiii, xv, 6, 15, 16, 26, 40, 43, 112, 120–127, 158. *See also* Justice; Savigny, Friedrich Carl von
Ius, xvii–xviii, 13, 15, 29. *See also* Natural law; *Recht*

Jaguar, 133, 149
Jakobs, Horst, 156
Jhering, Rudolf von, 107, 137–141, 147, 153–155, 166–167; Leibniz, 139. *See also* Savigny, Friedrich Carl von
John, Michael, 104–106
Justice, ix; justice as fairness, efficiency, and legitimacy, x–xii, 152–153, 154, 155, 160; justice and transcendence, x, xii–xiii, xvi, 139, 155, 159; activity of justice, x, 10, 16; justice beyond the rules, xi–xii, xvi; divorce from law, xiii, 141, 160; extinction of, xiii; transformation of, 5–6; science of, 14–15. *See also* Force of justice; Insight; Law; Science of law
Justinian. *See* Roman law

Kant, Immanuel, ix, x, 52, 68, 84, 89–91, 125, 167
Kiefner, Hans, 166
Kiesow, Rainer Maria, 171n14, 187n14
Klein, Ernst Ferdinand, 76–77, 79, 86
König, Peter, 164, 179n42, 182nn5,6

Lasser, Herman Andrew, 54
Lavintheta, Bernardus de, 39

Law: versus justice, ix, 15, 16, 89–91; as rules, ix; transformation of, xv, 10, 15–16, 157–158; product of science, xv, 6–7, 9, 10, 19–21, 32, 108, 118, 135, 155, 157, 159, 160; force of, 19. *See also* Positive law; *Recht*; Science of law
Law and economics, 9
Legality, 8–9, 83–86, 91, 101, 157
Legal order, 145–148, 149
Legal science. *See* Science of law
Legitimacy, x–xii, 10, 152–153, 154, 155, 160. *See also* Justice; Luhmann, Niklas
Leibniz, Gottfried Wilhelm, 1, 7–8, 10, 67–70, 88, 101, 144, 145, 147, 154, 160, 163; codification efforts, 11–12, 27, 54–56; legal science, 12–16, 18–25, 26–27, 54, 107–108; geometry and mathematics, 17–25, 26, 32–33, 42–43; force, 19, 28–29, 45–53, 62–63, 64; natural law, 21–25; positive law, 23–25, 108; elements of law, 25, 28–42, 54, 60; charity of the wise, 27, 39, 56, 64–66; monads, 28–29, 42–43, 45, 48; *Systema Iuris*, 55–66; and Savigny, 107–108, 110–111, 120, 130, 135–136, 137; double source thesis, 109–111, 138; and Jhering, 139. *See also* Force of justice; Principle of sufficient reason; Science
Lex. *See* Positive law
Locke, John, 93–94, 101
Loemker, Leroy, 14, 163
Luhmann, Niklas, 171n14
Luig, Klaus, 134–135, 164

Maitland, Frederic William, 142
Mandate, 36–38, 40
Mistake, 132–135. *See also* Savigny, Friedrich Carl von
Moll, Konrad, 164, 172n9
Motive to the BGB, 146–147, 148, 166

Napoleon, xii
Natural law, xiv, xvii–xviii, 4, 7, 21–25, 29, 53, 65–66, 81–83, 88–98. *See also Ius*; *Recht*
Neighbor, xi–xii
Newton, Isaac, 36
Nietzsche, Friedrich, 10, 52, 71, 72–73, 159, 167, 187n4, 204n14, 209n94
Nobility. *See* Danckelmann, Adolf Albrecht Heinrich Leopold von; Friedrich the Great; Nietzsche, Friedrich
Nonet, Philippe, 169n3, 174n17, 187n4, 190nn50,55, 209n1
Nörr, Dieter, 166
Numa, xii

Order, 91, 92, 93, 95, 101, 154–155
Otte, Gerhard, 37

Paul, 41. *See also* Roman law
Plaisted, Dennis, 178n41
Planck, Gottlieb, 140–141, 148, 152
Plato, x, 17, 160, 167; geometry, 18
Positive law, xiii–xvi, xvii–xviii, 1, 2, 3, 4–8, 15, 29, 49, 53, 81–82, 109–110, 116, 119, 156. *See also* Science of law
Posner, Richard, 5, 199n65, 209n85
Power, active or passive, 46–48
Principle of sufficient reason, 7, 15, 19, 44, 49–53, 130
Product of science. *See* Law; Science of law
Pufendorf, Samuel, 23, 111

Rawls, John, 169n6, 171n11
Recht, 68, 70, 92, 93, 94, 100, 101; relation to *Gesetz*, xvii–xviii, 84–85, 92–93, 94, 100, 119, 155, 158. *See also Ius*; Law; Natural law
Rechtsstaat. *See* Rule of law
Riley, Patrick, 13–14, 22–23, 52, 163, 164
Roman law, xii, 11, 24–25, 33, 34, 40–41, 120, 124, 134
Rousseau, Jean-Jacques, x
Rückert, Joachim, 107, 115, 165, 166
Rule of law, x, 84, 94–101

Index

Savigny, Friedrich Carl von, xvi, 9, 68, 105–108, 110–112, 137–138, 147, 148, 160, 165–166; legal science, 111–112, 115–125, 127–128, 135–136; *Volksgeist*, 112–117; *Recht*, 114–115; insight, 120–127, 128, 129; historical school, 121–124, 128; Christianity, 130–131, 135; doctrine of mistake, 132–135. *See also* Leibniz, Gottfried Wilhelm
Schelling, Friedrich Wilhelm Joseph von, 52, 125
Schiedermair, Hartmut, 24, 164
Schneider, Hans-Peter, 13, 60, 164
Schonborn, Johann Philipp von, 29, 54
Schwennicke, Andreas, 165
Science of law, xiii–xiv, 1–8, 9, 10, 14–16, 63, 66, 135–136, 141, 156; failure of, 6, 10, 155, 159; gift of, 10, 16; versus geometry, 17–19, 25, 38, 48; Leibniz, 19–21, 27, 28–29, 48–49, 51–53, 54–55, 81–83; legislative, 53; versus custom, 66, 68; Savigny, 111–112, 115–125, 128–129; Jhering, 137–141. *See also* Law; Leibniz, Gottfried Wilhelm; Principle of sufficient reason
Sebok, Anthony, 169nn5,7
Security. *See* Order
Social contract, 91–94
Socrates, 10

Solon, 33
Sportsman, xi, xii
Stahl, Friedrich Julius, 109, 129
Stölzel, Adolf, 79
Svarez, Carl Gottlieb, 8, 75, 76, 77, 81–82, 87–98, 101, 139, 147, 155, 164

Technique, 6–7, 10, 108, 119–120, 141, 156, 157–158
Thibaut, Anton F. J., 106, 113
Thieme, Hans, 165
Thrasymachus, 5
Tocqueville, Alexis de, 104
Transcendence. *See* Justice
Trendelenburg, Adolf, 69
Tuhr, Andreas von, 146, 166

Ulpian, 40, 41. *See also* Roman law

Weber, Max, 8, 85–86, 155, 157–158, 167
Whalen v. Union Bag & Paper, 169n4
Whitehead, Alfred North, x
Whitman, James, 105–106, 137
Wieacker, Franz, 68, 165
Wilhelm I, 73
Windscheid, Bernhard, 107, 145–146, 147, 148, 152–153, 166
Wolf, Eric, 77
Wolff, Christian, 21